Reminiscences

of

Vice Admiral Kent L. Lee

U.S. Navy (Retired)

Volume I

Copyright © 1990
U.S. Naval Institute
Annapolis, Maryland

Authorization

The U.S. Naval Institute is hereby authorized to make available to libraries and other repositories of its choosing the transcripts of four oral history interviews concerning the life and career of Vice Admiral Kent L. Lee, U.S. Navy (Retired). The four interviews were recorded on 29 September 1987, 9 October 1987, 29 October 1987, and 16 November 1987 in collaboration with Paul Stillwell for the U.S. Naval Institute.

During the lifetime of the undersigned, permission must be obtained from the undersigned in order to cite or quote from the transcripts of the interviews in any published work. The tape recordings of the interviews are and will remain the sole property of the U.S. Naval Institute. The copyright in both the oral and transcribed versions of the interviews shall also be the sole property of the U.S. Naval Institute.

Signed and sealed this 12th day of January 1990

Vice Admiral Kent L. Lee,
U.S. Navy (Retired)

Preface

Although he could hardly have foreseen all of its possibilities at the beginning, Kent Lee's naval career was in a sense the fulfillment of a boyhood dream. As a youngster growing up on a farm in South Carolina, he had a knack for making and fixing things with his hands. He also developed an intense interest in aviation, fueled by a brief flight at a local fair when he was a teenager. As war clouds loomed in 1940, he enlisted in the Navy and greatly enjoyed a tour as an aircraft mechanic because it combined his interests in aviation and working with his hands.

One thing led to another, including training as an aviation cadet and designation as a naval aviator in 1943. He wound up in Commander David McCampbell's famed Air Group 15 on board the carrier Essex and contributed to its success during the Central Pacific operations of 1944. Initially he flew in Bombing Squadron 15 and has fond recollections of the training and administration provided by the squadron commanding officer, Lieutenant Commander James Mini. Later he switched to Fighting Squadron 15 and shot down a Japanese Betty bomber while flying an F6F Hellcat.

After the war, he returned to being a bomber pilot and went through the lean, disorganized times of the postwar Navy. The Navy provided him subsequently with the college education he missed by enlisting right out of high school, and he went on to serve as both a staff officer and attack pilot during two combat tours in the Korean War. A subspecialty in nuclear weapons and their effects developed after that, leading to his service as an instructor in a nuclear weapons school.

In the mid-1950s, he got into testing and development work and subsequently commanded VA-46, a squadron of A4D attack planes, which was a considerable challenge after replacing a popular and charismatic skipper. As the decade of the 1960s got under way, he was one of the bright young men dispatched by the Navy to work with the Strategic Air Command on nuclear weapons targeting. It was a difficult relationship, because nuclear targeting up to then had been dominated by what he calls the "SAC fanatics."

The capstone of Lee's flying career came when he commanded the air group embarked in the Navy's first nuclear-powered aircraft carrier, the USS Enterprise. He was on board for a demonstration cruise to the Mediterranean and later helped plan the bombing attacks that might have been executed if the Cuban Missile Crisis had not been resolved peacefully.

Without meaning to, Lee was drafted into Vice Admiral Hyman Rickover's nuclear power program. After a year of instruction in nuclear power, Lee took command of the amphibious warfare ship Alamo as the United States got involved in the Vietnam War. His success in that ship proved to be a stepping-stone to command of the Enterprise, which he discusses in the forthcoming second volume of this memoir.

Throughout the recollections contained in this volume, Admiral Lee demonstrates over and over the enjoyment he received through naval service. He provides useful descriptions of many of the Navy's tactical aircraft from the 1940s to the 1960s in this volume. He also offers insights into factors such as leadership, maintenance, safety, and flying ability. The reader watches as Lee steadily acquires more experience and polish, making the transition from farm boy to successful naval officer.

The transcription of the interviews contained in this volume was done by Ms. Joanne Patmore of the oral history staff. Admiral Lee and I both did a considerable amount of editing to the verbatim transcript in the interests of accuracy, conciseness, and clarity. This version has his full blessing. Mrs. Lee has also been of considerable help in the editorial process from raw transcript to finished volume. Ms. Susan Sweeney of the oral history department did the detailed index for the volume.

                                             Paul Stillwell
                                             Director of Oral History
                                             U.S. Naval Institute
                                             January 1990

VICE ADMIRAL KENT LISTON LEE
UNITED STATES NAVY (RETIRED)

Kent Liston Lee was born in Florence County, South Carolina, on 28 July 1923, son of R. Irby and Hettie Floyd Lee. He enlisted in the U.S. Navy on 15 August 1940 and became an aviation cadet (V-5) on 12 November 1942, entering the flight training program on that date. Completing flight training at the Naval Air Station, Corpus Christi, Texas, he was designated naval aviator and commissioned ensign, USNR, on 7 August 1943. He was promoted to lieutenant (junior grade) to date from 1 November 1944, and on 8 July 1946 was appointed in that rank in the U.S. Navy. He subsequently advanced in rank to that of vice admiral, to date from 29 January 1972.

After receiving his wings in 1943, he had duty at the Naval Air Station, Jacksonville, Florida, and the Naval Auxiliary Air Station, Cecil Field, Florida, until March 1944. He then joined Bombing Squadron 100 and in June 1944 transferred to Bombing Squadron 15, operating off the USS Essex (CV-9). On 19 August 1944 he was assigned temporary additional duty, to fly with Fighting Squadron 15, but remained on the roster of Bombing Squadron 15. He was awarded the Air Medal for participating in numerous strikes against enemy positions and shipping at Marcus and Wake in the Marianas, the Bonins, Palau, and Philippine Islands during the period 19 May to 24 September 1944, and a gold star in lieu of the second Air Medal for destroying an enemy plane in the vicinity of Formosa on 12 October 1944. He is also entitled to the ribbon for, and a facsimile of the Presidential Unit Citation awarded the USS Essex.

Detached from Bombing Squadron 15 in December 1944, he next joined Bombing Squadron 151, and in September 1945 transferred to Bombing Squadron 17. In August 1946 he was assigned to Attack Squadron 5B. Undergraduate instruction with the Naval Reserve Officer Training Corps unit, Columbia University, New York, New York, August 1947 until May 1949, was followed by a year's instruction at the General Line School, Newport, Rhode Island.

In May 1950, he reported for duty on the staff of Commander Carrier Division 15, and "for meritorious service as Flag Lieutenant and Aide . . . during operations against the enemy in the Korean Theater from August 3, 1950 to January 15, 1951 . . ." was awarded the Navy Commendation Medal. In February 1951, he transferred to the staff of Commander Carrier Division 17. Assigned in May 1951 to Attack Squadron 115, based on board the USS Philippine Sea (CV-47), he was awarded a gold star in lieu of the third Air Medal for completing 20 missions against enemy aggressor forces in the Korean area of hostilities during the period 8 February to 2 June 1952. He is also entitled to the ribbon with bronze star for the Navy Unit Commendations awarded the USS Badoeng Strait (CVE-116) and the USS Sicily (CVE-118).

Detached from Attack Squadron 115 in June 1952, he was a student for two months at the Naval Schools Command, Treasure Island, San Francisco, California, then continued his studies at the U.S. Naval Postgraduate School, Monterey, California, from which he received the degree of master of science in physics in June 1954. Duty with Air Development Squadron Three until April 1956 was followed by an assignment for duty in the Weapons Section, Fleet Training Center, Norfolk, Virginia. In May 1958, he assumed command of Attack Squadron 46, and in September 1959 became technical aide nuclear physics, Power Branch, Material Sciences Division, Office of Naval Research, Navy Department, Washington, D.C.

During the period November 1960 until March 1962, he served as operational planner, Single Integrated Operational Plan Division, Joint Strategic Target Planning Staff, Offutt Air Force Base, Nebraska. After a brief tour of duty on the staff of Commander Carrier Air Group Four, he assumed command of Carrier Air Group Six in June 1962, embarked in the USS Enterprise (CVAN-65). In 1962, he ejected from an A4D Skyhawk while participating in operations during the Cuban quarantine. From March 1963 until March 1964 he had instruction in Nuclear Propulsion at the Atomic Energy Commission, Washington, D.C. He next commanded the USS Alamo (LSD-33) and in May 1965 reported as executive assistant and naval aide to the Assistant Secretary of the Navy (Research and Development).

In July 1967, he assumed command of the USS Enterprise (CVAN-65) and from 3 January to 26 June 1968 also served as Commander Task Unit 77.1. He was awarded the Legion of Merit for the ". . . detailed planning and execution of extensive and sustained combat air strikes against extremely hostile and heavily defended areas in North Vietnam . . ." He is entitled to a facsimile of the Navy Unit Commendation awarded the USS Enterprise and is entitled to a second star on his Navy Unit Commendation Ribbon.

In August 1969, he was assigned to the Bureau of Naval personnel, Navy Department, and in November of that year reported as Assistant Commander for Logistics and Fleet Support, Naval Air Systems Command, Washington, D.C. He became Director of the Office of Program Appraisal, Navy Department in August 1970, and in January 1972 assumed duty as Deputy Director of the Joint Strategic Target Planning

Staff, Offutt Air Force Base, Nebraska. "For exceptionally meritorious conduct . . ." in that assignment, he was awarded a gold star in lieu of the Second Legion of Merit. The citation continues in part:

> ". . . Responsible for exercising direct supervision over the activities of the Joint Strategic Target Planning Staff, Vice Admiral Lee was highly influential in the formation of policy and in giving direction to the policies established by the Joint Chiefs of Staff (JCS) and the Director, Strategic Target Planning, leading to and governing the development and maintenance of the JCS Single Integrated Operational Plan and the Coordinated Reconnaissance Plan . . ."

On 31 August 1973, he became Commander Naval Air Systems Command, Washington, D.C., and held that billet until relieved on 31 October 1976. He was officially placed on the retired list of the U.S. Navy on 1 November 1976.

He was also awarded the Distinguished Service Medal for duty as Commander Naval Air Systems Command on 31 October 1976. His other awards include the Legion of Merit with gold star, the Air Medal with two gold stars, the Navy Commendation Medal, the Presidential Unit Citation Ribbon, and the Navy Unit Commendation Ribbon with two bronze stars, Vice Admiral Lee has the American Defense Service Medal; American Campaign Medal; Asiatic-Pacific Campaign Medal; World War II Victory Medal; National Defense Service Medal with bronze star; Korean Service Medal; United Nations Service Medal; Vietnam Service Medal; and the Philippine Liberation Ribbon. He also has the National Order of Vietnam Fifth Class, the Gallantry Cross with Palm from the Republic of Vietnam, the Philippine Republic Presidential Unit Citation Badge, and the Korean Presidential Unit Citation Badge.

He is married to the former Mary Edith Buckley, of Piedmont, California, and they have three daughters, Nancy Carolyn Lee, Barbara Ann Lee Eisenson, and Marion Denny Lee Leonard.

Lee #1 - 1

Interview Number 1 with Vice Admiral Kent L. Lee,
U.S. Navy (Retired)

Place: Logon Farm, Admiral Lee's home near Gordonsville, Virginia

Date: Tuesday, 29 September 1987

Interviewer: Paul Stillwell

Q: Admiral, I had a pleasant drive through the rural Virginia countryside, and that leads to a first question. Are you descended from the famous Lees of Virginia?

Admiral Lee: No, I'm not. As a matter of fact, I've been asked that question many times. After I retired from the Navy in 1976, I got interested in just where the South Carolina Lees came from. My wife, at the time, was researching some of her forebears. I went over to the National Archives with her, where the records for the Census Bureau are kept. The first census in the United States was taken in 1790. And I followed the Lees of South Carolina--my family--back through the years looking at census reports every ten years to 1790.

My Lees had been in the same area, probably on the same land, from at least as early as 1790. I grew up in the Twenties and Thirties on this family farm. One of the interesting things for me was that my great-grandfather, who was a Lee, of course, made his mark on the census. This meant that he was illiterate, because census reports back in those days would list father, mother, all children, and ages. If the man could sign his name, he would sign. Otherwise, he'd make his mark. But just how long the Lees had farmed this particular piece of land before 1790, I never found out. I sort of dropped it at that point, because I then realized that the Lees didn't come down from North Carolina; that was folklore. Where they came from to settle in that area, I don't know. They were small yeoman farmers for generation after generation in South Carolina.

Q: Was your wife in any way inspired by Alex Haley and his Roots saga which came out at that time?*

Admiral Lee: No. My wife is very family-oriented. Her mother came from the Eastern Shore of Maryland. She was very interested in various parts of her family that came from the Eastern Shore. And just for fun I went over with her. It took several days, chasing back through the census reports, because the counties have changed through the years. But it's amazing how you can chase a family--chase is probably a better word than trace--down through the years through the census. You can see the children added,

---
*Alex Haley, Roots (Garden City, New York: Doubleday, 1976). Haley, a retired Coast Guard chief petty officer, traced his ancestry back to a slave ship that brought one of his forebears from Africa to Annapolis in the 18th century. In 1977 the story was shown as a television miniseries and spawned a great interest in genealogical research.

children dropped off. There were some names which appeared before the Civil War which never appeared again. And I suppose the Lees from down there were in both the Revolutionary War and the Civil War, but there are no records to show that.

I was born on July 28, 1923, on the family farm. This particular farm is 17 miles from Florence, the county seat, and about six miles from Coward, which is the nearest town and has the high school. My mother's uncle, Dr. L. C. Floyd, was the delivering physician. I was born in the farmhouse, which was the custom in those days. In my family there were six children--two boys and four girls-- and I was number three. When I was born, my brother was four, and my older sister was two.

We lived on what was called in those days a two-horse farm, which meant that we worked it with two animals--two horses or two mules, or one of each. Cotton and tobacco were the main crops, and other than those, we grew corn, hay, soybeans, and food crops. We had a milk cow, hogs, chickens, turkeys, and, of course, grew all the vegetables that we ate. We had peach trees, apple trees, and the like.

Since both cotton and tobacco were labor-intensive, we always had one sharecropper. The sharecropper and his family and our family worked the farm together. We would normally have about six acres of tobacco, and 10 to 12 acres of cotton. Both of the money crops were picked by hand.

Q: Was there a town nearby where you purchased things that you couldn't produce yourselves?

Admiral Lee: The market town for the area was Lake City, about nine or ten miles away. It had a bank--later on, two banks. It's where the tobacco was sold, where the cotton was sold, and where most of the provisions were bought. But back in those days, farmers really didn't buy many provisions.

The Twenties and Thirties were tough years on the farms. And besides that, the South had been treated by the North as more or less a colonial possession for many years after the Civil War. So the South really hadn't fully recovered. It was a very poor area: not much money, no electricity. We didn't have an automobile until '37 or '38. No telephones, no paved roads. About the only thing I can say about it is that we never lacked for food, because the land was fertile.

My father got as far as the eighth grade, then dropped out of school. He was not a good manager and not too energetic. He was very content to run a subsistence farm. My mother was a high school graduate, which in that part of the world at that time was not remarkable but unusual. And she was very intelligent, ambitious for her children, and with tremendous energy. She really was the family manager.

For the first and third grades, I attended a small two-room, two-teacher school called Salem. We walked to school, about two and a half miles through the woods, since it was closer to go through the woods than around by the dirt road. For the second, fourth through eleventh grades I went to Coward High School and rode a school bus.

In those days rural school districts were small, mostly two-teacher schools within walking distance of students. We were on the edge of a third district, Pleasant Grove. My mother refused to send her children to Pleasant Grove. She had us transferred to Salem. She then worked for several years to have the Salem and Pleasant Grove districts incorporated into the Coward District. In the summer of 1932 she succeeded. Hence, we were bussed to Coward, a first through eleventh grade consolidated school. Bless my mother. We are all greatly indebted to her.

As was typical in the South in those days, there were schools for the whites--not very good but schools--and then in the later years, in the Twenties and Thirties, there were school buses. But for the blacks all around us, the sharecroppers, there were no school buses and no schools. The blacks had no opportunity, by and large, to learn to read and write. My grandfather, who had 12 to 15 black families on his farm, did build a two-teacher school for his blacks in the Twenties. But that was an exception.

Q: How much contact did you have with black contemporaries when you were growing up?

Admiral Lee: In Florence County I don't know the exact numbers, but I daresay we had about 40% blacks and 60% whites. We grew up with them; we played with them; we saw them every day on the farms, in town. We knew them as friends. Black and white children played together, which was normal, every day. They were just playmates, and later on we worked with them in the fields. But there was that line of separation. They didn't go to school, and we didn't go to church with them. It was a very harsh world for the blacks.

Q: Did you reflect on that at the time, or is that more through the lens of hindsight?

Admiral Lee: I daresay it's more through the lens of hindsight than otherwise. It seemed normal at the time; it was part of the culture. But as I look back on it, I can see how very unfair it was. But that aside, throughout the South and especially in our part of the country, there wasn't much for anybody. And whatever there was, the whites usually managed to latch on to it one way or

Lee #1 - 7

another. The blacks, by and large, were relegated to the farmhand role.

Q: There were still some Civil War veterans around at that time. Was there a legacy of bitterness in the area where you lived?

Admiral Lee: There was never a legacy of bitterness between blacks and whites where I lived. I would say it was more paternalism, that the white farmers and landowners looked after and took care of their blacks. I never detected any bitterness on either side. I'd say it was a very good relationship by and large.

Q: An accepted way of life on both sides.

Admiral Lee: An accepted way of life on both sides is a good way to put it. There were some Civil War veterans, of course. My great-grandfather Floyd on my mother's side was a Civil War veteran. But the only bitterness that was around when I was growing up was bitterness towards the North and the Yankees. And that was prevalent; that was common. I had a schoolteacher in the seventh grade, and one day we started singing, for one reason or another,

"John Brown's Body" in school.* He got up and walked out. But that was the South in the Twenties and Thirties: great bitterness about the Civil War.

Q: How much part did religion play in your family's life?

Admiral Lee: My mother was very religious, Southern Baptist, as just about everybody was. I'd say the best people in the South were Southern Baptists and Methodists. The rednecks and lower classes were the fundamentalists. The blacks had their own churches, essentially Protestant Fundamentalists.

Religion was always very important in the South. The churches were social centers. It's where the boys and girls met. It's where the parties were organized, the church socials. The churches were the center of activities for the rural South. My father was never very religious, although he got very religious in his 60s and 70s. But when I was growing up, he was not too much of a churchgoer. He would go once in a while. But for my mother, church was very important.

---

*John Brown (1800-1859) was a fanatic who was obsessed with the idea of abolishing slavery by force. In October 1859 he and his supporters seized the federal arsenal at Harpers Ferry, Virginia (now West Virginia), intending this as a signal for a general insurrection on the part of slaves. He was captured, convicted of treason, and hanged. Northern sympathizers regarded him as a martyr and commemorated him with the song "John Brown's Body."

Lee #1 - 9

Q: How early did you get out into the fields?

Admiral Lee: I daresay the average youngster starts working on the farm as soon as he can move around--five or six years old--depending on what the task is. We gradually worked into the more difficult jobs and chores. We always worked on the farms after school. We would get home about 1:00 or 1:30 in the afternoon and work on the farm, also work on Saturdays. The smaller children would be assigned chores which they would do every day, such as feeding the chickens, or separating good leaves of tobacco from bad leaves. And then as the children grew older, they were expected to do more difficult things, more tiring things. But I daresay it's standard in most farm families, the children start right out on the day they can understand and walk and talk, helping on the farm. It's a way of life. And it's not bad. It's good. Farm children learn discipline early on.

Q: Parents nowadays try to impart a work ethic for their children. That was no problem in the period you're describing.

Admiral Lee: It was part of growing up. In comments on the farm and farm life, I didn't realize how poor we were. I had no sense of being deprived, primarily because our family was about as well off as other families. There weren't any wealthy people around. It wasn't that one family had electricity and automobiles, and another did not.

In a family such as ours, there's always a division of labor. I was the farm mechanic and carpenter. My father wasn't a very good mechanic, nor a carpenter, nor was my brother. So I kept barns repaired, and built things, and kept the machinery in running order. We built our toys, of course, and we had lots of recreation. A river flowed through the countryside about one and a half miles away. We went to the river swimming in the summertime, two or three times a week in the late afternoons. We'd have fishing parties at night, and rice and fish stews on the banks and spend the night on the river. So we had lots of recreation.

When I was about 12 years old, I went to the Florence County Fair and saw a Ferris wheel. I decided that we could build a Ferris wheel on the farm. And so I did. We built a Ferris wheel, a two-seater, all from farm materials, things that could be picked up around the farm such as axles from farm vehicles and two-by-sixes and two-by-fours and so forth. The midpoint of this Ferris wheel was about 12 feet high, and the top seat would swing up to about 16 or 18 feet. It was a great center of entertainment for local youngsters. It was turned by hand. But every once in a while, some youngster would go home with a bruised arm or a bruised hand, or worse. When the child's mother found out about the Ferris wheel, that youngster wasn't allowed to come over and play anymore.

But, anyway, I would say that by and large these farm years were happy years. Lots of big families in the countryside in those days. We had six children. The family on the next farm had 11 children. There was never a shortage of playmates. And there was always enough work. If there was a problem, it was money. There was never any hard cash. Buying necessities, such as shoes and clothes, was always very difficult, and especially with big families.

One of the high points in my early life came in the summer of 1938 or '39. The local paper announced that a Ford Trimotor airplane would be at the fairgrounds for a day, using super XX gasoline.* Rides were 60 cents. I persuaded my father that at least we ought to see it. We had never seen an airplane on the ground. He agreed. I was a frugal boy, and had just enough change to afford a ride.

At the fairgrounds, after watching the Trimotor take

---

*In the late 1920s and early 1930s, the airplane division of the Ford Motor Company built two versions of this monoplane airliner, one for 11 passengers and one for 14. The plane had a corrugated metal skin, one engine on the front of the fuselage, and one engine under each wing.

off and land two or three times, I told my father I was going for a ride. He was taken aback, but didn't say no. I handed over my hard-earned 60 cents and climbed aboard. There were about a dozen passengers. The takeoff run was short and bumpy; the noise was absolutely deafening. The Trimotor took off, circled Florence, and landed, about ten minutes and 500 feet. I was thrilled. The noise, the power, the exhilaration. I was also hooked. I wanted another ride but lacked the 60 cents. Never mind, some day I would fly my own!

I graduated from high school in June of 1940 and had maybe a B, B-plus average. I looked up my grades not long ago just to see what I'd done. I was probably in the upper 25% of the class. There were only 17 in the graduating class. There were just 11 grades. We had started with 55 in the eighth grade, and 17 graduated. We were also working on the farms, and very few of us did much homework. Scholars were not overly popular in the rural South. Good ol' boys were.

Thus far I have not mentioned girls and dating. The countryside was filled with attractive young farm girls, at school, at church, and on neighboring farms. As was the custom in rural America, girls tended to marry quite young. Many of the dropouts got married. I did have a girl I dated and corresponded with from about 1936 until 1944. She was an attractive young lass from Coward, one year behind me, who went on to Winthrop College after graduation. She gave up on me in 1945 and married a telephone man. These Navy men!

Q: Did it make a difference that your mother had the education and the ambition for her children?

Admiral Lee: I think it made a tremendous difference. It made all the difference, because she insisted that we all go to high school. She insisted, as much as she could, that we do our homework and do well. She was tremendously ambitious for her children. I really wanted to go to college, but, as I say, there just weren't the dollars. Also, there were no prospects, because at the age of 17, jobs were just about impossible to come by.

My older brother had joined the Navy in 1939 after one year at Clemson College, so I decided to enlist. I say sometimes that one of the reasons I joined the Navy was that I was a failure picking cotton by hand. About the best I could do was 75 pounds a day. A good cotton picker could tool along the rows and turn out 200-250 pounds a day.

I immediately ran into a problem when I tried to follow my brother's example. The Navy had a minority enlistment program up until sometime in 1940.* It was canceled with the onset of World War II and the desire for longer enlistments. I turned 17 on July 28, 1940, and the Navy was apparently closed to me for another year. I wasn't fully grown at the time. I was five feet, nine inches tall and 133 pounds--just a boy. But I claimed I was 18, namely that I was born on July 28, 1922, and so enlisted for six years in the Navy on August 15, 1940. The Navy seemed happy enough about that.

Q: One other thing I'm curious about from those years is how much awareness you had of the developing world events, both the impact of the Depression in this country and the dictatorships growing overseas.

Admiral Lee: Quite aware. We got a battery-powered radio in 1939. We took a daily newspaper starting about 1935, and I was a great reader, always. I was totally aware of what was happening in Europe--that Hitler seemed about to overrun all of Europe. I was well aware that the Navy was being expanded. I was also aware that very likely we would get into the war.** We were not living in a vacuum down

---

*Under a minority program, an individual enlists shortly before his 18th birthday and is released from the service just before he turns 21. Thus he completes his military duty while still a minor.
**World War II began in Europe in September 1939.

there. From my experience then and now, I daresay farmers follow world events much more closely than city people. They'd discuss it in the churches. They'd discuss it at the markets. Politics and discussion are a big part of rural life.

Q: Was there anything beyond your brother's example that led you to the Navy?

Admiral Lee: Yes. No local jobs for a 17-year-old. It was about the best thing I could do at the moment because I had no other good prospects. At age 17 I didn't want to become a sharecropper or stay on the farm. My plan was to enlist in the Navy, save my money, get out, and go to college. So I joined the Navy. I was given a physical examination in Raleigh, North Carolina, on 15 August 1940, immediately sworn in, and sent by train to Norfolk--my first train ride.

At Norfolk, I was taken to the Naval Training Station. Boot camp training was a major part of the Norfolk Naval Operating Base (NOB) in 1940. There was a huge drill hall (since torn down), about a dozen two-story brick barracks, and, of course, a parade field. This was all between the administration building (still there) and the main gate. Also, of course, a mess hall.

I was assigned to Platoon 107. Our platoon commander

was Chief Gunner's Mate Ray C. Burkett. Burkett was short (about five feet, three inches), wiry, tough, and hardbitten. He was also intelligent and hardworking. He made chief in less than 14 years in the old Navy (prior to World War II). As a matter of fact, he later became a lieutenant commander during World War II.

When I talk about Burkett, I'm reminded of a story about Secretary of the Navy Chafee. Chafee went through Marine Corps boot camp.* On a trip to San Diego as secretary, a Marine aide approached him and said, "Mr. Secretary, your DI is retired and living in the San Diego area.** Would you like to have lunch with him?"

Mr. Chafee said, "No, I guess not. I was not all that fond of the bastard." That's sort of the way I felt about Burkett.

Boot camp was a cultural shock. All Southerners are born with good manners. Politeness and courtesy are part of the culture. Boot camp was a different world. First, our heads were shaved. Then we were given a seabag of ill-fitting clothes, a series of shots, assigned a barracks, and turned over to the tender mercies of Chief Gunner's

---

*John H. Chafee served as Secretary of the Navy from 31 January 1969 to 4 April 1972. Chafee enlisted in the Marine Corps at age 19 and in February 1942 began boot training at Parris Island, South Carolina.
**DI--drill instructor, a senior Marine enlisted man who had frequent, often unpleasant, contact with the recruits he was training.

Mate Burkett. Also, we were placed in quarantine for two weeks.

Burkett issued us an old Springfield rifle, demonstrated how we were to dress, stow our lockers, and make our bunks. Then the training began. A typical day was reveille at 5:30 A.M. (0530), breakfast at 0630. At 0730 the day of drills, classes, and tests began. Burkett used The Bluejackets' Manual as a text.* We were each issued a copy.

For those few who were averse to lessons in personal hygiene, Burkett put a recruit and his entire seabag in the showers. For minor infractions of rules, we marched several hours with rifles. For more serious offenses, recruits were required to run with rifles held overhead.

Burkett had pet names for most of us. Mine was Dopey Sue. Burkett taught and drilled, drilled and taught. I marveled at his energy.

Before the nine weeks of boot camp were over, I had about decided the Navy was not for me. But even so, I survived Burkett and boot camp.

In each platoon the recruits that scored top grades on the battery of tests given by the Navy were sent to the class A schools--aviation machinist's mate school, electrician's mate school, bakers' school--depending on

---

*Published in a number of editions since the turn of the century, The Bluejackets' Manual is the basic handbook for enlisted personnel on a wide variety of naval topics.

their preference. I did well on the tests, so I was sent to the aviation machinist's mate school at Naval Air Station Norfolk, and this was for four months. The first two months we had academics all day long, and the last two months we worked for half a day in the overhaul and repair shops.

The Navy was just getting started with the A schools.* We didn't have adequate textbooks. I think the instructors we had were men who were failures as mechanics. We didn't have training aids. I think it was a very marginal school. Later on, especially during World War II, those A schools were developed into some of the most progressive and finest schools in the world, with marvelous training aids, first-class instructors.

Q: You mentioned the role of the test scores. Was your going into that specific rating a matter of choice?

Admiral Lee: Yes. One of the reasons I joined the Navy was to get into aviation. It was the only thing I applied for: aviation machinist's mate school. There were 65 recruits in our platoon, and of that number, about 20 went

---
*In the hierarchy of Navy schools, the A school provided the initial training in a specific enlisted rating. Following completion of A school, an individual had sufficient professional training to become a petty officer third class. Later in an individual's career, he might get more advanced training in B and C schools.

Lee #1 - 19

to the A schools. The other 40 were sent to various ships as seamen.

Q: What was the method of instruction in the school, given the drawbacks that you've cited?

Admiral Lee: We had an aviation machinist's mate second class as an instructor. Our text was a 1940-type book that was used to study for third class aviation machinist's mate. We would read through that book, chapter by chapter, and would be asked questions on it.

Q: Was there much practical experience with it?

Admiral Lee: None. We had no practical experience except in the last two months. We went down to the overhaul and repair shops for a half day. We were rotated there. But even that wasn't very satisfactory. We were assigned as helpers to civilian mechanics. For one two-week period I sanded the top of a PB2Y wing and for two weeks I worked in the engine overhaul shop.*

Q: Had you developed, once you got into a specific rating, more of a feeling for the Navy, that you would like it

---

*The PB2Y was a four-engine flying boat manufactured by Consolidated; it was a later model than the well-known PBY patrol bomber.

after all?

Admiral Lee: Yes. In March 1941 I graduated from aviation machinist's mate school and was sent to Naval Air Station Miami, Florida, which provided advanced training for aviation cadets. We had carrier squadron airplanes--the obsolete types--F3F fighters, BT dive-bombers, F4Bs, SBCs, F2As.* Aviation cadets were trained there for about three months, completing their flight training, and were commissioned.

I was put into the maintenance division. For the first year I was there, I was in a rigging check crew which nowadays we would call airframes. Airplanes were brought in for maintenance after 30 hours of flight time, 60 hours of flight time, 120 hours of flight time. I joined one of the check crews in airframes initially.

At Miami I discovered what the Navy could really be like. Miami was a first-rate naval air station. The commanding officer was Gerald F. Bogan, who later became a vice admiral, and World War II carrier admiral.** The executive officer was Commander A. O. Rule, and my division officer was Lieutenant W. S. Butts, USN, who later also

---
*The F3F was Grumman's last biplane fighter for the Navy; the Northrop BT was a monoplane scout/dive-bomber; the F4B was a Boeing biplane fighter; the Curtiss SBC Helldiver was a dive-bomber, the last combat biplane produced in America; the F2A Brewster Buffalo was a monoplane fighter.
**Captain Gerald F. Bogan, USN. Bogan's oral history is in the Naval Institute collection.

became a rear admiral.*

Q: Did you have any personal contact with Bogan?

Admiral Lee: Never any personal contact with Admiral Bogan until I became captain of Enterprise, and he sailed with us from San Diego to Hawaii in 1968. I talked to him about Miami. It was a very well-organized, very well-run station. Bogan and Pirie were interested in flying cadets as much as possible and keeping the airplanes in good condition.** Having been the farm mechanic and handyman for so many years, I fitted right in.

Not only that, but we had some absolutely first-rate chief petty officers. I've never seen better. I still remember some of the names. My first boss was a fellow by the name of N. M. Ruth, who was a chief aviation machinist's mate. Others were Chief Petty Officers Harry Dabb, William Bottenhorn, and Harry Crawford. Most of these chiefs became warrant officers and temporary officers during World War II. Those prewar chief petty officers really carried the maintenance load in naval aviation during the war. Without them, we would have had a much more difficult time during World War II. They were good

---
*Commander Adrian O. Rule, Jr., USN; Lieutenant Whitmore S. Butts, USN.
**Lieutenant Commander Robert B. Pirie, USN. Pirie retired as a vice admiral; his oral history is in the Naval Institute collection.

leaders, they were good mechanics, and they were good people.

I was at Miami from March 1941 until October 1942, which is something over 18 months. Happiness is a very difficult thing to measure. But I would say it was one of the happiest periods of my naval career, this time as a mechanic. We had good people. There was enough work to go around, because we went to a seven-day flying schedule towards the end of 1941. We put in a lot of hours, but it was good work.

Q: What specific things did you do?

Admiral Lee: The first year I was there, I worked on airframe check crews--typical example, an SBC or an F3F would come in for a 30-hour check. We did the maintenance checks and repairs. After a few months I was given a check crew of my own. Many of the control surfaces in those days--and the fuselages in some airplanes--were made of fabric. We used a baseball stitch to repair tears.* We replaced control surfaces, control cables, did riggings-- many of the planes were biplanes. There were cables which held the wings in proper position. Adjusting these cables was called rigging. We replaced landing gears and brakes

---

*When a baseball is manufactured, two pieces of horsehide are sewn together with a pattern of V-shaped stitches that produce a continuous seam where the edges meet.

and tires. We did the work which kept the airframe in good and flyable condition.

After about a year on the airframe crews, I moved over, at my request, to an engine check crew. A good mechanic needs to know both airframes and engines. When I had an engine check crew, we did all the maintenance on engines. An airplane would go out on a flight, and the pilot would come back and say, "The right wing tends to droop," or "The right brake doesn't hold," or whatever. We would do the troubleshooting and repairing. Engines, the same sort of thing.

We'd do the routine checks. We'd change spark plugs every 60 hours, for instance, and check the timing, check the carburetor, and check the propeller. We changed propellers periodically. If the compression was low on a given cylinder in those big radial engines, we changed the cylinder. There was a tremendous amount of work to do. It was interesting work. We had good tools, and good equipment, and good manuals to learn how to do things.

Admiral Bogan was never a spit-and-polish type, nor was Lieutenant Butts. They expected you to do your job. They didn't worry too much about your haircut. And they didn't worry too much about your dungarees. But they worried about the maintenance you were doing, repair work and so forth. And, of course, that sort of attitude came down through all the troops working on the hangar deck. It

Lee #1 - 24

was very important work, and I think we did a good job.

Q: I've talked to Rear Admiral Jackson Parker, who was a shipboard machinist's mate at that same time.* He said that the chief petty officers did not have a very deeply grounded theoretical knowledge of what made a ship's engineering plant work. But they had superb practical experience so that they could operate it well, maintain it well, and repair it well. Would that characterize the chiefs you encountered?

Admiral Lee: Yes, very much so. None of them were more than high school graduates. So they had very little theoretical knowledge, but they had great practical knowledge. As an example, I daresay there are any number of aeronautical engineers who couldn't troubleshoot a problem with a 1535 radial engine, whereas, one of these chiefs who'd been troubleshooting this engine for ten years could listen to it on the flight line and immediately tell you what the problem was and how to fix it.**

Q: Did these chiefs also have the sea daddy role for you--bringing you up in the ways of the Navy?

---
*The oral history of Rear Admiral Jackson K. Parker, USN (Ret.), is in the Naval Institute collection.
**Various models of the Pratt & Whitney R-1535 engine were used in a number of U.S. Navy planes of the 1930s and 1940s. The cylinders were arranged radially, like the spokes of a wheel, around the circumference of the engine.

Admiral Lee: No, very little of that in aviation. We worked very hard at Miami because of the workload. We were working six days a week, had one day off. And that day off wasn't necessarily Sunday, because we were operating seven days a week. I think the sea daddy role was more appropriate aboard ship than at a naval air station.

Of course, Lieutenant Butts and the chiefs looked after their good people. I think this happens throughout the Navy. A typical example, all seamen--nowadays they're called airmen--have to take their turn mess cooking for three months. But in our division the youngsters who were good mechanics never went mess cooking.

I think it's very interesting to look at promotions back in those days. I enlisted in the Navy on August 15, 1940, and was an apprentice seaman for four months, and then was automatically promoted to seaman second. As an apprentice seaman, I got $21.00 per month. As a seaman second, I got $36.00 per month. I took an examination and was promoted to seaman first on April 1, 1941, and I got $54.00 a month. Then another examination, and on September 1, 1941, I was promoted to aviation machinist's mate third class, after roughly one year in the Navy. Third class got $60.00 a month. On July 1, 1942, I was promoted to aviation machinist's mate second class at $72.00 per month.

Lee #1 - 26

Those people who were in the check crews and good performers also got flight pay, another sea daddy bit. But I think from the time I was a seaman first, I always got flight pay. Flight pay in those days was 50% of your base pay. We had to fly four hours a month with the aviation cadets in whatever they were flying. So that made my pay $81.00 for seaman first; $90.00 for third class; $108.00 for second class. I thought I was a rich.

Q: Again, it's relative.

Admiral Lee: Yes.

Q: There was a romance and mystique associated with aviation, and it wasn't nearly so commonplace as now. Did that play a part in your enjoyment of what you were doing?

Admiral Lee: Yes, I would say so. And what I wanted to do more than anything else was to go to flight training. I planned to go one way or another. The Navy had an enlisted flight training program at the time, but I didn't have enough time in the service to apply for it. I had that in mind. But I looked at these aviation cadets as they came through Miami and talked to several of them. I decided they didn't have a lot more to offer than I had, and that I could do it, too. What I really wanted to do was fly one of those airplanes I was working on.

But I would say that Naval Air Station Miami was a happy time. Miami was a very interesting town--Miami and Miami Beach. I bought an automobile, a 1936 Chevrolet, for $250.00. It was a good automobile. We met a lot of nice girls and other people around Miami and were made very welcome. We went to the beaches, had picnics, saw movies, went roller skating, all the things young people did. We also were invited on fishing trips by local people who had boats. We also went to local bars and dance halls. At 17 and 18, I was never carded. There was enough action for everyone.

In the summer of 1942--I don't remember the exact date--the Navy reduced requirements for aviation cadets from two years college to high school graduates. Then in August of 1942, the aviation cadet selection board from, I think, the Jacksonville district, came down to Miami. A number of us took the battery of tests and a physical exam, and we applied for aviation cadet training.

At about the same time, the Navy started an internal program of selecting qualified enlisted men for the aviation cadet program from all ships and stations. The aviation cadet selection board from Jacksonville then confined its efforts to the civilian area. The Jacksonville board required references, transcripts, much paperwork. The internal Navy program was run by each command. Very little paperwork was required. We applied, were recommended by our chiefs, were interviewed by our division officers, and that was it. The flight physical that I had taken for the Atlanta board was used for the internal program. A number of us then applied for the naval aviation cadet program at Miami.

Eventually about 20 became aviation cadets. It was a happy day when I was told that I'd gotten one of the spots. A friend of mine by the name of Spence Matthews, aviation machinist's mate third class, got the first spot and was sent to St. Mary's College preflight school to begin training in late October 1942.* Another friend by the name of H. M. Reid, aviation structural mechanic third class, and I got the number two and three spots. We were to begin aviation cadet training on November 12, 1942, at St. Mary's College.**

Q: Had you considered going to the Naval Academy at all as an option?

Admiral Lee: Yes, I had, as a matter of fact. The Navy had a program at the time for enlisted to enter Annapolis. When I was in boot camp, I talked to Chief Burkett, the platoon commander, about this. He wasn't too enthusiastic,

---
*Herbert Spencer Matthews eventually retired from the Navy in the early 1970s as a rear admiral. He has been interviewed as part of the Naval Institute's oral history program.
**St. Mary's College, Moraga, California.

but he sent me over to see a lieutenant in the training command headquarters. The lieutenant asked me how much math I had had. I answered two years of algebra in high school and one year of plane geometry. He asked me if I'd had quadratic equations. I said I didn't remember.

He said, "Well, the Naval Academy is about 90% math. Maybe you just ought to go to aviation machinist's mate school." They had a special program for people who qualified for the Naval Academy. They were sent to sea on battleships, tutored, and then sent back to the prep school. He didn't think I had the academic background, so he sent me to the aviation machinist's mate school instead, which was probably just as well.

Do you remember what quadratic equations are?

Q: I don't know about those either.

Admiral Lee: Equations with variables of the second order, i.e., X^2. I had forgotten, too. If I had explained quadratic equations at that time, I might have had a very different career but I don't think a more enjoyable one.

At any rate, in late October 1942, I sold my automobile. H. M. Reid also had an automobile, so he and I drove his vehicle from Miami to Oakland, California, and stopped along the way to see the Grand Canyon and other great sights. I must confess--I just couldn't wait to get started at preflight school. I checked in on 11 November, and on 12 November, I was discharged from the U.S. Navy as an aviation machinist's mate second class and reenlisted as a V-5 aviation cadet.*

I was them 19 years old, six feet tall, and weighed about 160 pounds. So, you see, I had really grown up from my five-nine and 133 pounds. I also had a great inferiority complex. I was in battalion 12; every two weeks a battalion was formed of about 250 young men. Many of them were from the upper Midwest, and almost all except Reid and I were college men. The high school graduates hadn't yet gotten as far in the pipeline as preflight school. There were a few, but not many. In my battalion, there were about ten ex-enlisted men out of about 250--two from Naval Air Station Miami. I was very worried. I thought, "Well, this is my great chance, and I'll really give it a college try."

Preflight schools were started in about June-July of 1942. It was the boot camp for naval aviation, with an accent on conditioning. In preflight schools, cadets spent a half day in athletics and a half day on academics. In athletics we had football, boxing, swimming, basketball, track, and the obstacle course. In academics were Navy

---
*One of several Naval Reserve training programs during World War II, V-5 involved aviation and produced Naval Reserve ensigns and Marine Corps Reserve second lieutenants.

regs, principles of flight, physics, algebra, and subjects such as recognition, that would get an aviation cadet ready to enter primary training.

Then in addition, there was the military part of it, the Springfield rifle close-order drill, the firing range, inspections, i.e., boot camp. And if you've seen <u>An Officer and a Gentleman</u>, that's preflight school.*

Q: Was it as harsh as that movie depicts?

Admiral Lee: No. I enjoyed every minute of it. We were graded on academics, and that was an objective grade. The military grade was one given by the platoon leader: close-order drill, inspections, and all the 1,001 things that have to do with military--your "grease mark," in other words, as they say at the Naval Academy.

We were also graded in athletics. By that time they'd had enough people go through the training that they knew what an average man ought to do in a 100-yard dash or the obstacle course, and so forth. If you hit the average, you got a 2.9. I had no trouble with athletics. And I found out that I didn't have too many problems with the military part, because I'd been through Burkett's boot camp.

---

*The film <u>An Officer and a Gentleman</u> was released by Paramount Pictures in 1982. It depicted the training program at Naval Aviation Officer Candidate School. Richard Gere starred as an officer candidate, Debra Winger as his girlfriend, and Louis Gossett, Jr., as a tough, shrewd Marine Corps drill instructor.

Lee #1 - 32

Q: And you were a second class petty officer.

Admiral Lee: I had been a second class petty officer, so I didn't have any trouble with the military--any part of it. And not only that, my platoon leader was a fellow by the name of Lieutenant Jorgensen, USNR. He was a St. Mary's College graduate and football player, had played professional football as a tackle.* He was one of these great big guys, about six-four, 220 pounds, a nice gentle giant. You've seen the type. And, of course, everybody loved him. He was a genuinely nice guy. He thought his platoon could do no wrong. We worked hard for him.

The academics I didn't find half as difficult as I had imagined. I worked at it. I wasn't going to fail. And the athletics, I never had so much fun. We didn't have much in the way of athletics in the high school where I grew up: a little baseball, a little basketball. Also we had a number of youngsters who couldn't get over the obstacle course. You'd be surprised at how poorly conditioned some were. For them it was very tough.

I had the shock of my life at the end of the course. At graduation I came in number one in the battalion, which I never even dreamed of. I was number one in academics at 3.65 and had a 3.43 overall average. I don't know what I

---

*Lieutenant (junior grade) Carl Jorgensen, USNR; tackle for the 1934 Green Bay Packers and 1935 Philadelphia Eagles.

Lee #1 - 33

had in military and athletics, but I did fairly well. So for the first time in my life that I came in number one in something. I kind of liked it.

Q: You were living up to your mother's expectations.

Admiral Lee: Yes.

There was another event which you might find interesting. St. Mary's College is in the Moraga Valley, which is a beautiful valley east of Oakland. After the first month, we got one day a week off and were bussed in to the trains and had liberty. We could go to San Francisco or Oakland, wherever. We had no discipline problem. In our platoon we had a good group. Also Jorgensen would have been very, very hurt if we had gotten into trouble.

On Saturday, December 26, 1942, I went to the Leamington Hotel officers' club, right in downtown Oakland. Many of the young ladies from the Oakland area came out to entertain the aviation cadets on weekends. On this particular Saturday, December 26, 1942, I met a young lady whose name was Mary Edith Buckley. She was 18 years old, a freshman at Wellesley College in Boston, Massachusetts, and home for Christmas. She lived in Piedmont, which is a residential area up above Oakland, beautiful homes, that kind of place. To make a long story short, I saw her a number of times during the holidays, and six years later, almost to the day, I married her. And we have been married for these 40 years.

Q: Quite a contrast in backgrounds.

Admiral Lee: Wasn't it?

Q: All this was quite foreign to the experience of your parents. Did you keep them up to date on your progress as you went along?

Admiral Lee: Oh, yes. You know, one of the things that I've tried to tell my children is, "Never forget your roots. They're important." They had a saying for this down South, "Never get above your raising." But, oh yes, my mother was very pleased and very proud of my progress thus far. But, anyway, when I met this young lady, marriage was far from my mind. And I lost contact with her for several years, but we got back together again when I was at Columbia after she had graduated from Wellesley. But there was a dramatic contrast in backgrounds in 1942.

Q: What was the next step then after you wound up number one at St. Mary's?

Admiral Lee: You were given a choice on your next assignment, depending on your rank in the class at graduation from preflight school, within the choices available, of course. And those choices had to do with becoming a navigator or an aviator, and what primary base you would like to go to. And since I was pretty high up on the list, I chose Los Alamitos, which was a naval air station primary training base just outside Long Beach. I reported to Los Alamitos the first week in February. I was in class 2-A. Classes were designated by month number and letter. I was in the first February class.

Q: Were you commissioned at that point?

Admiral Lee: No. I was an aviation cadet until completing flight training. Nowadays I think they commission them on graduation from preflight school. But in those days we had to complete flight training and then were commissioned. So I went to Los Alamitos as an aviation cadet. Los Alamitos was not very different from preflight school in terms of the daily schedule. We had a half day of ground school and a half day of flying. We flew the standard N2S Yellow Peril.*

---

*The Stearman N2S Kaydet was a biplane trainer that got its nickname from the standard yellow paint scheme. It had a maximum speed of 124 miles per hour at sea level, service ceiling of 11,200 feet, and a range of 505 statute miles.

I was assigned an instructor by the name of Lieutenant McLaughlin, USNR. After about ten dual flights, he gave me an upcheck for a solo flight. But then I got my first setback. We had to get two upchecks. The next day I went up for my second upcheck with an instructor by the name of Ensign Cox, USNR, and got a down. The following day I tried again and got an up. And the next day, which was about the middle of February, I soloed in an N2S. Southern California was a new experience for me--the orchards, the sunshine, the beautiful countryside, Long Beach. We had school for a half day and flying for a half day. I thought I was in heaven.

Q: Was flying something that you adapted to pretty readily?

Admiral Lee: Well, I had flown at Miami. I'd flown in the back seats of various types of aircraft for perhaps 100 hours and gone dive-bombing and formation flying with cadets. So flying itself was nothing new, the experience of going up in an airplane. Having the controls was new, of course, but I didn't seem to have any trouble learning to handle the airplane. And I remember I couldn't wait to get out to that airplane every morning. I would always get there 15-20 minutes early. If I did that, I could always get started before the scheduled time. Also I could land about 10 minutes late and thus get in a few extra minutes of flight time, and a few more landings, or a few more practices in whatever we were doing.

The primary training took place at Los Alamitos and lasted roughly three months--February, March, and April. I got roughly 100 hours of flight time in the N2S, or Yellow Peril, which all flight training students flew in those days.

Q: Some pilots particularly revel in the exhilaration of flying. Did you find yourself in that category?

Admiral Lee: Yes, I thoroughly enjoyed flying. I thoroughly enjoyed maneuvering the airplane; I thoroughly enjoyed every aspect of it--taking off, landing, acrobatics.

Q: I guess you'd gotten over your inferiority complex by then.

Admiral Lee: Yes, as I said a moment ago, I thought I was in heaven. You know, I would have paid to do this.

Q: How much attrition was there along the way--both in preflight and in flight training itself?

Admiral Lee: I don't know. I rather think it was fairly high, but I never saw any numbers. Training time and flight time were not wasted on those who did not do well. There was no shortage of people. If a cadet got two downs, he was looked at, his progress reviewed. Cadets in preflight school failed because of athletics or academics or military. My friend H. M. Reid didn't make it through; I don't know why. I had another friend from Miami who didn't make it through either. I never saw any numbers on what the attrition was.

Q: Well, not only that, but they were probably saving lives that would otherwise have been lost.

Admiral Lee: Yes. Yes. So not too much time was wasted on an individual who was having trouble. I had no problems in either the flying or the ground school. I think the only memorable event was that Admiral Byrd, the polar explorer, came in one day, and he gave me a few choice words for flying through a cloud.* He'd been out flying in an N2S, and he met me on the ground and very strongly disapproved of what I had been doing. And that was my only experience with Admiral Byrd.

---

*Rear Admiral Richard E. Byrd, Jr., USN (Ret.). In 1926, as a lieutenant commander, Byrd had flown over the North Pole with Chief Machinist's Mate Floyd Bennett, the first time the feat had been accomplished. In 1929 Byrd and three companions became the first men to fly over the South Pole. He commanded several expeditions to Antarctica.

Q: What did he disapprove of?

Admiral Lee: My flying through clouds. I had not yet learned to fly on instruments; we were taught that later on.

Q: So you were still pretty much in the basics as far as airmanship.

Admiral Lee: All basics--dead engine landings, acrobatics, formation flying, taking off and landing--the fundamentals of flying.

Q: How would you characterize the quality of the instructors at that phase of the war?

Admiral Lee: I would say flight instructors were very good. One type were plowbacks, people who'd gone through flight training, and for one reason or another, were kept on as instructors. And I'd say they were adequate instructors. Another type were people like my original instructor, Lieutenant McLaughlin, who was an aviator in civilian life. He was at least 30, so I thought of him as an old man. But he had flown in civilian life and had gotten a commission as a lieutenant, I assume, and came in as a flight instructor.

I thought the instruction at preflight school was excellent--academic, athletic, even military. And I thought the ground school instruction in primary training was first-rate, primarily because by then the Navy had gotten professional teachers into these jobs. The Navy had recruited; preflight school was staffed by college and high school teachers and professors. And the primary training, essentially the same. So people teaching navigation, weather, engines, and so forth, were very well qualified. I thought the instruction was of a very high level.

Q: Were you getting any instructors who had fleet or combat experience?

Admiral Lee: None in primary and none in advanced. We did have combat experienced instructors in operational flight training, which I will tell you about later.

Q: How much emphasis, other than this chance encounter with Admiral Byrd, was there on safety?

Admiral Lee: You know, one of the strange things about safety is that the Navy apparently didn't learn about safety until about two-thirds of the way through World War II. There were no safety officers. There was emphasis on safety but not as such. Later on, you know, the Navy launched a tremendous safety program, and it paid very great dividends. Each squadron had to have a safety officer. And we checked in great detail all the items having to do with safety, and checked each pilot off.

The one thing that was taught in great detail was called survival in World War II. In preflight school and primary, all the way through, survival was stressed. It was a form of safety. The Navy really didn't have an aviation safety program until towards the end of World War II. And we didn't get it all organized until the Fifties, when the accident rate got out of hand with the early jet aircraft. We then began to put the emphasis where we should have had it all these years. But, you know, we had to learn.

After primary flight training, I was sent to Corpus Christi, Texas, which in 1943 was the center for what was called basic and advanced training. My first stop in the Corpus Christi area was Cabaniss Field, where I flew the Vultee Vibrator in May and June of 1943 for about 45 hours.* And, once again, the schedule was about the same--one half day of flying, one half day of ground school. I didn't have any problems in either ground school or flying there.

---

*The Vultee SNV Valiant was a monoplane trainer that had seats in tandem for instructor and pupil. It had a maximum speed of 166 miles per hour.

Lee #1 - 42

The next stop was the Naval Air Station Kingsville, Texas, where advanced training took place, and where we had no ground school. The basic instrument training which took place at Cabaniss essentially ended the ground school. About the only ground school we had at Kingsville was the necessary instruction for each phase of flying, such as bombing, ordnance, gunnery, and so forth.

At Kingsville we flew the AT-6--or in those days we called it the SNJ.* Very nice trainer plane. My section got there around the end of June, and we flew 90 hours during the month of July. I looked in my logbook this morning--we completed the last flight on July 31, 1943. I was then graduated from advanced training, commissioned an ensign, U.S. Naval Reserve, on August 7, 1943, with the date of rank of August 1, 1943. I had 235 hours of flight time.

Q: How did the advanced training differ from the basic and primary that you'd been through?

Admiral Lee: In primary training we flew a little airplane called the N2S Yellow Peril. The first 20 hours of primary training were used to learn to fly the airplane. Then we

---

*The North American SNJ Texan was a monoplane trainer that could accommodate a pupil and instructor in tandem. It had a maximum speed of 205 miles per hour at 5,000 feet, a service ceiling of 21,500 feet, and a range of 750 statute miles. AT-6 was an Army Air Forces designation.

went into such things as minor acrobatics. Then we did dead-engine landings, and then into formation flying. All this took time. So after I racked up my 100 hours in primary training, I went to basic training. Then in basic training, we stepped up to a bigger airplane. We also began a little formation flying, but most basic training was devoted to instrument flying. We flew with an instructor, and we learned how to fly instruments.

Q: Was there a hood or something to keep you from peeking?

Admiral Lee: Oh, yes, there was always a hood when we flew in the rear seat. And we had Link trainer flying, practice on the ground in flight trainers, simulated flying. That was basic and instrument training at Cabaniss Airfield. At advanced training in Kingsville the first phase was checking out in the airplane, learning to fly a new machine. After a few familiarization flights, we did aerobatics, formation flying, and some night flying, then into gunnery and bombing. The SNJ was an admirable airplane for this. It had a single .50-caliber machine gun which fired through the propeller. We took turns towing an aerial target around the gunnery range and shooting at it. Somewhat to my surprise, I was a good gunner with a bomb rack on one wing. We practiced glide and dive-bombing.

I'd say it was the first tactical flying--formation flying, cross-country flying, acrobatic flying, air combat flying, gunnery, dive-bombing.

After that, once again, we had a choice as to what our next duty would be. Earlier in the war, the Navy had planned its flight training program so that all aviators went through primary flight training. Then a split was made. Those who were going into transport flying and patrol plane flying went one route, and those who were going into carrier aviation went another route. The only flying I could even think about was carrier planes, because that's what I'd worked on as an aviation machinist's mate.

Q: Were the transport and patrol communities viewed as sort of second class at that time?

Admiral Lee: Not necessarily. I'd say the young tigers wanted to get into fighters and dive-bombers and go win the war--the young tigers and young idiots maybe. Others opted for patrol planes and transports. There were some cadets who didn't like fighters and dive-bombers. It's a pretty vigorous, energetic type of flying, you know. I don't know how the division was made. Probably not very different from what happens today. If you graduate number one in your flight class, you get first choice. So, by and large,

Lee #1 - 45

I daresay the top aviators go into carrier aviation--not always. Some very top aviators elect to go into VP, because it's a personal choice.

Q: Well, this was really a specialization brought on by the war, because before that pilots had alternated back and forth.

Admiral Lee: Yes, before the beginning of World War II, naval aviators were given training in both multi-engine and carrier types. They went back and forth. I know Admiral Moorer flew off carriers, and he was also in VP squadrons.* That was the common practice.

Q: Indeed it was.

Admiral Lee: Beginning with World War II--I don't know exactly when it happened--but fairly early it was decided we couldn't waste time in training young aviators to be both. We never went back to the old way after World War II. I understand that it took about 18 months to get through flight training prior to World War II. The new way got it down to less than a year.

---
*Admiral Thomas H. Moorer, USN, served as Chief of Naval Operations, 1967-70, and Chairman of the Joint Chiefs of Staff, 1970-1974. His oral history is in the Naval Institute collection. VP indicates patrol aviation in the Navy.

I started on November 12 and finished flight training the following August 1. I was very fortunate, because I went to Los Alamitos, and then to Corpus Christi, Texas. The weather was ideal at both stations. Some of my classmates from preflight school went up to Pasco, Washington. They were four and five months at Pasco. I finished ahead of them by two or three months--just the breaks of the game.

Q: Well, after you decided you wanted to be a tiger, then what was the next step?

Admiral Lee: I applied to go into the dive-bomber business. Naval Air Station Jacksonville was the center for operational flight training, and Cecil Field was the center for dive-bomber training in those days. They had the SBD Dauntless, which, of course, was the standard fleet dive-bomber until mid-1943, when it began to be replaced by the SB2C Helldiver.* The SBDs then were sent to the training commands, and that's what we had at Cecil Field.

---

*The Douglas Dauntless had a wing span of 41 feet, top speed of 245 miles per hour at 15,800 feet, range of 1,100 statute miles, and a gross weight of 10,855 pounds. The Curtiss Helldiver had a wing span of 50 feet, top speed of 295 miles per hour at 16,700 feet, range of 1,165 statute miles, and gross weight of 16,616 pounds.

And, of course the SBD scored a great victory for the Navy and the United States at Midway, because it's the dive-bomber that sank those four carriers.*

My instructor was a Lieutenant (j.g.) Muller and he was a combat experienced pilot. He was a fine instructor, one of the best I ever had. At Cecil Field the senior instructors were lieutenants or lieutenants (junior grade) who had come back from a first combat tour. Each senior instructor had an assistant instructor, and I had a Lieutenant (junior grade) Loren Nelson, USNR, who was a plowback. He graduated and they kept him on. The assistant instructors were kept for about six months, and then sent to sea.

I was at Jacksonville August, September, and October, and I got about 120 hours in the SBD. I had my first accident while taxiing out to take off. The man in front of me stopped. I put on the brakes too suddenly and nosed up an SBD. I was required to carry around my neck for three days one of those Dilbert signs. It was terrible, but I survived.

The last thing on the docket was eight carrier landings on USS Sable in the Great Lakes in an SBD.**

---

*Four Japanese carriers, the Kaga, Akagi, Hiryu, and Soryu, were sunk by carrier-based SBDs in the Battle of Midway in early June 1942.
**The USS Sable (IX-81) was a former Great Lakes passenger steamer that had been fitted with a flight deck and commissioned in the U.S. Navy on 8 May 1943 in order to provide a landing platform for carrier qualifications. Being in the Great Lakes protected her from enemy attack.

Lee #1 - 48

When the orders came out, much to my chagrin, I was detained at Cecil Field as an instructor, assistant instructor. And I wanted to win the war!

Q: I'd be interested in your recollections both of the SBD and those first carrier landings.

Admiral Lee: The SBD was a marvelous airplane. Since that time, I've had considerable experience with airplanes and some technical training. In my time in naval aviation, I've flown three or four airplanes that I thought were perfect designs. By a perfect design, I mean it has a good airframe. The airframe is not treacherous, has good stall qualities, good high-speed qualities, good landing qualities, and is easy to maintain. It also must have a good engine, and the engine is properly mated to the airframe. There were not and are not many airplanes built like that. The SBD was one, except for one factor. It was also a marvelous dive-bomber. You could maneuver it in flight. The SBD was a very responsive airplane at low speeds and a good carrier plane.

The one exception, it was underpowered. If the SBD had had a more powerful engine, it would have been a far better airplane for '43 and '44 than the SB2C, which was the dog of all dogs. Even so, the SBD was a marvelous design and a great airplane. At Naval Air Station Miami, I had previously flown in the predecessor to the SBD. It had a Pratt & Whitney 1535 engine and was called the BT. The BT was the predecessor to the SBD, built by Northrop, and then Douglas took over the design. As I said a moment ago, it wouldn't carry too much load, because it didn't have large wings, and it didn't have much power. It had a Wright 1820 engine in it, with about 1,000 horsepower.

Before the first carrier landings, we, of course, had carrier landing practice at Cecil Field. I thought carrier landing practice was great fun. Then we were given one field carrier landing practice drill at Naval Air Station Glenview, Illinois. I got the one flight there and then flew out to the Sable, which was operating in Lake Michigan from Naval Air Station Glenview, Illinois.

I think for the first carrier landing, all pilots are on automatic. Later on, after a certain number of carrier landings, you get so you can observe everything that's going on. You can fly the airplane down to the deck. You see the deck. You feel the airplane. I don't think this is true for the first carrier landing or the first few carrier landings. It's all on automatic. It's all so strange. And I think that's why field carrier landing practice is so important. You've got to get all of these things that you do in landing on a carrier to the point where they're reflex action.

Q: Conditioned response.

Admiral Lee: Conditioned response. And that's exactly what landing on the Sable was like. It was conditioned response. And it was all a blur. Later on, after I'd made, say, 30 or 40 landings on a carrier, the deck became something other than a blur. You knew what you were doing all the way until you hit the deck. You knew when to wave off, but not initially. I was too young and immature to be terrified. But I thought it was a good experience. The Sable could handle only one plane at a time. They pushed you back to the end of the deck with about 20 crewmen. The air officer was on a bullhorn, and he was heckling these troops who were pushing the airplanes back. And he'd tell them, "Not fast enough. Too much liberty last night."

I made eight carrier landings on Sable in one flight and in one day and didn't feel that I was really all that well qualified in carrier flying. But they marked me qualified, and away I went.

Q: Did you rely a good deal on the LSO during those landings?*

---

*The landing signal officer (LSO) stands at the rear end of the flight deck and gives signals to the pilot to indicate what sort of approach he is making and what corrections, if any, are needed.

Admiral Lee: Those first landings you were 100% in the LSO's hands. Before the days of the mirror landing system and angled decks, the pilots were all in the hands of the LSO. The LSO was <u>the</u> man. And you followed everything he said or signalled to you. There were no radio communications then. With the angled deck and mirror landing system, pilots do, I'd say, 90% of it themselves. They never hear from the LSO. In those days, I'd say it was about 90% LSO and 10% pilot for that type of a landing.

Q: Did you have to condition yourself to the fact that your plane is to the point of stalling, and you have to drop it onto that deck?

Admiral Lee: Not only then but later on in flying other types of airplanes from a carrier--I never felt that I was very close to a stall. I always felt that I had good control. And you can be very close to a stall. You can stall if you don't handle it properly. With a properly executed approach to a carrier landing, there is still adequate margin.

Q: The <u>Sable</u>, as I have read, was really a deck put on an old passenger steamer, so there was no hangar deck, no place to put those planes except to just push them back and take them back off again.

Lee #1 - 52

Admiral Lee: They just handled one at a time. I think they had three or four wires on the Sable. And it was just long enough to make a takeoff. But it was adequate; it saved a lot of time and effort. It was dedicated to qualifying all the young aviators coming out of the operational training command. It did a good job.

Q: Did you ever have any dive-bombing practice while you were in the SBD?

Admiral Lee: Oh, yes. I didn't go into this in great detail, but I'd be happy to. The training at Cecil Field was very comprehensive. We had all the training that one would need for going into combat. We got about 110 or 120 hours in the SBD. We had at least 10 or 12 flights in dive-bombing, very good instruction. And we had a man calling the hits so that you knew where you dropped. We had 10 or 12 flights in gunnery, shooting at towed targets. We had night flying, formation flying, glide bombing, cross-country flying. I thought it was very fine training.

I think we could have gone to war in SBDs fairly soon after that. As it just so happens, the SBD was being pulled out of the fleet at this time and being replaced by the SB2C. And for those of us who went to the fleet a few months later, we had to transition to the SB2C. But to answer your earlier question, I thought the SBD was a marvelous design. And its successor, also built by Douglas, was a big SBD. It was called the A-1 or the AD Skyraider, designed by the same man.*

Q: Ed Heinemann.

Admiral Lee: Ed Heinemann.** He was the SBD man, and then he also designed the A-1, AD. It had adequate power, had a bigger wing, carried a bigger load. Just as marvelous in every way--high-speed performance, low-speed performance, carrier work, and had a fine engine--a Wright 3350, with about 2,000 horsepower. What we really needed in World War II was the A-1.

When I think about properly designing an airplane, with all the things that I just described--having a good engine which matches the airframe; having enough power; having an airframe that's good at all speed regimes; a good carrier plane; tough; capable of taking high G's; is maneuverable in a dive with speed brakes out. The AD in all of those things was just about perfect. The number one airplane that I flew in all of my years in naval aviation, from the standpoint of design, was the A-1.

---

*Before 1962, the Skyraider was designated the AD, afterward the A-1.
**Edward H. Heinemann and Rosario Rausa, Ed Heinemann: Combat Aircraft Designer (Naval Institute Press, 1980). This book contains the memoirs of a man who was a noted designer for the Douglas Aircraft Company (later McDonnell Douglas Corporation) for many years.

Lee #1 - 54

Q: It had a good deal of longevity as well because of those qualities.

Admiral Lee: Lasted forever. We still had it in the Vietnam War. It was a marvelous design in every way. Just about every airplane that I flew in my 36 years in naval aviation had some problem which prevented it from being a great airplane, with the exception of two or three. The SBD could have been if it had had more power. The A-1 had it all. The F-18, I believe, has it all too.*

Q: That's interesting because the F-18 has had a lot of critics.

Admiral Lee: I know it.

Q: What were the differences in technique in hitting a land target and a ship in your dive-bombing?

Admiral Lee: For hitting a land target--if you have no wind, you calibrate your sight on a dive-bomber, such as the SBD, an A-1, or an SB2C, so that you can dive pipper (sight center) to pipper (target center). You dive down to some predetermined altitude, such as 3,000 feet, release

---

*The F/A-18 Hornet is a Navy fighter-bomber developed in the mid-1970s when Admiral Lee was Commander Naval Air Systems Command. He discusses the plane in considerable detail later in this oral history.

your bomb, pull out--and your bomb should hit the target. It's all worked out ballistically and aerodynamically, so that the bomb should hit the target. That's the theory.

Now--wind. The wind that counts most is the wind where you release your bomb. The wind moves your airplane. So on a land target, if you've got ten knots of wind from the north, you have to know how many feet that ten knots of wind will move your bomb in dropping from 3,000 feet to the target. You look at your tables, and you see that you've got a wind from the north. Then you move your sight over and correct that much. Your pipper might be on some imaginary circle, 100 feet to the north of the target. And if everything is going right, you press the pickle and you hit the target. That's for a land target. The only correction you have to make if your dive is right, your angle is right, your speed is right, you've got the right ballistics on your bomb, is for wind.

Now, hitting a moving ship, you have two corrections to make. You still have to make that wind correction, if there is any wind. And you have to make a speed correction for the ship. If the ship is stationary, the only thing you have to worry about is the wind. And you make the wind correction just as you do for a land site. In hitting a ship, you look at the ship, you look at the wake, and you estimate what sort of lead to allow for ten knots. It's the same as wind, the sort of correction you need--you've got that in your head. So you lead the ship by that much, for the speed of the ship. And then you have to know the wind, and every good naval aviator can look at the water and read the wind. Say you want to lead the ship by 200 feet, and your rings on your scope will give you that. Then you would make the speed correction for the ship and then the wind correction. You've got to make them both. We used to dive-bomb towed targets off Jacksonville in operational flight training. After you've done it for a period of time, you get so it's sort of automatic. And you do it, say, to the closest five knots for wind and for target speed.

Q: That's like seaman's eye in ship handling.

Admiral Lee: Same thing. And then after you've done it enough, you don't do the calculating; you just know where to put it, based on the circumstances. Same thing. That's the way dive-bombing works.

Q: How do you know when to pull out of that dive?

Admiral Lee: Good pilots try to pull out at the same altitude every time. And in that way they can improve their dive-bombing. You check your altimeter in the dive.

When that altimeter passed 3,000 feet, that was my check. I watched it coming up to 3,000 feet, and I tried to be in smooth flight, which is very important; you don't want to be in a skid. I tried to be in smooth flight and have my aim point at the proper position. And as soon as I got that done, which would take a fraction of a second after passing 3,000 feet, I would pickle and pull up. And chances are, if you did that, you might be releasing at 2,500 feet, or something like that, or maybe even a little lower. And you never wanted to pull out very high, anyway. So you release your pickle, bring in your speed brakes, and head for the water, sort of a modified pullout.

Q: And you probably wanted to achieve consistent dive angles also.

Admiral Lee: You'd be amazed at how consistent you can be. You'd be amazed. You can be very consistent in dive angles. You go to ranges where they can tell you what your dive angle is. You use the target to set your dive angle. You would bring the target in to the wing roots. And if you're at 12,000 feet or 14,000 feet, you bring it in to a certain point, where you know if you begin your pushover there, you're going to be at a 70-degree dive angle. And after you've done it enough, you can feel when you're too steep, or when you're not steep enough. If you're not

Lee #1 - 58

steep enough, you can pull up and push over again and get a little steeper. If you're too steep, there's not much you can do. You just have to recognize it, correct your aim accordingly and hope like hell.

Q: Were you, during this time, also learning how different planes can work cohesively as a unit?

Admiral Lee: Yes, very much so, tactics.

Q: Any examples that come to mind?

Admiral Lee: During operational training, we never really got into squadron tactics or group tactics where we worked together as a whole squadron. We only had, say, a maximum of six planes at a time. And we did fly formation, but that sort of training came at a later time.

I did the first, you might say, divisional dives--12 and 15 and 20 planes in combat--with VB-15.* We didn't do that sort of training in operational flight training in World War II. We didn't have the numbers of planes or the facilities. We worked on the fundamentals of the things I've described.

Q: But I gather as time went on, you were getting

---
*VB-15--Bombing Squadron 15, in which Lee served in combat on board the USS Essex (CV-9).

increasingly comfortable with the techniques that a dive-bomber pilot uses.

Admiral Lee: Yes, I thought by the time I graduated from operational flight training I was reasonably proficient.

Q: Unless you've got anything else, maybe that's a logical place to break.

Admiral Lee: All right.

Lee #2 - 60

Interview Number 2 with Vice Admiral Kent L. Lee,
U.S. Navy (Retired)

Place: Logon Farm, Admiral Lee's home near Gordonsville, Virginia

Date: Friday, 9 October 1987

Interviewer: Paul Stillwell

Q: Good morning, Admiral. We got you last time through your operational training, and we're ready to resume at that point, please.

Admiral Lee: After operational training, I went up to the Great Lakes and made the standard eight carrier landings on Sable. And at that time I was ready to go to the fleet, I thought. However, it was customary at the operational flight training centers to bring back young ensigns as assistants to the lieutenants, who normally had fleet experience and who led groups of young aviators through operational training. My bombing records, gunnery records, and carrier landing records were fairly good, so I was brought back as assistant instructor.

My duty was to be Lieutenant Dopuch's assistant for operational flight training in the SBD and instrument instruction in the SNJ.* We would take about a dozen pilots at a time through introduction to the SBD Dauntless, familiarization, formation flying, gunnery, dive-bombing,

───────────────
*Lieutenant (junior grade) Dan Dopuch, USNR.

glide bombing, cross-country flying. We taught them all the techniques, all the tactics that a young aviator would need to know in joining the fleet.

As you can imagine, I was very disappointed at being returned to Cecil Field as a plowback. I was just 20 years old and wanted to get out there and win the war. I thought I was a reasonably good instrument instructor. But I think overall I was not a success as assistant instructor. I was too young. I was too immature and too inexperienced. So I think all that made me a little bit shy and a little bit uncertain, especially in operational flight training, since I'd never been to the fleet.

Q: Did you discuss that problem with the officers you were working for?

Admiral Lee: No, I didn't. It's not something you discuss. You do what you're told, and perhaps some of this is hindsight.

Sometime around February 1944, I guess, I had a midair collision with a student--nobody hurt, both planes landed safely.

Q: What were you flying then?

Admiral Lee: I was flying an SBD Dauntless, and the

student was also flying a Dauntless. We had a collision on a rendezvous, and he ran into my tail. I think the powers that be at Cecil thought that I didn't handle it very well, in terms of letting him run into me.

At that time Cecil Field periodically sent, about once each six months, a group of assistant instructors to the fleet, people who had been there normally about a year. I requested to go with the next group. In March I was detached from operational flight training and sent out with four other pilots.

I was an ensign, and I was sent with Lieutenant (junior grade) Loren Nelson, who was truly an outstanding aviator--and I'll talk a little bit more about him later--and Lieutenant (junior grade) Earl Mallette to the Pacific.* They were both very good people; they'd stayed at Cecil about a year as assistant flight instructors and I think were perhaps more successful than I was. They were both older and more mature. We flew to San Diego on commercial DC-3s, and made many stops.** We stayed there a week or so and then rode a jeep carrier--my first experience at sea--from San Diego to Pearl Harbor.***

---

*Lieutenant (junior grade) Loren E. Nelson, USNR; Lieutenant (junior grade) Earl C. Mallette, USNR.
**DC-3 was the commercial designation of a Douglas-built cargo-passenger aircraft. The Navy version was designated R4D, and the Army Air Forces version was designated C-47.
***Jeep carrier was the standard nickname for a small escort aircraft carrier, designated CVE, that was used primarily in support roles such as transporting spare pilots and planes to the fast carriers.

Q: What ship was that? Do you recall?

Admiral Lee: USS <u>Midway</u>, commanded by Captain F. J. McKenna.*

There were three squadrons at Barbers Point, which is just to the west of Pearl Harbor. The mission of these squadrons was to hold and train replacement pilots for the Pacific Fleet. At this particular time, in April of 1944, we had built up, in a period of about six to nine months, to eight or ten big carriers in the Pacific--built up very rapidly. VB-100, VF-100, and VT-100 were formed at Barbers Point to keep them supplied with airplanes and with pilots.** So I joined VB-100 in late April and immediately checked out in the SB2C Curtiss Helldiver, which had replaced the SBD, the Douglas Dauntless, as the dive-bomber in the fleet.

Q: Was this squadron comparable to the RAG squadrons that came along a number of years later?***

---

*The USS <u>Midway</u> (CVE-63) was renamed USS <u>St. Lo</u> on 10 October 1944 so that her original name could go to a large new aircraft carrier, CVB-41. On 25 October 1944, two weeks after being renamed, the ship was sunk in the Battle of Leyte Gulf. Captain Francis J. McKenna was the commanding officer from commissioning to sinking.
**VB-100--Bombing Squadron 100; VF-100--Fighting Squadron 100; VT-100--Torpedo Squadron 100.
***RAG--replacement air group, a type of squadron responsible for training aviators in a specific aircraft before they were assigned to fleet squadrons.

Admiral Lee: VB-100, in a sense, could be comparable to one, but all the pilots reporting to VB-100 had gone through operational flight training. The operational flight training squadron at Cecil Field was more comparable to today's RAGs. But it just so happened that the squadron at Cecil Field still flew SBDs.

Q: So the stop in Hawaii served that useful purpose for you.

Admiral Lee: Yes. We had had the operational flight training and qualified in SBDs, but now they were flying SB2Cs in the fleet. So we checked out in the SB2C, flew dive-bombing runs, all the same type training we had at Cecil Field. And then, finally, we had carrier qualifications in the SB2C, on a jeep carrier out of Pearl.

Q: How would you compare it with the SBD, both as a dive-bomber and in bringing it in to the carrier?

Admiral Lee: I could talk about it now, if you wish. I have a fair amount of information on the SB2C, and this would be a good time to talk about it.

I talked last time about the Douglas Dauntless as a dive-bomber, and I said that it was a marvelous plane--

pilots could maneuver it in a dive, and its bombing scores were very good. It didn't have enough wing area, and it didn't have enough power. It wouldn't carry a big load. And once you got a load on, it would climb very slowly.

Its replacement was this Curtiss Helldiver, and the Curtiss Helldiver was, I daresay, the worst dive-bomber ever built. I was reading Samuel Eliot Morison's history of World War II, and he even commented on the poor bombing scores by the Curtiss Helldiver.* I chuckled a little bit as I read it. The man really got around. The Curtiss Helldiver was also underpowered; it had a Wright R-2600 engine in it with about 1,700 horsepower, which was a very good engine.

The airplane itself was big and clumsy, not very maneuverable, was slow, had a low climb rate. And one of the problems was that it had a bomb bay which made the fuselage big, and hence added to the drag. Worst of all, it was a poor dive-bomber. In dive-bombing, pilots fly up to the pushover point at 12,000 to 16,000 feet. The pushover point is something you learn by experience.

---

*S. E. Morison, New Guinea and the Marianas: March 1944-August 1944 (Boston: Little, Brown and Company, 1953), says the following on page 317 in assessing the June 1944 Battle of the Philippine Sea: "In the matter of planes, the F6F Hellcat fully sustained its high reputation, and the two types of Avengers did well when given their proper weapon, the torpedo; but the new Helldiver (SB2C) was outshone by the two remaining squadrons of Dauntless dive-bombers (SBD). Unfortunately, nothing could be done about it, since the production lines were rolling with Helldivers; here the Dauntless fought her last battle."

You're never exactly on because of wind, the movement of the target, and so forth. And you need to be able to make corrections in the dive. The Skyraider and the Dauntless were both very maneuverable in the dive. If you weren't on the target after you pushed over and lined up, you could maneuver in order to get on to the target. In the SB2C, it was just about impossible to maneuver to get on the target. If you weren't fairly close, you weren't going to hit it. You could pull ahead, and you might even steepen your dive a little bit, but if you were off to either side, it was very difficult to maneuver it over and onto the target.

Q: So that would make the pushover point a lot more critical.

Admiral Lee: The pushover point was very critical. I found out later on in flying the SB2C that if I could make two or three dives on a specific target, say a land target, and adjust so that I knew exactly where I had to push over with relation to the ground, I could get fairly good bombing scores. But in the real world, you get only one pushover. So the SB2C was not a good airplane. And not only that, it required a lot of maintenance. It had plumbing that was unnecessary. It didn't have a powered control system, which it needed. And hence it was heavy on the controls, which explains why you couldn't maneuver in a dive. But, even so, it was the airplane we had in the fleet at that time.

Q: Captain McCampbell said that Commander Mini had trouble in his first carrier landings with the SB2C, because he had a tendency to bring it in high.* Did you have adjustments to make in that phase, also?

Admiral Lee: No, I thought the SB2C was a reasonably good carrier plane. It had one fault. I know what McCampbell is talking about. I wasn't a member of VB-15 at the time. Later on, when I'd had maybe 100 landings in the SB2C, the same thing happened to me. The SB2C, when it was light, had a tendency to float. You'd come in for a carrier landing, and you definitely had to push over to hit the deck. If you didn't do that, if you just cut the power and didn't ease your nose over, you could float up the deck and hit the barrier. And that happened to me two years later. I know exactly what I did. I watched it at other times.

Sometime before I got to the squadron, VB-15's initial commanding officer was relieved, Commander Dew.** The squadron thought he was a good man. Commander Mini was his

---

*Captain David McCampbell, USN (Ret.), has been interviewed as part of the Naval Institute's oral history program. As a commander, he was Commander Air Group 15 in 1944. Lieutenant Commander James H. Mini, USN, commanded Bombing Squadron 15 (VB-15), part of Air Group 15.
**Lieutenant Commander Irvin L. Dew, USN.

relief. Commander Mini had not flown the SB2C before. Air Group 15 was left at Pearl Harbor while Miles Browning's ship picked up another air group and went on to the war zone.*

While at Pearl Harbor in training, Commander Mini, in his very first carrier landing, floated over the deck and got a barrier, which was sort of standard for the course. I don't think Commander Mini was the world's best aviator. I would say he was an average aviator but very qualified. So that, I think, was just one of those things. It happens to everybody sooner or later.

Anyway, on about the first of June, Loren Nelson, Earl Mallette, and I were put on a jeep carrier in Pearl Harbor with a load of replacement airplanes. We also had pilots from VF-100 and VT-100, and hence we had SB2Cs, TBFs, and F6Fs.** We were going out to join the fleet, to deliver these airplanes, and replacement pilots as needed. The CVE

---
*Captain Miles R. Browning, USN, was first commanding officer of the USS Hornet (CV-12). He had command only a short time in combat before being relieved for cause.
**The Grumman TBF Avenger was the standard torpedo plane in the fleet in 1944, although it was also used at times as a dive-bomber; it had a wing span of 54 feet, gross weight of 15,905 pounds, and maximum speed of 271 miles per hour at 12,000 feet. The Grumman F6F Hellcat was the Navy's top carrier fighter during the last half of World War II, compiling a superb record in air-to-air combat; it had a wing span of 42 feet, gross weight of 15,413 pounds, and maximum speed of 380 miles per hour at 23,400 feet.

was USS Breton, Captain F. M. Trapnell, USN, Commanding.*

Q: Did you have any specific duties en route?

Admiral Lee: No duties en route. We were just passengers. And we, of course, were briefed on what to expect. We were briefed on a catapult shot, because the jeep carrier wasn't long enough to launch these airplanes in a deck run. So each jeep carrier had one or more of the old hydraulic catapults. We were previously catapulted from the jeep carrier, USS Copahee, that we had qualified on in the Pearl Harbor area. We had an uneventful transit of the Pacific and joined the fleet in the vicinity of Guam on June 19th.

Q: An interesting day to arrive.

Admiral Lee: June 19th was the day of the Marianas "Turkey Shoot."** We joined the fleet refueling group. On June 20th, Essex was sent over to refuel.*** And the day before

---

*Captain Frederick M. Trapnell, USN, was later commanding officer of the USS Coral Sea (CVB-43) and a skilled director of the Navy's flight test program. He eventually retired as a vice admiral.
**In aerial action that day, U.S. Navy fighter planes shot down more than 300 Japanese aircraft, thus giving rise to the nickname that has stuck ever since.
***The USS Essex (CV-9) was the first ship of the principal class of fast aircraft carriers that fought in World War II. She was 872 feet long, had a beam of 93 feet, speed of 33 knots, and standard displacement of 27,100 tons when completed. She was commissioned 31 December 1942 and first went into combat in November 1943 at the Gilbert Islands.

had been a very active day for all air groups in Task Force 58 when VF-15 from Essex shot down 30 or 40 airplanes.* Dave McCampbell got seven. June 20th was the day of the fleet strike--that is, U.S. planes against the Japanese fleet.

Well, on June 20th, we were all suited up and launched to the various carriers in the area. Loren Nelson, Earl Mallette, and I landed on Essex, and I think all of us were very lucky to make a safe landing, because maintenance people in the jeep carrier had loaded the empty rear seat of the SB2C with a lot of heavy armament gear and other spare equipment. And the plane was very tail-heavy.

Q: Had you known they were doing that?

Admiral Lee: Yes, I knew it, but as inexperienced as I was, weight and balance of an airplane didn't mean a lot to me, because the airplanes that we flew didn't require a lot of weight and balance calculations. It was very difficult to get it out of whack. Later on, it became easier.

Air Group 15 had been aboard Hornet with Captain Miles Browning. Browning was unhappy with the air group and he had taken aboard a different air group, which was available at Pearl Harbor, and had left Air Group 15 at Pearl. Air

---

*Task Force 58 was the fast carrier task force, a principal component of the U.S. Fifth Fleet engaged in the Central Pacific offensive. VF-15--Fighting Squadron 15.

Group 15 was at Pearl, as I understand it, about two or three months. On May first, Essex picked up Air Group 15 and headed west. And from May first until June 20th, they had been in a number of actions and had lost several planes and several pilots. So VB-15 decided to keep us as replacement pilots. And, of course, we had brought three planes. VF-15 also kept some replacement pilots, but I don't think VT-15 did.*

Q: How did it come about that you were allocated specifically to that ship and that air group from the jeep carrier?

Admiral Lee: I don't have the faintest idea. The air officer who ran things on the jeep carrier merely designated the three of us to go to Essex. And that was it. We took off and went. I think they had gotten a message from Essex saying, "Send us three airplanes." And, of course, it took three pilots to send three airplanes, so we went. We weren't necessarily going to stay with Essex and VB-15. It depended on their need for pilots. And there was some discussion after we got there about whether or not we would stay. I think Commander Mini looked at our records. We'd all been assistant instructors in operational flight training. We had a little more flight

---
*VT-15--Torpedo Squadron 15.

time than most. He interviewed us, and I think he liked us--Mallette, Nelson, and Lee--and decided to keep us as replacement pilots.

This, as I explained a moment ago, wasn't always the case, because squadrons kept replacement pilots only when they needed them. Usually they lost more airplanes than pilots. Later on, during the course of the cruise, we got replacement planes but no pilots. Sometimes we sent our own pilots after them if we didn't need pilots.

But, anyway, on June 20th, we joined VB-15 in USS Essex. The air group commander was Commander David McCampbell, who during the course of this particular cruise, shot down 34 Japanese airplanes and was subsequently awarded the Medal of Honor.* The captain of the ship was a man by the name of Ralph Ofstie, who later became Deputy Chief of Naval Operations for Air.** The executive officer, previously the ship's air officer, was David McDonald, who later became the Chief of Naval Operations.***

---

*For a book-length account of the air group's operations during its time on board the Essex in 1944, see Edwin P. Hoyt, McCampbell's Heroes: The Story of the U.S. Navy's Most Celebrated Carrier Fighters of the Pacific War (New York: Van Nostrand Reinhold Company, 1983).
**Captain Ralph A. Ofstie, USN; he later served in the rank of vice admiral as Deputy Chief of Naval Operations (Air), 1953-54, and Commander Sixth Fleet, 1955-56. His career was cut short by his death from cancer in November 1956.
***Commander David L. McDonald, USN, eventually reached the rank of four-star admiral and served as Chief of Naval Operations, 1963-67. His oral history is in the Naval Institute collection.

My commanding officer in VB-15 was a Commander James H. Mini, Naval Academy Class of 1935, and, in my view at the time, the world's best commanding officer. I thought VB-15 was an exceptional squadron. And I had a very good basis for comparison, because as I will relate later, I also flew with VF-15. In VB-15, we had an executive officer by the name of Lieutenant Roger Noyes, who was also a very good man.* We had a flight officer by the name of Lieutenant R. H. Mills, who later worked for me in Omaha, Nebraska, and a maintenance officer by the name of Lieutenant J. D. Bridgers.**

The first thing Commander Mini did was put us in a training program. Lieutenant Bridgers spent a number of hours with us on the airplane to make sure that we understood all the systems, safety and survival procedures, and problems they'd had with the airplane. This training took a period of a week to ten days with the squadron. And it was absolutely first-rate in every respect. Lieutenant Mills took us through tactics that were being used. The ordnance officers went over all the ordnance, how it was used, the fusing, how to drop it, from rockets to bombs to the machine guns.

Q: This was essentially classroom training?

---
*Lieutenant Roger Noyes, USNR.
**Lieutenant Richard H. Mills, USNR; Lieutenant John D. Bridgers, USNR.

Admiral Lee: Both classroom and going to the airplane. It was a very thorough checkout, even though we had qualified in the SB2C at Pearl. This training that we were being given by the VF-15 was an order of magnitude better, excellent training in every way. The instructors, so to speak, were squadron pilots who had some combat experience.

We got a fair amount of survival training: bailing out, parachuting to the water, how to survive once you hit the water, the life raft. The officer responsible for a particular part of the squadron--whether maintenance officer, flight officer, operations officer, ordnance officer, or survival officer--was in charge of that segment of the training. And Commander Mini made sure we were thoroughly qualified and checked out in every area. In all the years I was in naval aviation, I think he was probably the best administrator as a commanding officer that I ran across. He had a thorough grasp of what training was all about and how vital it was. Commander Mini was not one of our outstanding aviators, which David McCampbell was. But even so, we need a lot of Commander Minis in our Navy, because they make the place go.

Q: As a by-product of this training and orientation, did you get into the esprit and solidarity of the squadron as well?

Admiral Lee: Yes, I thought VB-15 was a very cohesive unit. They had a lot of squadron spirit, a talented group of officers. And they, I thought, did a creditable job. We had a lot of all-squadron briefings, which covered intelligence and every other aspect of the operations coming up. It was probably the best informed squadron in the fleet, the best trained, and the best organized. After every flight, there was always a very good critique--what went right and what went wrong.

Q: Sometimes new guys get a bit of hazing. Did you go through any of that?

Admiral Lee: No hazing to speak of. The only hazing I got on Essex was when we crossed the equator. No, Jim Mini was not the hazing type. This was very serious business. People were losing their lives every day out there, and there wasn't time for that.

Q: This is to make you productive squadron members as soon as possible.

Admiral Lee: Yes. We didn't fly for the first week or so while we went through this training period. Our first flying was done in the Guam area. At that particular time, the ground forces were invading Guam, and Tinian, and bypassing Rota.* Our job was to fend off any Japanese that came around, to give close air support to the men ashore, and to run missions of opportunity--such as railroads and shipping. We did that through June and July.

Q: Had you gotten specific training along the way in close support of ground troops?

Admiral Lee: No. And I'm not sure that the squadron itself had previously done any close support of ground troops. We were given detailed maps of Guam, Saipan, and Tinian. We were taught how to use a grid system to designate specific locations ashore. We would fly over to Guam and go into orbit until the ground controller called us in on a specific target. He would describe it to us and then give us the coordinates. When we had the target in sight, we would attack it.

Q: What kind of emotional reaction did you have when you finally got into combat?

Admiral Lee: The first couple of nights before I went into

---

*Invasion dates for the Marianas were as follows: Saipan, 15 June; Guam, 21 July; Tinian, 24 July. Rota was used only as a bombing target and remained in Japanese hands until the end of the war.

combat, I didn't sleep very well. As you can understand, I was very uptight and nervous. And as normal, I think, for most people--you go through this until the time you man your airplane and rev up the engine, and then all of that nervousness leaves you. At least it did me. And I found that was true throughout World War II. The night before the first flights following a period of rest and recreation, I was always very nervous and didn't sleep very well. Once we manned the airplanes, revved up the engines and were ready to go, it was all business. I don't ever remember being very nervous about that.

Q: You focus on the job, and that drives away the other thoughts.

Admiral Lee: You're so busy that you don't have time to be afraid, was my impression.

I have one little story I'd like to tell about the SB2C and bombing. I was out one day with a flight of six SB2Cs during this period, and we spotted a Japanese merchantman. He was about a 10,000 tonner--not a big ship. We thought, "Oh, great, we've got ourselves a good target. Six of us--I was an ensign and probably the sixth man on the flight--made a dive on this merchant ship. And I doubt that the beam was more than 60 feet, maybe 300-400 feet long. We dived from about 12,000 feet and each of us released a bomb on him. Not one hit. But that was sort of standard for the SB2C. Not a very good dive-bomber.

We then strafed with our 20-millimeter guns, and that was also a problem with the SB2C, which I didn't mention earlier. It had two 20-millimeter guns, one in each wing. And they were prone to jam. I daresay the 20-millimeter guns jammed 50% of the time. So from my experience with it, it was a very unsatisfactory combat airplane. I didn't know so at the time. But later, flying much better airplanes, I realized what a dog the SB2C was. But that was sort of typical for the SB2C. Six SB2Cs dived on one lone ship, and we all missed him. We then strafed him, but he was still steaming along when we left.

Q: How much coordination did you have with the rest of the air group?

Admiral Lee: We had a lot of coordination with the rest of the air group. If the target was defended, we always went in in what is called a group grope--torpedo planes, dive-bombers, and fighters all went together. The fighters provided fighter cover. The dive-bombers went in high to make a dive-bombing run, and the torpedo planes went in low to make glide-bombing runs. With a few exceptions--and I was never on one of those--the torpedo planes carried bombs, because it wasn't often that we had a ship to torpedo. The TBF wasn't a dive-bomber, but it could make 40-degree glide-bombing runs and do pretty well, about as well as the SB2C in glide bombing. The SB2C was a better glide-bomber than it was a dive-bomber.

In mid-August, after my first combat experience, our part of the fleet went into Eniwetok Atoll for rest and recreation. After we had been in for three or four days, we were called into the ready room by Commander Mini; that is, we had a squadron pilot meeting. We were told that the fleet commander had decided to reduce the number of SB2Cs on each of the carriers and increase the number of fighters. If we did that, we would have some extra pilots in VB-15.

The thinking was that we should train some of our SB2C pilots in the F6F on Eniwetok, while we were in, and take them back to sea as fighter pilots. These pilots all had had two or three months of combat experience, a number of carrier landings. They could partially solve VF-15's problem of getting additional pilots and also solve VB-15's problem of having extra pilots.

Commander Mini asked for volunteers, nine SB2C pilots to check out in the F6F and go over to VF-15. There were six volunteers, and I was one of the six. I think Mini hesitated a moment about letting me go, since I'd been in the squadron only about two months. I wasn't privy to their conversations about it, but I understand they were reluctant. I think if there'd been more than six volunteers, I wouldn't have been allowed to go. But, anyway, I was accepted.

Q: What was your motivation for wanting to make the switch?

Admiral Lee: That's a very good question. I don't know. More action, I suppose. I often think that I was very foolish to volunteer for such a thing--not having all that much experience, all that much flight time. But I did. And I think it was the idea of, "I've seen what flying a dive-bomber is like. And that's pretty exciting, but I'd like to try a fighter plane. Maybe I'd get myself a Japanese plane."

Q: Were you motivated at all by the fact that the F6F had a better reputation than the SB2C?

Admiral Lee: No, not really. The grass is usually greener on the other side, and I wanted to fly the F6F. But at that particular time, I was happy with the SB2C, having no problems with it. I think it was just a challenge. That's probably the best way to put it--a challenge. And at 21 years old, a young man wants a challenge.

Lee #2 - 81

Q: He thinks he can do anything.

Admiral Lee: Yes. So I volunteered with five other pilots. Someone decided that we needed a lieutenant. So a lieutenant by the name of Dutch Kramer--this was his second combat tour--was drafted.* So seven of us moved ashore to Eniwetok Island, lived in tents, and checked out in the F6F. I got 12 flights in eight days, two field carrier landing practice flights, and the other six pilots got about the same. Then we went back aboard ship as fighter pilots and joined VF-15.

Q: Did you get any liberty on Eniwetok in the midst of all this?

Admiral Lee: Of course. Ashore was liberty--beer every night. We were living in tents at one end of the island. At the other end was the officers' club. You know, the first structure built on any one of those atolls as the fleet went in was an officers' club. After flying, we would go down and have a few beers and a few drinks. Pilots from the air group were coming ashore every day, going to the officers' club and swimming in the atoll. The officers' club was opposite a beach. We went swimming almost every day. Our tent was right opposite the beach.

---
*Lieutenant Henry H. Kramer, USNR.

The island was not very wide. The runway was in the middle of the island, and we were on one of the islands of the atoll. The buildings, such as maintenance hangars, tents, and living quarters, and so forth, were built along the edge of the island, next to the ocean. It really was very pleasant. And, as I say, we had a great time flying those F6Fs around Eniwetok.

We spent the bulk of our time after the initial flights in dogfights with each other. I had a friend by the name of Lieutenant (junior grade) Gunter, who was from VB-15, of course.* He and I used to have a dogfight every day in the F6F. Then the last day in August we went to sea again.

Q: Had your tactical training come in the form of these dogfights?

Admiral Lee: That was about the extent of our tactical training.

I'd now like to comment on VF-15 and its organization. The first commanding officer was Commander David McCampbell, and I believe Lieutenant Commander Charlie Brewer was executive officer.** Jimmy Rigg was, perhaps, the operations officer.*** A fellow by the name of George

---
*Lieutenant (junior grade) Monchie M. Gunter, USNR.
**Lieutenant Commander Charles W. Brewer, USN.
***Lieutenant Commander James F. Rigg, USN.

Duncan also was in the squadron, and also Wayne Morris, the movie actor.* The first group commander was relieved by David McCampbell. Charlie Brewer became the commanding officer of VF-15, and Jimmy Rigg became executive officer. Commander Brewer was killed on June 19th, and Commander Rigg became commanding officer. Lieutenant Commander George Duncan, a Naval Academy graduate, 1939, became executive officer.

I was absolutely amazed at the contrast between VB-15 and VF-15. We got absolutely no indoctrination and no training in VF-15. We had had enough experience in VB-15 to know the things we ought to learn. So we had our own little training sessions.

Q: More of a do-it-yourself thing.

Admiral Lee: More of a do-it-yourself thing, because the commanding officer and the department heads organized nothing for us. We were assigned to various flights, and the first day out of Eniwetok all seven of us were launched. I got four carrier qualification landings in the F6F, in four flights. That was the extent of our training. We then went to sea as fighter pilots.

---

*Lieutenant Commander George C. Duncan, USN. Lieutenant Bert DeWayne Morris, Jr., USNR. For a summary of his movie and flying careers, see Barrett Tillman, "Wayne Morris: Actor, Naval Aviator and Fighting 15 Ace," The Hook, summer 1984, pages 48-49, 51.

Our first combat out of Eniwetok was on 8 September. The Marines were invading Peleliu. I was sent over to bomb and strafe with Lieutenant Kramer, also from VB-15. I flew wing on Lieutenant Kramer on this particular mission. We got to Peleliu, and there was lots of fire, smoke, bombs going off, and so forth. We made an attack in our assigned area, dropping bombs and strafed. As we pulled out, Lieutenant Kramer was hit in the right wheel well. We pulled up to 2,000 or 3,000 feet, and I told him that he was on fire and to get out. But he never opened the canopy, never made a move. He just rolled to the left, and went right in. His only combat flight in the F6F was at Peleliu.

Q: That gives one pause.

Admiral Lee: Of those seven VB-15 pilots that went over to VF-15, we lost two of them, Ensign Gaver and Lieutenant Kramer.* But that was my introduction to combat in VF-15.

After Peleliu we took part in the initial raids in the Philippines. We stayed in that general area of the Pacific for about 30 days. We were involved in air-to-air combat with Japanese planes, hitting shipping, hitting military installations, and whatever was needed in softening up the

---
*Ensign Henry C. Gaver, USNR.

Philippines for MacArthur's invasion, which was to come off fairly soon.

Q: What are your recollections of air-to-air combat?

Admiral Lee: I'm going to describe three or four events during the course of this. One of the things that a fleet normally does is send out scout planes. We were in the vicinity of Formosa, and these scout flights were usually made up of one SB2C and one F6F Hellcat. They went out 250-300 miles at 2,000 or 3,000 feet looking for the Japanese fleet or planes.

On October 12 I was sent on one of these. We were out perhaps 200 miles. It wasn't an overcast day, but there were low-level to mid-level cumulus clouds as you so often see in the Pacific. There were quite a few of them, maybe 4/10 cloud cover, cumulus clouds from about 2,000 feet up to 12,000 feet, scattered around.

As we were nearing the end of our sector, I spotted a Japanese Betty, a twin-engine bomber with a turret on top of the fuselage. I alerted my SB2C partner, who happened to be Dave Hall.* Of course, I knew him because I'd been in VB-15. I told him, "Let's catch that Betty." Well, the Betty had sighted us, and he had made for the clouds. I went to full power, and the SB2C, of course, couldn't keep

---

*Lieutenant (junior grade) David R. Hall, USNR.

up with me. I was going to give him a shot at it too. SB2Cs don't get many chances to shoot a Japanese plane.

But the SB2C couldn't keep up, and I didn't want to let the Betty get away. But before I could catch him, he'd gone into a cloud. I went in right behind him. He came out the other side of the cloud, obviously. I was right behind him. I started right on his tail, but he opened up with that turret. I could see the tracers going by me. So I decided that wasn't such a good idea. By then I was running at 2,800 RPM and 54 inches, full power.* I pulled up to an altitude about 1,500 feet higher than the Betty, on his righthand side, and made what aviators call a high-side run and pulled in on him at about a 30-40-degree angle from above and the side.

Q: Were you using the wing root as a point of aim?

Admiral Lee: Yes. The F6F had six .50-caliber machine guns, and they always worked--the best armament the Navy ever bought. I turned all six guns on, and when I got within range, I let all six go, and hit him in the starboard wing root. His wing root and engine caught fire, and he then spiraled down to the ocean. The plane hit the water, there was a big flash of fire, followed by black

---

*Power in World War II aircraft engines was measured in revolutions per minute and manifold pressure. The figures for full power were 2,800 RPMs and 54 inches.

smoke. I followed him down to the ocean. The SB2C pilot could see the smoke and came to join me. We made one circle and then resumed our search, but we didn't see another Betty that day.

Q: Was there a sense of exhilaration in your first kill?

Admiral Lee: Yes, the adrenaline was flowing freely. Having cornered this Betty and shot him down first pass, I thought I'd accomplished a great deal. The SB2C pilot was just about as excited as I was.

Let me talk a little about the F6F. The fighter plane the Navy had during the early part of World War II was the F4F, also built by Grumman.* It was not very maneuverable, didn't have a lot of power, and was inadequate to fight Zeros. The F6F Hellcat entered the fleet in great numbers in 1943. The F6F was a barrel-shaped airplane, had folding wings, and had a Pratt & Whitney R-2800 engine--a very fine engine. But the F6F was heavy. It didn't have a high climb rate, and it wasn't nearly as maneuverable as the Zero, not nearly as maneuverable as some later planes that we had, such as the

---

*The F4F Wildcat had a 1,200-horsepower Pratt & Whitney R-1830 engine, wing span of 38 feet, gross weight of 7,952 pounds, maximum speed of 318 knots at 19,400 feet, and an initial climb rate of 1,950 feet per minute.

F8F.* However, it was rugged. It was tough. It would take a lot of punishment. And I think plane-on-plane, the Zero could maneuver around the F6F very well. But for the type of fighting we did, in teams, the F6F did very well against the Zero.

The best fighter we had in World War II in the Pacific was the F4U.** It was a better fighter than the F6F--had the same engine. But it had more wing area, was more maneuverable, and had a better climb rate. The Marines used the F4U, because the first F4Us were not good carrier planes. They had trouble landing aboard. I wasn't a party to that, but I understand that's why we bought the F6F rather than the F4U for carrier duty.

Some other experiences I had in combat--we were in the Formosa area during this period. And one of the first things that was done when entering a new combat area was called a fighter sweep. The first thing in the morning, a big flight of fighters from each carrier is sent in on the attack. They fly over and sweep the airfield, try to catch the enemy airplanes on the ground, and shoot them down there in the air.

---

*The F6F's initial climb rate was 2,980 feet per minute. The Grumman F8F Bearcat had a 2,100-horsepower Pratt & Whitney R-2800 engine, wing span of 35 feet, top speed of 421 miles per hour at 19,700 feet, gross weight of 12,947 pounds, and an initial climb rate of 4,570 feet per minute.
**The Vought F4U-4 Corsair had a 2,100-horsepower Pratt & Whitney R-2800 engine, wing span of 41 feet, top speed of 446 miles per hour at 26,200 feet, gross weight of 14,670 pounds, and initial climb rate of 3,870 feet per minute.

It wasn't often that VB-15 replacement pilots in VF-15 got to go on fighter sweeps. Fighter sweeps could be good hunting. The senior pilots claimed their rights. VF-15 pilots were a very aggressive lot, led by Commander McCampbell, and Rigg, and Duncan--very good pilots, very aggressive. I'll have to give them credit for that. VF-15 had 26 aces--pilots who shot down five or more Japanese planes.

Anyway, on October 13, 1944, for one reason or another, I was assigned to a fighter sweep, fourth man in our division of four planes. There were 30 or 40 F6Fs altogether on this fighter sweep. There was always cloud cover over Formosa especially on the east side. Most of the built-up areas in Formosa were on the western side; mountains were on the eastern side. We crossed the mountains above the cloud cover and dropped down through the broken clouds--and it was perhaps 8/10 or 9/10 cloud cover--and attacked airfields. There were Japanese fighters flying around just beneath the cloud cover. It was very difficult to spot them. I don't think we shot down any Japanese planes that were in the cloud cover.

Our mission was to destroy the airplanes on the airfield, anything that was movable--tank trucks, vehicles, people, buildings, airplanes--on these airfields. That we did. Coming away from the airfields, we were attacked by these planes that had been flying around in the cloud edges. My division leader, of course, was using lots of power and flew into the clouds, which everybody was doing, and I was supposed to hang onto him. I lost him as he went into the clouds. And when you're flying wing on another pilot, and not looking at your own instruments, when you lose him, you've lost your point of reference. It's very difficult to regain your orientation from the instruments in your cockpit.

The next thing I knew, I was pretty much out of control dropping out of those clouds. I could see those Zeros heading for me. I got my plane straightened out, went to full power, and right back into those clouds. And I must confess I wasn't much of a hero that day. But I think the true heroes are those who know when they're licked and live to fight another day. I climbed into the clouds, went on through, and rendezvoused with my flight back over the ship. We were heading for home when this happened. And I knew how to get home, obviously. The other pilots thought I had been shot down.

Q: It might be worth explaining just how you knew the way to get home. Was that from the homing signal?

Admiral Lee: Yes. I'd be happy to explain it.

We had two methods of navigation from a carrier. Method number one was a plotting board. Each airplane had a rack for a plotting board. A plotting board is a navigational device for plotting course and speeds, called dead reckoning. You estimate the wind by reading it from the water. And after many flights over water, such as we had in the Pacific, you get pretty good at dead reckoning. Good enough so that you can get yourself home most any time, just plain DR-ing, because you always know approximately where you are if you're a good navigator. And Commander Mini insisted that we all work at problems like that, daily almost.

The second device was what was called ZB. The 360-degree sector around the ship was divided into pie-shaped segments. And a different letter of the alphabet was sent out by radio in Morse Code in each segment. For instance, from dead north to 015 degrees might be A today. Pilots were issued a little wheel which would show what the sectors were for the day, and if a pilot tuned in ZB, got a Morse Code F, he would look for the F sector, and then could determine where the ship was. We always tuned in our ZB coming home from flights to make sure we were coming in in the right sector.

Now the other reason this was important is that we had assigned sectors, and they were different every day for approaching the ship. Today we might approach the ship from sector M. Tomorrow it might be sector F. This is because of possible attacks by the Japanese. Any airplane that didn't come in in the assigned approach sector was shown no mercy; it was automatically shot down. So that pilots had a very good reason for tuning in their ZB and making sure that, first of all, they knew where the ship was, and also to come in in the right sector.

Q: And that would be varied so you wouldn't establish a pattern.

Admiral Lee: Varied every day. Every day a different wheel, and the sectors would be changed. But it was a very effective system.

Anyway, I'd just gotten back to the ship. I'm going to talk about two more incidents during this tour. On another day, November 6, 1944, four F6Fs were sent over Manila to bomb and strafe. Our assigned area was the waterfront this particular day, four F6Fs. This was when the invasion was in progress down south in Leyte. We arrived over Manila. And lo and behold, there was a Japanese destroyer out into the stream doing 20 or 25 knots, obviously hoping to escape, as we came onto the scene. We each had one 500-pound bomb. Of course, our six .50-caliber machine gun magazines were filled. We dived on this destroyer, and the three people in front of me released their bombs, and all three missed. I figured I had him. I had him right in my sights, pickled the bomb,

Lee #2 - 93

and nothing happened. I pulled out, and my division leader saw I hadn't dropped my bomb. And I could just see what he was thinking: "That dumb-ass ensign."

So I persuaded him, "Let's make another run. Let me drop my bomb."

I double-checked all my switches, and we went in again on this destroyer. He was smoking a little bit where we were hitting him with the .50-calibers. Another run, released it--was just positive that I had a hit--pulled out, no explosion. About that time the division leader had had it. So we didn't make any more strafing runs on him, and the three had missed. We then made some runs on our shore-based targets and headed back to the ship. I tried to jettison my bomb, which is the procedure because you don't like to land aboard with a bomb on--but it wouldn't jettison. So I got back aboard ship, inspected the airplane with the ordnance man. The bomb rack was not hooked up. Otherwise, I would have gotten myself a destroyer.

Q: All that effort foiled by one little thing.

Admiral Lee: Yes, bomb rack not hooked up.

I think the other exciting event of my combat tour in Essex happened during the Battle of Leyte Gulf. You might remember that we were landing in Leyte Gulf when the

Japanese launched a two- or three-pronged attack on us. They sent some carriers down from the north--carriers without airplanes, for the most part--as decoys.

Q: That was Admiral Ozawa's group.*

Admiral Lee: Admiral Halsey bit.** We had literally dozens and dozens of amphibious ships landing troops in the Leyte area. And the Japanese, meantime, were sending a battleship force through San Bernardino Strait which was no small feat navigating through those islands at night. And the Japanese didn't have radar. I always admired them for their navigational feats in World War II without radar. Remarkable. But, anyway, Halsey took the bait and headed north after the Japanese fleet. We launched an attack on the Japanese fleet up north and did considerable damage.

Towards the end of the day, which happened to be 25th of October, 1944, I was launched to escort a photo plane. The Japanese fleet at this time was perhaps 150 miles away. It was just a little short of dusk when we were launched. We approached the Japanese fleet, which at this time was heading north--and some ships were burning, some ships were smoking. And when we appeared on the horizon, they started shooting at us with everything they had. My photo pilot

---
*Vice Admiral Jisaburo Ozawa, IJN, Commander Mobile Force.
**Admiral William F. Halsey, Jr., USN, Commander Third Fleet.

took pictures of the Japanese fleet as it was retreating to the north, in its beaten and battered condition. I stayed with him. When we got back to the Essex, an hour or so later, it was dark. I had never made a night carrier landing, nor had any night carrier landing practice. Just wasn't done. I followed the photo pilot around and there was the landing signal officer in his lighted suit. He brought us aboard very nicely--my first night landing.

We were in the Formosa area, the Philippines area, the Western Pacific area, until near the end of November 1944. And at this time the Japanese were very definitely on the run. And towards the end of our tour, we really didn't see many Japanese planes. VF-15 had shot down more than 300 airplanes.

Towards the end of November, we headed back to Eniwetok. And around the first of December, Air Group 15 was relieved by Air Group Four. Essex stayed out to continue the war. Air Group 15 then was transferred to Bunker Hill.* We came home on the Bunker Hill, stopping at Pearl Harbor for two days. Bunker Hill steamed into Seattle. We got home in time for Christmas in 1944. So that, in my own case, I had left Pearl Harbor around the first of June, and got back sometime in early December. While in the Western Pacific, I had flown 71 flights and

---

*The USS Bunker Hill (CV-17) was a sister ship of the Essex.

flights, combat air patrol over the force, and antisubmarine patrol.

When we arrived in Seattle, we were given a choice of next duty: West Coast or East Coast. I chose the East Coast. The government would pay my transportation. Otherwise, I'd have to pay my way east and back again.

Q: Before we get to that, I'd like to ask a few more questions to wrap up the combat tour. You talked about the one mission where you shot down the Betty. Were there any others where you shot down Japanese planes?

Admiral Lee: No. I never got a shot at a Japanese plane other than that Betty. I always flew what was called "Tailend Charlie," the last man in a flight. I flew once or twice with David McCampbell. But I never personally got a shot at another plane, which was a big disappointment. The flights where enemy planes were usually encountered were the fighter sweeps and the like.

I did strafe a lot of planes on the ground but never any air-to-air combat. I observed David McCampbell shoot down one or two airplanes. If we were in the air, it was understood that the group commander, Commander McCampbell, would get first crack at the enemy, and he usually brought them down.

Q: What was your view of him as a group commander?

Admiral Lee: I thought David McCampbell was a very fine aviator, very aggressive. I think from that point of view, he was a great group commander, because that was his job, to be the leader. And if the leaders, namely, the group commander and the commanding officers of the squadrons, hold back, you're not going to have much of a combat group. So from the standpoint of being a combat leader, and willing to go every day to meet the Japanese, David McCampbell didn't have a peer. I thought as an organizer and as an administrator, I didn't see that he did very much.

I have compared VB-15, under the leadership of Commander Mini, and VF-15 under the leadership of Commander Rigg. It may be that I'm a little unfair to Commander Rigg, because at this particular time the character of the squadron was set. They had finished their training, and they, I suppose, didn't feel like embarking on a training program for replacement pilots. But I think one squadron was properly organized and administered in every way, and the other was not. But in time of war, we need David McCampbells.

Q: You talked about this mission when you shot down the

Betty. You had a combination of a scout bomber and a fighter. Why that particular combination?

Admiral Lee: The idea was that the scout bomber was a better navigator. I happened to come from the VB squadron and thought I was a pretty good navigator. But the fighter and the SB2C were paired together because these were long search missions. The primary job of the SB2C pilot was navigation. The F6F pilot was to fight any combat necessary. And, of course, they could both attack freighters and the like.

Q: But this combination is viewed as better than sending out two of one or the other?

Admiral Lee: Yes. At that time it was considered better. And it was a pretty good combination. We could put wing tanks on and go out to 300-350 miles maximum. And every day searches like this were sent out.

Q: You, having been in both squadrons, are in an interesting position to compare how they differed in such things as airmanship, radio discipline in the air, aggressiveness, and their overall nature.

Admiral Lee: VB-15 was a very disciplined squadron.

Flight discipline was excellent. Air discipline was excellent--just about as good as you're going to get. I thought in the fighter squadron, it was more or less every man for himself--not a great deal of discipline, not compared to the VB squadron. VF-15 lost seven pilots in operational accidents. That's an indication of lax discipline.

There is one interesting bit that I would like to comment on. Our ship, the Essex, got back down south in time for the SB2C squadron to be launched against the Japanese ships which had come through San Bernardino Strait. And in one of these attacks, Commander Mini's SB2C was hit. He limped home but couldn't see. His windshield was covered with oil. His wingman on this particular flight was Lieutenant (junior grade) Nelson, the replacement pilot, who led Mini home to the ramp for a carrier landing. Commander Mini thought that Lieutenant Nelson was just about the finest aviator around after that. And, of course, Nelson was a superlative aviator. On that same series of missions, Lieutenant (junior grade) Mallette was lost. I corresponded with his mother until her death just a few years ago.

I would also like to comment on Essex. Essex was, perhaps after World War II's Enterprise, the finest ship in the Navy. I think the Essex-class carrier was just about an ideal design. Of course, it had been designed and redesigned about six times before it was actually put into production. The Navy had a very difficult time getting enough money to build aircraft carriers in the Thirties, but we had built several, including Yorktown, Hornet, and Enterprise. All the thinking that went into those designs eventually became the Essex, which was CV-9 and the first of its class.

I thought the Essex-class ship had just about ideal characteristics: a very livable ship, good wardrooms, good ready rooms, marvelous engineering plant, well designed, well laid out, a ship that was good in rough seas, and very maintainable. I believe the Essex-class carrier is one of the finest ships the Navy ever bought. I went through two typhoons aboard Essex. In one typhoon we lost two or three destroyers, capsized. But that is a horrendous experience, going through a typhoon. They just seemed to go on forever.

Q: What do you recall specifically about the typhoon?*

Admiral Lee: Well, as an ensign in the VF squadron. I never saw the weather charts that weathermen ought to see. And later on, when I became captain of a ship, we had learned to avoid typhoons. Actually, we knew how to avoid

---

*In mid-December 1944, while operating in support of the invasion of the Philippines, the Third Fleet got caught in a typhoon that sank three destroyers and damaged a number of other ships.

typhoons in 1944. We could have avoided those typhoons. As a matter of fact, Admiral Nimitz and Admiral King launched an investigation after we went through those two typhoons.* Admiral Halsey was severely criticized, because instead of keeping track of the weather and possible typhoons and moving the fleet to avoid them, which was quite possible, he elected to let the ships weather the typhoons. I never saw the report of the investigation. But the typhoons were terrible.

We were told we were approaching a typhoon. All aircraft were secured with double chains, hangar deck and flight deck. The ship went to essentially steerageway, just enough way on to keep control of the ship. A typhoon will typically last two or three days. There was no sleeping. The bow would rise up, seem to stall out like an airplane, and then come crashing down. The ship would roll 20 and 30 degrees. And then we'd start going up again, rise up and crash down. Fortunately, Essex sustained no damage. We had our airplanes soaked with salt water, but I don't remember that we had any losses of men or damage to the ship.

Q: You talk about the Essex as a physical structure. She

---

*Fleet Admiral Chester W. Nimitz, USN, Commander in Chief Pacific Fleet and Pacific Ocean Areas; Fleet Admiral Ernest J. King, USN, Commander in Chief U.S. Fleet and Chief of Naval Operations. The second typhoon hit the Third Fleet in June 1945 and damaged several ships.

also has hundreds and hundreds of men on board. How was the relationship between the men of the air group and of the ship's company?

Admiral Lee: I thought relationships were excellent. The air group went out for about six months' combat, whereas the ship stayed out there for the entire war. I think being a member of the ship's company was very difficult. When Air Group 15 joined Essex, Essex had had one combat tour of six months with Air Group Nine. We replaced Nine, and were with Essex for roughly six months, perhaps seven months altogether. Then we left and Essex got another air group. Essex had three consecutive air groups, each aboard for perhaps seven months. While this third air group was aboard, Essex got hit by a kamikaze plane.*

But Essex was a very professional ship. The captain when I was aboard was Captain Ofstie. And the executive officer was David McDonald.

Q: Do you have specific memories of those two?

Admiral Lee: Only that I saw Commander McDonald in the wardroom every day at dinner, and he visited our ready room once in a while. He was a courtly southerner, as you

---

*On 25 November 1944, a Japanese suicide plane hit the Essex, killing 15 and wounding 44.

probably know. And Captain Ofstie talked on the 1MC, which is the ship's loudspeaker system, periodically. I never personally talked to Captain Ofstie. He was a very popular captain.

Q: What was the atmosphere like in the wardroom? You had these active periods when you were flying, but you also had a chance to relax in between.

Admiral Lee: Ships at sea are like a big prison, except there are no handcuffs. We had movies. There were bridge clubs, reading, and we did have an exercise room. I thought relations were surprisingly good aboard ship. We had a lot of professionals aboard, both USNR types and regular Navy types. And they were there to do a job, and they did. And the idea was that whatever had to be done to further the war, that's what we did. And with Captain Ofstie and Commander McDonald, of course, Essex was very much a "can do" ship. I thought living conditions were great aboard ship. I lived in a bunk room, so-called "boys' town." But we had clean sheets every night, no foxholes, and stewards took care of our laundry. Wardroom--I thought the food was excellent, a lot of rice. Sometimes we ran out of fresh provisions, but that was no great hardship.

I think fighting a war from an aircraft carrier is

fighting it in style.

Q: You told a story at lunchtime that bears repeating about Wayne Morris in the wardroom.

Admiral Lee: We did have one famous aviator in Air Group 15, the movie star, Wayne Morris. Wayne at this time was, I would guess, in his early 30s. He was a friend of the group commander and had not gone through normal flight training. He was what was called an AVT aviator--namely, a person who was given a commission and wings for a specific purpose, such as training, say, in primary flight training. So Wayne Morris must have done some private flying before he got into the Navy.

David McCampbell, as squadron commander of VF-15, in 1943, somehow or other persuaded the Navy to transfer Wayne Morris to VF-15. He was a very good pilot, shot down several Japanese planes, and pretty much a regular fellow. I can remember one time sitting by him in the wardroom for dinner. This particular night we had fish. And Wayne always had a nice sense of humor. Wayne ate his fish from around the bones of the fish so that the skeleton was lying on his plate when he'd finished. One of our stewards came around, and Wayne picked up his plate and said to the steward, "How about a refill?"

But that was Wayne Morris, a very fine person.

Q: Did you in both squadrons spend a lot of time in the ready rooms?

Admiral Lee: Yes. The ready room was our home. We played bridge. We read. We had briefings. We had two places where we could stay, really. One was the wardroom, which is the officers' living room and dining room. The other was the ready room. We spent much of our time in one or the other of those places.

Q: How would you describe the routine in a ready room on the day of a mission?

Admiral Lee: On the day of a mission, priority in the ready room was given to those flights that were going out. Pilots not on the flight schedule were expected to clear out, or sit in the back of the ready room. The squadron had two or three intelligence officers. They would get all the information on the missions--maps, descriptions, everything that was known about the missions--and the air intelligence officers would brief the flights as to what to expect and what they would see. The flight leader then would brief on the entire flight--takeoff, rendezvous, altitudes, attack, what we do if we're attacked, then the route home, the approach sector to the ship. He would go over every phase of the flight in great detail. Normally we'd finish with all our briefings five or ten minutes before man airplanes. We normally manned airplanes 30 minutes before launch.

Q: How long would the briefing take?

Admiral Lee: An hour and a half. We manned the ready rooms two hours before a combat flight and manned aircraft 30 minutes before launch. We had two adjacent ready rooms and immediately after the flight, all pilots would meet in the other ready room and have a debriefing. The air intelligence officers would be there. We each filled out a form and described what we saw and what we had done. These were all put together by the air intelligence officers. A combat action report for that day would be submitted by each ship: number of airplanes sighted, number shot down, number of losses, number of ships attacked, close air support missions run. It was very well organized and very well done.

Q: I would think that sometimes--in the heat of battle and excitement--that different people would perceive the same event differently. How were those things ironed out back in the ready room?

Admiral Lee: I suppose, for the most part, they weren't. It's very true that in the heat of battle people see different things. And it's just about impossible to tell who got what hits in a bombing run, for instance, if 10 or 12 planes are diving on one target. It was much easier, of course, in fighter combat, because you can usually tell who shot down an airplane. The way we operated, only one plane at a time could shoot at another individual plane. But I think if there were any doubts about what happened, the air intelligence officers sort of smoothed it down and evened it out. We merely reported what we saw, what we did.

Q: It was up to somebody else to resolve it.

Admiral Lee: Right. We didn't try to resolve any differences.

Q: Was that pretty much standard doctrine, that only one fighter would be allowed on an individual target?

Admiral Lee: I don't remember that it was standard doctrine, but it's pretty difficult for two fighters to shoot at one target--targets that were small in those days, such as an opposing fighter. Because the time span when you can shoot at an enemy airplane is so small. If you're making a run on another airplane, whether it's a fighter or a bomber, you have a time frame of perhaps three seconds, when you can get off an effective attack. By then you're past. If it's a high side, or an overhead, or a head-on, it's just about impossible physically for two fighters to shoot at the same target, if they're coming from roughly the same direction. It could happen if they're attacking from different directions. But in a case like that, there's a great chance of a midair collision. And we did have a midair collision in the VF squadron. Two fighters collided, and we lost both planes and both pilots.

So, as a matter of tactics, the fighters were divided into four-plane divisions--two two-plane sections. And it was understood that the leader of the four-plane division led the fight. The second section and his wingman were there to protect him. They didn't normally shoot. So the people who became the aces were the division leaders, which I didn't have any argument with.

Q: Because presumably they were the most experienced.

Admiral Lee: They were most experienced, and our job was to protect them. You would follow them right through, whatever attack they were making.

Q: You talked about the incident in which you were being fired at by the turret from the Betty. Were there other occasions on which you were shot at?

Admiral Lee: We were always being shot at. The Japanese put up a pretty good fight. We saw lots of flak, wherever we went almost: in the Marianas, in the Philippines, Peleliu, Formosa. You'd see these burst at your altitude or thereabouts. And the planes we lost never saw what hit them. So in aviation, you either came home safely or you didn't come home.

Q: Do you develop somewhat of a fatalistic attitude toward that as you fly into it?

Admiral Lee: You know, I think it's a common human failing. You figure it won't happen to you.

Q: Just like when you get out in your car.

Admiral Lee: You think that all those other people will get shot down, but I won't. I'll get back. We had two or three pilots shot down and picked up by submarines, or in the Philippines, picked up by Filipinos, and who later got back to the ship. So all pilots who were shot down were not lost. Maybe we got back half a dozen.

Q: Well, indeed, I've heard that extraordinary efforts

were made to recover them, just to boost morale.

Admiral Lee: Yes.

Q: You talked about the one instance in which the bomb rack was not hooked up, so you couldn't drop your bomb. Was that an exception to the normal maintenance quality?

Admiral Lee: Yes. I would say maintenance was excellent.

I'm going to talk about this later, but back in those days, every ship and every naval air station had its own maintenance crew. A squadron in an air group consisted of the pilots, the ground officers, and a handful of enlisted men; VB-15 had no maintenance people. The maintenance people belonged to the ship, Essex. And the same thing was true ashore. The maintenance was done by air station people, because that made logistics so much simpler. Now that's an expensive way to do it. In peacetime each squadron has its own maintenance people. We inspected our planes monthly in VB-15. Each pilot was given an airplane to inspect, and we went out and gave it a very thorough inspection. In VF-15 that was never done. But maintenance was, in general, very, very good. The maintenance crews worked very hard.

Q: You develop a pretty close relationship with your

Lee #2 - 111

mechanic, because your life is in his hands.

Admiral Lee: Yes, I think that's one of the unfortunate parts about World War II, because we didn't really know our mechanics. I didn't know one maintenance person on Essex, because I never saw them. They were always working on the hangar deck, and they weren't a part of the squadron. I never met one of them, unfortunately. Even the plane captains belonged to the ship. Having been an aviation machinist's mate, I looked forward to knowing some of these people, but it wasn't possible in those times.

Q: You couldn't go down to the hangar deck, and just talk to these guys?

Admiral Lee: I could have, but they were all so very busy. We went down and inspected our planes, but I didn't know any maintenance people on Essex.

Q: We touched briefly on the liberty situation there at Eniwetok, when you were converting to the fighter. What do you recall of liberty at any other places, such as Ulithi?

Admiral Lee: I believe we went into Ulithi between the Philippines and Formosa. Ulithi was not very different from Eniwetok. It had a big officers' club. And we all went over and drank booze, went swimming, and so forth. They had a racket on Ulithi. I wondered why the Navy put up with it. In order to buy drinks at the bar and so forth on Ulithi, we each had to join the club. And to join the club cost one dollar. So that whoever was running the club must have made a fortune. The entire fleet went through there, one dollar tribute from each officer. I wonder whatever happened to all that money.

Q: Makes one wonder. What about the mail situation? That's always a highlight for people at sea. How often did you get that?

Admiral Lee: I thought mail wasn't bad. A replenishment ship that was designated to come alongside Essex would be given Essex's mail. And Essex would get 100 or 200 bags of mail about once every week or two weeks. Of course, mail call was always a very exciting time aboard ship. And I'd say mail delivery was very good. I believe the mail was flown from the States out to Hawaii. Then I believe it was flown from Hawaii out to one of the lagoons, Ulithi or Eniwetok, and there it was put aboard replenishment ships which then brought it out to us. I daresay 20-30 days from the States to the ships was about par for the course.

Q: How good was logistic support for the aircraft in the

squadrons you were in?

Admiral Lee: Logistic support was excellent. We didn't worry too much about planes in those days. If we had a plane that hit a barrier or was badly damaged, we would salvage what parts we could from the plane and push it over the side. We couldn't afford to devote the space to a wrecked airplane and bring it back. But I think a fair amount of cannibalization went on. If we didn't have a spare propeller, why, we'd take one off a plane that was down. But logistics support was excellent, surprisingly good, I think, for everything.

We had tenders in all the fleet anchorages. We had teams of technicians who could go from ship to ship, repair airplanes or ships themselves. Airplanes were fairly simple in those days. A good mechanic with a set of hand tools could repair 99% of an SB2C or an F6F. No electronics to speak of. No powered flight controls. No radars. Guns were simple. Hydraulic systems were simple. The engines were not all that complicated. We didn't need complicated test equipment. All you'd need was a hoist to change an engine now and then.

And, of course, we also had metalsmiths, people who were good working with metal, riveting and the like. We had welders. We had electricians. And none of them had sophisticated equipment, because it wasn't needed. The

Lee #2 - 114

availability rate on airplanes was very high, perhaps about 70% or 80%.

Q: You mentioned briefly the one instance where you floated in the Helldiver. Could you talk about that more specifically, and then generally about landing operations?

Admiral Lee: The SB2C was a reasonably good carrier airplane, had a good engine, but when it was lightly loaded, it had a tendency to float. If you were coming in to make a landing and the signal officer gave you the signal to cut, that meant cut your engine. The SB2C's nose wouldn't just automatically drop and touch down on the deck. When you cut your engine, you had to consciously drop the nose.

Q: With the stick.

Admiral Lee: Push over and then flare in the SB2C. And if you didn't do it right, the airplane would float. I've seen SB2Cs many times float just above the wires. The barrier's a great big steel cable, stretched across the deck from about three feet up to eight or ten feet high. The airplane would fly right into it.

This happened to me in an SB2C in 1945. I was requalifying, floated, and I ran into the barrier. Not much damage done, just an engine change. The F6F, on the other hand, almost never floated into the barrier. Because it had, I suppose, a high wing loading as opposed to the SB2C. When you chopped the power on an F6F, the nose dropped. You chopped the power on an F6F as you were coming over the ramp, on signal, and about all you had to do was flare. But the SB2C was different--you had to make sure your nose dropped and then flare, because it wouldn't drop itself especially if you were a little fast.

Q: So that was one definite advantage you got, shifting from one squadron to the other.

Admiral Lee: Yes.

Q: Well, I think that about exhausts my questions on that combat tour. We're ready to get you back to the East Coast then.

Admiral Lee: Yes. Let's go back to the East Coast. I was home for Christmas in 1944 and then in January reported to Air Force, Atlantic Fleet. I then was sent on up to VB-97 at Naval Air Station, Glenview, which was a holding squadron. And then in February 1945, I was assigned to VB-151.

Q: Had you expressed a preference to get back into a bombing squadron?

Admiral Lee: Yes. I had a choice when I got back. I could have gone into a fighter squadron or a bomber squadron. Of the people who switched from VB-15 to VF-15, I think at least two of us went back to the SB2Cs.

Q: What was that choice based on in your case?

Admiral Lee: I liked dive-bombing. I liked to have a crewman along. And I'd had my fling as a fighter pilot. No great thought went into it. And this may sound odd, but I thought dive-bomber people were a more circumspect group. I seemed to be happier in the bomber squadron than in the fighter squadron.

Q: And that may have just been because of the two particular ones you were in.

Admiral Lee: Very possibly it was. But, anyway, I came back, and I had a choice. And I made the choice to go to an SB2C squadron. I was assigned to VB-151, and our forming and retraining were done at Naval Auxiliary Air Station Manteo, which was on a little island 20 miles from Kitty Hawk, North Carolina. The Navy had built a small air station, and it was used for forming of squadrons and retraining. There were two or three other squadrons reforming down there. We were at Manteo for two months, and there were about five or six of us from VB-15 in VB-151.

We got a new commanding officer, of course--a lieutenant by the name of Phil Cobb.* The executive officer was a lieutenant by the name of Walter Roach.** Both of them had had combat. We reformed at Manteo with about 20 planes and about 35 pilots. We went through the standard training--formation flying, dive-bombing, glide-bombing--and then moved up to Naval Air Station Oceana, where we joined the group.*** We then had two months of group flying. Our SB2C squadron joined an F4U squadron and a TBF squadron. We were Air Wing 151.

And I'd like to make a comment on this commanding officer, Philip Cobb. He was an ex-aviation cadet, chemical engineer from the University of Michigan. He was in the early battles--Midway and down in the Solomon Islands area, and so forth, and had been awarded the Navy Cross. He was a very fine aviator, but he didn't like to fly. He averaged four to six hours a month during the course of our training period. He claimed he was too busy doing paperwork. This had a very bad effect on the

---
*Lieutenant Philip W. Cobb, USNR.
**Lieutenant Walter Roach, USNR.
***Oceana Naval Air Station is in Virginia Beach, Virginia.

squadron, because in a squadron the skipper has to get out there and fly. He has to be number one in gunnery, bombing, night flying, and everything else; he has to be out front. And that's why I think the leadership exhibited by David McCampbell was so important.

Q: He was just the opposite of McCampbell, it sounds like.

Admiral Lee: Yes. Phil Cobb was a fine aviator, but I think he was just lazy, or didn't like to fly. I don't know if I ever went on a dive-bombing run with him or not. We had an adequate squadron, but for that reason alone, it wasn't a first-rate squadron.

Q: After what you'd been through on the Essex, almost anything would have been anticlimactic, but this was even worse.

Admiral Lee: Yes. Although we had a happy squadron, a good squadron. It was kind of a joke in the squadron that the skipper never flew. But we had enough people with enough experience. We had two lieutenants, the CO and XO. All the rest of us were jaygees. We got about 20 brand-new ensigns from the operational flight training command. Our job was to train them.

Q: Were you assigned to a carrier?

Admiral Lee: No. We trained two months at Manteo, moved up to Oceana, trained two months at Oceana as a group, and then headed west. In August 1945, we were at Naval Air Station Corvallis, Oregon, all set to go, when the war ended.

We had no real problems during the course of this retraining. The six of us from VB-15 had been assigned the usual department head jobs in the squadron, division leaders. And we had some fairly good young people. We weren't so old ourselves; I was 21. The new ensigns were about 20-21.

At about this time I was thinking about what I might do when the war was over. While I was home during the holidays, I visited North Carolina State University at Raleigh, North Carolina, made an application to study electrical engineering, and was accepted. Came the end of the war, which happened in August 1945. The Navy was under great pressure to let everybody out. About this time I had a choice to make--whether to leave active duty and go to North Carolina State or join the regular Navy.

The Navy came up with a program about that time for reserve officers. We could apply for a commission in the regular Navy. If accepted, then the Navy would supposedly send us to college. I didn't like shipboard duty very much, but I liked aviation. And so I elected to stay. I decided if I were not given a regular commission, I would then go on down to North Carolina State.

Well, as things worked out, I was given a regular commission and was assigned to Air Group 17 in Fallon, Nevada, at the end of 1945. I got a new commanding officer by the name of Heber J. Badger.* And my squadron was VB-17. The whole air group spent the winter of '45 in Fallon, Nevada. Commander William F. Bringle was the group commander. He later became well known and also later became commandant of midshipmen at the Naval Academy.

Q: Commander Seventh Fleet.

Admiral Lee: Commander Seventh Fleet. Very good man. We had three squadrons--VT-17, VB-17, and VF-17. We trained at Fallon through late 1945 into the winter and then were transferred to Brunswick, Maine. By about this time the Navy had become a shambles. The period from 1945 to 1947 was very difficult for the Navy. Officers were mustering out every week. Men were being discharged, either on points or the end of their enlistment. Squadrons had no maintenance people.

When we got to Brunswick, Maine--as a typical

---
*Lieutenant Commander Heber J. Badger, USN.

example--we had about 30 SB2Cs and maybe a dozen maintenance people. Since I had been a mechanic, I organized a program for the pilots to work with the mechanics on our airplanes so we'd have something to fly. Bringle thought that was great. We checked our airplanes, changed spark plugs, and did all the things we had to do in order to get some flying in.

The Navy was being withdrawn from around the world, and it took people to do the withdrawing. We were withdrawing from Australia, the Atlantic, and all parts of the Pacific. Personnel were being reassigned; ships were being mothballed; aircraft were being mothballed. We were trying to maintain some semblance of a navy. The Navy had enough people, but they were spread everywhere. We had to shift from air stations doing maintenance, and ships doing maintenance, to giving the maintenance people back to the squadrons. It was much more efficient. During the war every station and every ship had a full complement of maintenance people.

So for all of those reasons, the Navy would have had a difficult time to beat the Salvation Army in early 1946. In retrospect, I think things went amazingly well. Eventually hundreds of ships were mothballed. All the people were discharged who wanted to go. Bases were closed. It was decided in the spring in 1946, about June, that Brunswick would be closed. And we were then transferred down to Naval Air Station Norfolk.

Bowdoin College is in Brunswick, Maine. I decided to enroll for the spring semester in 1946. I took two courses--English composition and economics. The skipper of the squadron was very happy to see me do this. I enjoyed it. Bowdoin was a very nice college, very fine college. I had two good instructors. And the classroom was filled with veterans--people back from the Army, Navy, and Air Force to start college.

Q: I guess your flying schedule was flexible enough you could fit it in around your class work.

Admiral Lee: No problem. We had no planes to fly.

Q: That would solve that.

Admiral Lee: I took two three-hour courses. I arranged them so that I could go take two hours at a time, and I did my homework at night. I thoroughly enjoyed it.

The other thing I did--I had a friend named Mary Edith Buckley from 1942 down at Wellesley College. By 1946 she was a senior. While I was at Brunswick, I was always looking for recreation, so I went down to Wellesley for two or three weekends and saw this young lady that I'd met when I was an aviation cadet at preflight school. She and a friend of hers came up to Brunswick one weekend.

The executive officer of our squadron was a good friend of mine by the name of Walter Roach. He and I had a small apartment at that time. I talked him into taking Mary Edith Buckley's friend--her name was Anne Gottlieb--as a blind date for the weekend. They were seniors getting ready to graduate. We had a very nice weekend. I even took Mary Edith up in a small airplane, which I rented. She got sick, which wasn't all that pleasant. It was her first airplane flight. Walter Roach married his blind date two months later. Mary Edith graduated from Wellesley and went on back to California. More about her later.

Q: All right.

I'd be interested in more on Bringle also. He eventually became a four-star admiral, so I would think he had both the management, administrative talents, and the leadership abilities.

Admiral Lee: Yes. Bringle had it all. Bringle was a group commander in a very difficult period. He was a very energetic man, and was a great personality, wonderful smile. I've met only two or three people that I thought more attractive than Bringle. I'd say about the most attractive man I've ever known, greatest personality I've known was probably Jerry Miller--marvelous, just fun to be with the man.* But Bringle was not far behind.

Q: Bringle is not as warm an individual as Miller, I gather.

Admiral Lee: Very nearly so. He's a very warm man, very friendly. Ensigns could talk to Bringle, and did it all the time. Very fine aviator.

Q: Very polished too.

Admiral Lee: Very polished man. Bringle was a diplomat, and that means that Bringle was also a politician. You know, he always said the right thing at the right time. Very sophisticated, very polished, very smooth Southern boy from Tennessee. It was pretty obvious that Bringle would go places in this Navy.

Q: Did you get much chance to fly with him?

Admiral Lee: Never flew with him at all. He flew the fighters all the time, F4Us. We flew with him in group

---

*Vice Admiral Gerald E. Miller, USN (Ret.), is the subject of a two-volume Naval Institute oral history. Miller was graduated from the Naval Academy in the class of 1942, qualified as a naval aviator, and later commanded the USS Franklin D. Roosevelt (CVA-42) and the Sixth Fleet. In 1960 he and Lee were among the first Navy members of the Joint Strategic Target Planning Staff at Omaha, Nebraska.

attacks--group gropes, as they were called. I never personally flew with him, but people were all around me who did. He was very fine aviator.

When we were down at Norfolk, he was sent to the Naval Academy. He was a natural for the Naval Academy--well spoken, charmer, has the image. You know, he was a big handsome guy, football player at the Naval Academy. I saw him through the years many times, and I considered him a friend for the next 30 years.

In November of 1946, VB-17 was redesignated VA-5B at Naval Air Station Norfolk. The air group, which consisted of one SB2C squadron, one F4U squadron, and one TBM or TBF squadron--was designated Air Group Five. And we trained at NAS Norfolk.

In December of that year, 1946, I volunteered for an unusual assignment. The Navy decided to send six airplanes up to Newfoundland for cold-weather testing. We took two SB2Cs, two F4Us, and two F8Fs. These six airplanes stayed at Newfoundland about three weeks with another squadron. The squadron later went aboard a small jeep carrier out of Newfoundland, and we flew home overland. But while at Newfoundland, I checked out in the F8F. Having previously flown the F6F, I found it very interesting to fly the F8F. The differences were startling. The F8F had the same engine as the F6F, an R-2800 engine, Pratt & Whitney. The plane weighed about 4,000 pounds less, and instead of having a barrel fuselage, it had a very slim fuselage, so that the F8F was a great performer. It would have been the equal of the Japanese Zeros in World War II. It was a real hot rod. And I thoroughly enjoyed that.

Q: What else did you do while you were there? What was the reason for the mission?

Admiral Lee: Just to see how we could perform in Newfoundland in cold weather.

Q: What were the results of this?

Admiral Lee: It really wasn't much of an exercise. I sometimes wondered why we did it. We had our own small maintenance crew. The weather was cold, obviously, in Argentia, Newfoundland. But we had the facilities that were necessary--namely, a hangar and heaters to heat our engines. The runways were kept clean of snow and ice. We flew two or three flights a day out of Argentia and around the Newfoundland area. We had no problems whatsoever. The secret to cold weather operating, of course, is to take proper care of your engines.

Q: Did BuAer send engineers up to test the results?*

---

*BuAer--Bureau of Aeronautics.

Admiral Lee: No, they didn't. They just wanted to know how we did, and we told them. Small, short report. But the secret in any cold weather operations, whether it's with a tractor or with an engine, is to get your engine warm. If you've got some way to warm your engine before you try to start it, you're in great shape. Once you get it started and going, you're fine. The problem is getting them going in cold weather. If you plan properly beforehand with either a heated hangar, or if not a heated hangar, have some type of heating system, so you can blow air through for an hour or so to get them warm, batteries warm, engine warm, oil warm. We never had any problems, because we took proper care of our airplanes and engines.

Q: Did you have any problems with lube oil or hydraulic fluid in that weather?

Admiral Lee: No. You see, airplanes are designed to fly in cold air. Because, as you know, the air, the adiabatic lapse rate, I think it's called, is 3.6 degrees Fahrenheit for a 1,000 feet, or something like that. The temperature drops a certain number of degrees per 1,000 feet, so that airplanes, the engine oil, cowl flaps, hydraulic fluid--they're all designed to fly in cold weather, because the weather is always cold at altitude. The problem in cold-weather operations is what you do with them on the ground. The best solution is not to let them cool off. Put them in a heated hangar, even a tent where you can keep the air warm like this room.

Q: Is there a problem with the pilots in an atmosphere like that?

Admiral Lee: No. The cockpits were heated, and we wore our normal flight gear. We had no problems. If we'd come down, there would have been a problem. You know, we'd need exposure suits. But we wore exposure suits.

After we returned to Norfolk from this excursion to Newfoundland, VA-5B went on the shakedown cruise of Valley Forge, a new aircraft carrier.* We went to Cuba and stayed down there February, March, and April--in Guantanamo, flying both off the air station and off the ship, while the ship went through underway training, all the damage control exercises and so forth. We came back with her, and were off-loaded at Naval Air Station Norfolk.

Q: Did she have a relatively full crew during that training?

---

*The USS Valley Forge (CV-45), a near-sister of the USS Essex in which Lee had served earlier, was commissioned 3 November 1946.

Lee #2 - 129

Admiral Lee: Valley Forge was a brand-new ship, just commissioned, was given a full crew. We were only assigned to her for shakedown to Guantanamo. Standard operation. Nothing unusual about it. We were there to help them with their training.

Q: So it was more for the benefit of the ship's crew than the air group.

Admiral Lee: Oh, I'd say 90% of it was for the benefit of the ship's crew, because the Valley Forge was to do refresher training, come back to the Navy yard for whatever work needed to be done, and then go to the West Coast.

Q: She was one of the very few carriers in commission in the Pacific when the Korean War broke out.

Admiral Lee: Yes. These years, '45 to '47, were very difficult ones for the Navy. And they were very difficult ones for me personally. I was getting tired of flying the SB2C. I was getting tired of being in a squadron. I thought maybe I'd missed the boat, because I had decided to stay in the Navy, in aviation, and not go to North Carolina State. But my time eventually came.

In July 1947, I was assigned to Columbia University in

the Holloway plan.* The Navy's plan at this time for the education of former officers was that we would get five semesters--assuming two semesters as a year--at a college or university. These colleges and universities were those 52 that the Navy had at the time in the NROTC program.** Then we were to be sent to General Line School for a year to study subjects that normally are taught at the Naval Academy, such as seamanship, navigation, ordnance, gunnery, and the like--line subjects. Well, the college chosen for me was Columbia University in New York City.

Q: Did you have any choice?

Admiral Lee: No. I got orders to Columbia University, and I was delighted to get them. But I was a little shocked. I had never lived in a big city and up to this time had really led a fairly sheltered life: first, the farm in South Carolina, and then the Navy. The Navy is quite sheltered. And here I was going to New York City on my own, Columbia University, in a huge city--subways and millions of people--and I really didn't know what to

---
*The plan was named for Rear Admiral James L. Holloway, Jr., chairman of a panel that formulated it as a means of providing a sufficient number of regular officers for the post-World War II Navy. For a summary, see an article by the originator, "The Holloway Plan--A Summary View and Commentary," U.S. Naval Institute Proceedings, November 1947, pages 1293-1303.
**NROTC--Naval Reserve Officer Training Corps, a program by which individuals receive naval officer training while being educated at civilian universities.

expect. But, anyway, I arrived in New York City in August of 1947 and checked in with the professor of naval science.* And we were more or less on our own. There were maybe a dozen naval officers in my class. All except two or three were aviators. The aviators were assigned to universities that had flying facilities nearby, and we flew at Floyd Bennett.**

So I got a good look at New York City, a good look at Columbia. Then I decided I'd plan to complete all requirements for a degree, except a major, which I wouldn't be able to do in five semesters. Columbia, at that time, had specific requirements for a degree. I can remember them to this day. We had to have 12 hours of English; we had to have three college years of a language--Spanish, French, German, something. We had to have 12 hours of social sciences--history, psychology, economics, and so forth. We had to have 12 hours of science and math. Well, I planned my schedule so I could complete all of that and take as much math and physics as possible in the meantime.

Q: Did your work at Bowdoin count toward that?

Admiral Lee: Yes. Work at Bowdoin counted towards that,

---
*The professor of naval science was the head of the university's NROTC unit.
**Floyd Bennett Naval Air Station was in Brooklyn, named for the mechanic who accompanied Commander Richard Byrd on his flight over the North Pole.

both the English and economics. I just continued them at Columbia. During the course of five semesters there, I took one college year of Spanish in the summer term, Spanish all day. So I was able to complete the three college years of Spanish and get the language requirements qualification. And, of course, I did the 12 hours of English and the 12 hours of social sciences. And then I took as much science and math as I could. I took seven math courses, through integral calculus. I took three physics courses and engineering drawing. My years at Columbia and in New York City were happy years.

Q: Why do you say that?

Admiral Lee: I had plenty of money. I was a lieutenant with flight pay going to college. I had an automobile. Absolutely no restraints. Completely on my own. New York City is a marvelous place for a young man. You name it, it's there. If you like girls, there are plenty of girls at Columbia. If you like baseball games, they are there. Broadway, plays there--the subways. Fascinating place.

Q: Where did you live?

Admiral Lee: I lived on 76th Street and Broadway. I lived with another student there, who was best man at my wedding.

We had a small apartment, and a landlady by the name of Mrs. Flynn cleaned it for us. We did our own cooking, just the two of us. My friend and apartment-mate was Al Goodberlet.*

Our subway station was 76th Street. We'd take the subway up to Columbia every morning. It was only a very short ride; it ran frequently, I think we got out at 116th. It might have been 110th, depending on where we were going at Columbia. Columbia, I think, runs from 110th to 116th, from Broadway to Morningside Drive. That's Columbia-- several square blocks, and Columbia owns most of the real estate around it.

I think my exposure to New York City has been beneficial to me all my life and my career. In the first place, I didn't know what a big city was like. And I suppose, in the second place, having grown up in the South, I didn't know any Jews. I met one Jew as an aviator in World War II. But I really didn't know him. And, of course, at Columbia, it was about, I don't know, 60 to 70% Jewish. And New York City had, perhaps, four million Jews at that time. They're a very talented people. In almost every class at Columbia the top students were always the Jewish boys and girls.

I remember my first year there. In one of my classes was a very attractive Jewish girl who had black hair. She

---

*Lieutenant (junior grade) Alphonse G. Goodberlet, USN.

was a very good student. I asked her for a date, and she agreed. I was a little bit naive at the time. I got on the subway and rode over to Brooklyn, where she lived in an apartment house. But when Mama met me at the door, I began to get the message. She really wasn't enthusiastic about her daughter going out with me. Just on sight, she could see that I wasn't Jewish. And she didn't think that was such a good idea. So I never asked the young lady out again, but she was a very attractive person.

But I learned something else at Columbia, and I learned it quickly. Columbia, like most big universities, has a lot of instructors--people who teach courses, whether it's math, or English, or economics, or whatnot. They are graduate students and instructors who are working for Ph.D's. I learned very quickly--avoid young instructors who are working for Ph.D's like the plague. And, if you can, get the old professors--about 45 to 55, the guys who've been around--if you're really interested in learning something and being a good student. And I did that.

I would take classes any time, day or night, to get the old-timers and to avoid the young instructors. The young instructors, for the most part, were not interested in me. They were interested in getting their Ph.D and getting out. This was just a means for them to make a living while they were doing this. Some of them were fair, but some of them gave less than they should have. So I tried to get the old-timers, the professors who'd been around a long time, who'd seen a lot of students, and who had no axes to grind.

Columbia had some marvelous professors. I remember I took a course from one by the name of Callcott.* He was in the Spanish department. We talked about everything. One day he was talking to the class about race problems in the United States. He was about 50-55 years old, Spanish, been around a long time, and a very fine man. He said that we would never solve the race problem in the United States until we had completely assimilated the Negro, the black. He said, "Then you will have solved it. And you won't solve it beforehand." Coming from the South, I thought he was smoking opium. But, you know, he was right. He was right. I don't know how long it'll take. It looks like it'll take a long time.

We had lots of time off between semesters, holidays, and it was an absolutely great two and a half years, five semesters. And most of us worked pretty hard there. I think we gave it a college try. I know in my grades--in the seven math courses, I got seven A's. Physics I got two A's and a B-plus. And I think in the whole time I was there, I got two C-pluses, and all the rest were A's and B's. And the other five-term students were doing very well also.

---
*Dr. Frank Callcott, Associate Professor of Spanish.

Now another major event of that period came in the spring of 1948, after I'd been at Columbia a year. We had a break between the end of the spring semester and the beginning of the summer term. I wrote this young lady, Mary Edith Buckley, who was out in California, and told her I was driving down to South Carolina in June, end of the semester. I asked if she would like to come to New York and drive down to South Carolina with me. She wrote back and said she would love to. So she came east.

We took a leisurely trip down to South Carolina, stopped off at Patuxent and saw our friends, the Roaches, her Wellesley classmate. We drove on down through the Eastern Shore of Maryland to see some of her mother's relatives. On down to South Carolina, to the farm, to let her see what life was like down there. On down to Myrtle Beach and back up to New York, where we met her parents. Her father had come east on a business trip. He was in the wholesale whiskey business.

We decided to get married during the Christmas break in 1948. We made the decision in Raleigh, North Carolina. Then she went back to California, and I went back to school. During Christmas break in 1948, I flew out to California, and we were married. She came back to New York with me. And I moved out of my cozy little apartment, and we sublet a furnished place in the Bronx, very close to Yankee Stadium. We lived there for the spring semester of

Lee #2 - 137

1949.

Q: So now you were going south on the subway to get to Columbia.

Admiral Lee: Yes, now I was going south. And one of the odd things about Columbia--where we lived earlier on in New York, if I got on the subway at 76th Street, and I didn't get on the right subway, I'd get out at 116th Street, and I would be, you know, thinking about a physics problem, half in a daze, for one reason or another; 116th Street would come up and I'd get off the subway and start walking up. I'd look around when I got up to 116th Street, and it would be Harlem. It was like putting up a periscope--I only took one look around, and down again. Take the subway back to 96th, then back up to Columbia. You know, the subway split at 96th. If you take the wrong one--if you get on south of 96th, you will end up in Harlem. If you take the right one, you end up at Broadway and Columbia.

But I think Columbia was very important for me for a lot of reasons. I was very frustrated in not having gone to college earlier. And I wasn't really sure what kind of a student I would be, never having really gone to school. I thought Columbia was a good challenge. And they had, without a doubt, some of the world's great professors. I'm sure they do today. And I did a lot of growing up in New

York City, living as a civilian and going to Columbia.

Q: Did you feel a sense of awkwardness when you first got there?

Admiral Lee: Yes, very much so. New York City is a very sophisticated town. They don't have much time for country bumpkins, but I learned. We learned quickly. Nobody to guide us. We made a few mistakes, but, by and large, it was a very happy experience. Down South, you know, Jews were oddities. After two years at Columbia, it never even occurred to me, as I looked at my classmates or anybody out on the street, to think what they were. It just fades away. I find out that they're not very different from other people. We had very good friends of whatever religious persuasion.

Q: Then you're dealing with them as individuals rather than members of a particular group.

Admiral Lee: Yes.

Q: You mentioned the ball game opportunities. The Giants, Dodgers, and Yankees were all in sway then, and it was the golden age of New York baseball. Did you take advantage of that?

Admiral Lee: Oh, yes. We went to baseball games. We went to see the New York Yankees football team at Yankee Stadium.

Q: That would have been in the All-America Conference.

Admiral Lee: I've forgotten, but it was professional football, with Marion Motley.

Q: He was on the Cleveland Browns, so that they would have been on the visiting team.

Admiral Lee: We went to see football games and baseball games. And I saw my first Broadway play during this time, and, of course, a number of others. Went to Radio City Music Hall--you know, all the things you do in New York. As a lieutenant drawing flight pay, I had enough money to afford an automobile and fairly comfortable quarters.

Q: Did you wear your uniform to class?

Admiral Lee: No. From the time I left VA-5B in Norfolk, until the time I reported into Newport, Rhode Island, I wore it only when I got married and when I went flying.

Q: Did you have to check in at all with the professor of naval science?

Admiral Lee: Yes. The NROTC unit kept our records--medical records, personnel record--but that was about it. They didn't bother with us. They had the midshipmen, taught classes, and the only time he would bother with us was if we had a problem. We had one or two people who flunked out. Of course, the professor of naval science would be concerned about that. He was a Navy captain, a battleship captain, Wellings.* His brother made admiral, but he didn't. But he was a very fine old gentleman. And he wanted us to get the most we could out of Columbia and get good grades and study hard. But he wasn't breathing down our necks. We weren't given extra duty. He gave us all the freedom we wanted. And there was never a problem. It was a very, very wonderful two and a half years.

Q: Did you grow intellectually during that period in the sense of having broader concerns about the world?

Admiral Lee: I think so. For the first time I began to read The New York Times and The Wall Street Journal, during this period in New York. Before that I didn't know what they really were. Yes, your intellectual horizons expand

---
*Captain Timothy F. Wellings, USN.

remarkably going to school and living in New York City.

Q: Did you keep up professionally with Navy topics?

Admiral Lee: No. The only thing I did with the Navy was to fly four hours a month out at Floyd Bennett.* And we used to go out there and fly whatever was available, I didn't keep in touch with the Navy in any way at all. I considered my job at the time to be my education.

Q: Did you have a free hand in deciding which subjects you would take?

Admiral Lee: Yes. I think that was unfortunate. Not in my case, but it was unfortunate in many cases, I think. A lot of five-term students took the easy courses. I think a minimum should have been prescribed: physics, calculus, and so forth. I think we should have been required to complete the Columbia requirements for a degree. It was up to the professor of naval science in each institution. Ours didn't put any requirements on us. But I decided that I was not going to be content with just what I could get at Columbia. I wanted to go on and get a degree of some type. And the thing to do when I had this opportunity was to complete all the requirements for a degree, except a major.

---
*New York Naval Air Station, Floyd Bennett Field.

And it appeared to me that I could do it, which I did. And then all I had was to complete a major in math and physics. I had everything else.

Q: What was your specific objective at that point?

Admiral Lee: I planned to apply for graduate school for aeronautical engineering as soon as I became qualified. The Naval Postgraduate School had an aeronautical engineering program. And you didn't have to have a degree, but you had to have college physics and math through integral calculus, and you could be admitted, which was what I was aiming for.

Q: So you had that requirement in mind as you were laying out your program.

Admiral Lee: Yes. I intended to go to graduate school. That was my plan all along. And I thought in order to get into graduate school, I'd have to have good grades. And I had pretty good grades. I think I did about as well as I could in physics and math. I didn't intend to go there and fail. I thought it was the opportunity I would have. But I never expected to have such a great time there. It was fun.

Q: All that and New York too.

Admiral Lee: Yes, I'd like to go do that again. There was a huge building down the street from us. I lived on 76th; on 72nd or 74th was a place called the Three Arts Club, which was established by a very wealthy lady years ago. She sponsored young ladies who came to New York City to study the arts--singers, artists, musicians, and so forth. Young ladies from all over the country lived in the Three Arts Club. She subsidized the building; they could live there for reasonable prices. It was a very well run place, sort of like a big hotel with bars on it. They had matrons in charge and a dining room. It was like a college dormitory, a little better.

My first semester, there was a young lady from the Three Arts Club in one of my classes. I met her, and one thing led to another. We spent a lot of time at the Three Arts Club. And my roommate at Columbia and later best man at my wedding married one of the Three Arts girls that I introduced him to. And another good friend at Columbia married one of them. So Columbia and New York City were very exciting. And all these very interesting girls. One might be from Dubuque, Iowa--father a doctor, and she was there to study voice, or piano, or something. Very talented group of young ladies, and very attractive. So with all of that, I felt that my cup was running over, as

Lee #2 - 144

they say.

Q: Then it was back to reality at Newport.

Admiral Lee: Back to reality at Newport. In the summer of 1949, after finishing my five-term program at Columbia, I was ordered to Line School at Newport, Rhode Island. Now I had a wife and some baggage. Up to this point, I could move from one station to another with three bags and a parachute bag. But now we had lots of silver, and china, and all the things that married couples accumulate. So we went to Newport, and lived in the Anchorage, which provided quarters for students. And I went to Line School.

Line School was set up by Holloway to train officers who were not Naval Academy graduates in line subjects, modeled on the Naval Academy. We were taught, and had practical instruction in seamanship and navigation. They had small boats in Newport which we had to pilot around. We learned piloting, gunnery, and ordnance. They had various types of gunnery and ordnance there, and we had to operate it and learn about it and take exams. Legal and naval regs. They had a destroyer engineering plant, and we studied that. We'd fire it up, and run it, and that sort of thing.

I was in a section of about 30 students--about 80% of them naval aviators, 20% line. And we had a very nice year. The academics at Line School were really a breeze after Columbia. I'd say the academic level of the average student was much lower. Many of them had little math to speak of, for instance. Many of them had never had physics.

I learned all about naval publications, and all of the subjects which every line officer ought to know. Plus we had a lot of fun during the course of the year--sailing and various athletics. As a matter of fact, I played badminton almost all year. We had a tournament at the end of the year, and I was the badminton champion. But I did do one thing to further my chances in graduate school. I took differential equations after hours and checked off one more item in the math area. And also, while at Line School, I applied for graduate school. I applied for aeronautical engineering. However, I was told that I was not eligible, that I must go to sea. I'd had my three years of shore duty.

Q: A lot of the Navy-type stuff, to use that term, was probably new to you at that point, wasn't it?

Admiral Lee: Oh, yes, all new. Seamanship, navigation, celestial navigation, piloting a boat--all the things you have to learn in seamanship, the plotting board, the maneuvering board, the tactics of ships, gunnery, engineering. If you're going to be a line officer in the Navy, they are the things you ought to know.

Q: So even though you were on board ship in World War II, your focus was so narrow that it didn't really take those things in.

Admiral Lee: I learned very little about shipboard operations while on Essex and later Valley Forge, because aviation consumed almost 100% of our time, one facet or another. So that this was a very useful year.

Q: Who were the instructors in the line school?

Admiral Lee: About 90% of them were Naval Academy graduates, who had been in destroyers, battleships, cruisers, and submarines. There were a few aviators, but not many. But I'd say 90% were Naval Academy graduates and 90% were 1100s or blackshoes.* And they were very fine instructors. They, by and large, knew their subjects fairly well. We also studied electrical engineering, which was taught by a civilian. We also had math, but the math and the electrical engineering were both on a basic level.

---

*The officer designator for the battleship-cruiser-destroyer type line officer was 1100; the designator for aviators is 1310. "Blackshoes" is a nickname for the surface and submarine officers, while "brownshoes" is a nickname for naval aviators.

I wouldn't say that they were college-level courses. For most electrical engineering courses taught at the Naval Academy and at most colleges and universities, the students have to have math through integral calculus. I daresay no more than one out of ten had this background, so it wasn't taught at the rigorous college level. But it was still a reasonably good course.

Q: What about such things as steam engineering, damage control, and stability. Did you get into those topics?

Admiral Lee: We had all of those. Steam engineering--they had a destroyer plant. Damage control, stability and control. We had problems, exercises, and firefighting. They had the whole range of line subjects, and we did that for a year. I haven't looked at the various courses that we took for a long time, but I think it's everything taught at the Naval Academy. They just moved it all right up to Newport.

Lee #3 - 148

Interview Number 3 with Vice Admiral Kent L. Lee,
U.S. Navy (Retired)

Place: Logon Farm, Admiral Lee's home near Gordonsville, Virginia

Date: Thursday, 29 October 1987

Interviewer: Paul Stillwell

Q: Admiral, last time we got you through Line School, and now we're ready to put you into the Korean War.

Admiral Lee: Very good. That's just where I went.

In June of 1950 I graduated from the General Line School at Newport, Rhode Island. It was a good year of academics, training needed by a line officer. While at Newport, I applied for graduate school in aeronautical engineering, but was told that I'd had enough education for the time being and had to go to sea. I assumed I would go to a squadron, either East Coast or West Coast. But, much to my amazement, I was sent to the staff of Commander Carrier Division 15, which was a jeep carrier ASW group.* In this group were the Badoeng Strait and the Sicily.**

I arrived in San Diego, rented an apartment, and reported to the staff about the first of July. In late

---
*ASW--antisubmarine warfare.
**The USS Badoeng Strait (CVE-116) and USS Sicily (CVE-118) were small escort aircraft carriers, commissioned in November 1945 and February 1946 respectively. Each was 557 feet long, had a beam of 75 feet, displacement of 11,373 tons, and a maxium speed of 19 knots.

June--as a matter of fact, on the 26th of June--North Korea invaded South Korea. And around the Fourth of July, Carrier Division 15 was ordered to the Far East.

Q: Where had the staff been based? Was it embarked in one of the ships when you arrived?

Admiral Lee: When I arrived, the staff was in one of those small buildings on North Island.* The staff went aboard ship only when they had an ASW exercise. Sometimes only one carrier took part in the exercise. In that case, they'd go aboard that particular ship and run submarines, destroyers, and the carrier with ASW airplanes.

When I reported on 3 July, the staff was at North Island between exercises. I didn't know what my billet would be, but I found out very quickly that I was to be aide and flag lieutenant to a newly selected rear admiral by the name of Richard Ruble.**

As I said, the North Koreans invaded South Korea on June 26th. And Harry Truman, our President, decided that that couldn't be. So we were ordered to Tokyo. I believe we left on 5 July and went out and joined the staff of Commander Naval Forces Far East, which was headed by Vice

---
*North Island is a naval air station in Coronado, California, just across the harbor from San Diego.
**Rear Admiral Richard W. Ruble, USN.

Admiral Turner Joy.*

Q: Which ship did you go over in?

Admiral Lee: We flew to Tokyo with a stopover of two or three days in Hawaii. The Badoeng Strait and Sicily were in the San Diego-to-Hawaii area, and both of them were directed to load up Marine squadrons and head west. In the meantime, we were out in Tokyo learning about the naval forces and what was going on in the Far East.

Q: How large a staff was it?

Admiral Lee: We had a total of ten officers. It was an ASW staff, so we had a submariner, an aviator, a destroyer commander, Marine Corps colonel, CIC officer, weapons officer, and so forth.**

Q: The Marine colonel sounds odd for an ASW staff.

---

*Vice Admiral C. Turner Joy, USN, served as Commander U.S. Naval Forces Far East from 1949 to 1952. During that time his role expanded to encompass command of all United Nations naval forces in the Korean War, and he became senior U.N. delegate at armistice talks with North Korea.
**In addition to Lieutenant Lee, the staff officers were CAPT Henry T. Dietrich, USN, chief of staff; COL James Neefus, USMC, Marine rep; CDR Wilson Coleman, USN, ops officer; CDR Harry H. Greer, USN, submarine ops; CDR Burton H. Shupper, USN, surface ops; LCDR Vincent F. Kenney, USN, CIC; LCDR Martin Stack, USN, air ops; LCDR Thaddeus F. Rudnicki, USN, communications; LCDR John C. Doherty, USN, flag secretary.

Admiral Lee: Well, that's what we had, Marine Colonel James Neefus, a very nice fellow.

Our job in Tokyo was to assist Commander Naval Forces Far East until such time as the Badoeng Strait and Sicily got out to the Far East with their Marine squadrons.

Q: Do you have any impressions of Admiral Joy from that period?

Admiral Lee: I don't have any professional impressions, but he was a very nice man, very kindly man, and interested in everything that was going on. I met him only half a dozen times or so, and I never worked for him directly. I worked for Admiral Ruble.

We stayed in Tokyo about three weeks, maybe four weeks. During that time I decided to improve my mind, so I enrolled in a Japanese language class. Unfortunately, that lasted only about three weeks. I learned to say hello, goodbye, and a few odd words like that.

Q: How was the bulk of the time spent there?

Admiral Lee: We spent the bulk of the time in the Naval Forces Far East Headquarters helping however we could. We augmented the staff, and Admiral Ruble handled certain administrative details. For instance, we surveyed the airbase at Atsugi.* We helped set up Commander Fleet Air Pacific, who later came in and, I believe, was an admiral by the name of George Henderson, who was a World War I aviator.**

Q: Did you work mostly with their plans and operations people?

Admiral Lee: Our people did. I worked for Admiral Ruble, whatever he had going on for the day. An aide and flag lieutenant arranges transportation, arranges housing. He's the "go-fer." And I was a lieutenant, and that's exactly what I was.

Q: What are your memories of him, what kind of personality?

Admiral Lee: Admiral Ruble was an intelligent man. A Naval Academy graduate of 1923, he and Arleigh Burke were classmates, and he was a naval aviator.*** He was navigator of the Enterprise in World War II during those early battles and was later captain of the Valley Forge

---

*Atsugi Naval Air Station, near the U.S. fleet base at Yokousuka, was used by the Japanese during World War II.
**Rear Admiral George R. Henderson, USN.
***Admiral Arleigh A. Burke, USN, was Chief of Naval Operations, 1955-61. His oral history is in the Naval Institute collection.

Lee #3 - 153

during her around-the-world cruise.* His assignment just before Carrier Division 15 was as aide to the Secretary of the Navy, who at that time was Rowboat Matthews, from Nebraska.** He thought very highly of Mr. Matthews. Ruble was also an aeronautical engineer.

In any event, he and the staff were extra hands around Commander Naval Forces Far East for three or four weeks while additional staff people were sent out from the States, because the Naval Forces Far East staff wasn't large at the time this all started. This particular staff had to run the naval war part of the Korean War. Admiral Joy worked directly for General MacArthur.***

Q: Were people there still pretty much groping at that point?

Admiral Lee: Yes, very much so. Admiral Joy had a small staff on one or two floors of a building near MacArthur's headquarters. The first order of business was to get a new building, new staff and start planning, building, and

---
*The Valley Forge made a 1947-48 deployment from San Diego that took her around world before returning home.
**Francis P. Matthews was Secretary of the Navy from 25 May 1949 to 31 July 1951. His deprecating nickname resulted from the circumstances leading to his appointment. His predecessor had resigned in protest over the cancellation of the aircraft carrier United States. Critics charged that Matthews, an Omaha banker and attorney, didn't know about any vessel bigger than a rowboat.
***General of the Army Douglas MacArthur, USA, Supreme Commander Allied Powers Far East.

operating. It was chaos.

We had very few forces in the Far East at this time. I believe we had one aircraft carrier, the <u>Valley Forge</u>, and the British had one. The great effort at that time was to get forces out there--destroyers, carriers, airplanes, patrol planes, Marine squadrons, Marine troops. The whole thrust was to build up the effort, set up all the facilities that were needed for them--mostly planning, mostly getting buildings, setting up that airfield.

I went down to Atsugi with Admiral Ruble, as I said earlier. And at that time it was an abandoned field. We looked at the fuel dumps, at the runways, and the buildings. And, as you know, the Navy and Marine Corps came in and took over and carried on sizable operations from Atsugi during the course of the Korean War.

Q: How cooperative were the Japanese?

Admiral Lee: The Japanese were very cooperative. Whatever the U.S. Government wanted at that time was delivered quickly; General MacArthur was still the supreme commander. We had not signed a peace treaty. I saw General MacArthur drive by in his limousine a couple of times--my only exposure to the great man. But it was an interesting period of time.

Also, it was my first exposure to senior officers. I had been in school for three years, and before that I'd been in fleet squadrons. We had a lot of senior officers on the staff, and I was working with them and around them all day.

After three or four weeks in Tokyo, doing the things I've described which were involved in the buildup, we moved aboard Badoeng Strait. Badoeng Strait had come into Japan with a Marine squadron aboard. Sicily also came in, went out to Korea, and started operating with its Marine squadron in Tsushima Strait. Badoeng Strait went out and joined Sicily, and they operated as a task group.* We normally had four, five, six destroyers and two carriers. And at this particular time, the United Nations forces had been pushed back by the North Koreans, who came down in great force.

Our people were pushed into what was called the Pusan perimeter, which wasn't much bigger than Albemarle County.** Our two carriers and Valley Forge--because that's all there was at the time--gave close air support to the United Nations forces in South Korea. This went on for weeks and weeks. And finally the Pusan perimeter was stabilized. Our Marines were flying F4Us from dawn to

---

*Task Group 96.8 comprised the two carriers plus destroyer minesweepers Endicott (DMS-35) and Doyle (DMS-34) and destroyers James E. Kyes (DD-787) and Taussig (DD-746).
**Albemarle County, Virginia, which contains the city of Charlottesville, includes the farm where Admiral Lee lives.

dusk, every day--no night flying. But every day both carriers, from dawn to dusk, launched F4Us carrying full loads of ordnance--rockets, machine guns, bombs--and giving close air support to our troops.

Q: Did you stand watches during that time?

Admiral Lee: Yes. I was also aide and flag lieutenant, which meant I ran the flag mess, was in charge of the signal bridge, and handled transportation. I started out on the bridge, where I was assistant staff watch officer for, say, six weeks to two months. Since I'd just graduated from Line School, all the tactical publications were familiar to me, and I'd learned how to work the maneuvering board. I knew all the tactical formations, and the signals, and so forth. I qualified as a staff watch officer, and from that time on I took a regular turn on the bridge as a watch officer, directing the formation.

About the time the Pusan perimeter was stabilized, around the first of September, we went into Sasebo. Admiral Ruble and I flew from Sasebo to Tokyo in a PBM aircraft and landed in Tokyo Bay.* I went with him to the headquarters, and we stayed in the old Imperial Hotel. He went to a meeting with all flag and general officers

---

*The PBM Mariner was a twin-engine patrol flying boat built by the Glenn L. Martin Company.

that General MacArthur was hosting. The meeting was to plan the Inchon landings.

Q: How tight was security on that?

Admiral Lee: Security was very tight. I think the only people who knew were in this group that MacArthur called together. And the role, of course, of Ruble was to provide close air support for these Inchon landings.

We stayed in Tokyo about three days, and I had another good look at the city. And this time we lived in style. We were flown right back to Sasebo, thence back to sea on the <u>Badoeng Strait</u>. And we might have had two or three days of close air support work around the Pusan perimeter. Then we immediately set sail around South Korea, because we were operating in the Sea of Japan, just north of Tsushima Strait. We went around southern Korea, up into the Yellow Sea, and right up opposite Inchon.

Q: Off the west coast.

Admiral Lee: Off the west coast of Korea. And I suppose it took one or two days to steam around. It's not very far. And the landings at Inchon took place on September 15, 1950. And we were there for close air support.

Q: What are your recollections of that day?

Admiral Lee: Well, we were off the coast a little ways, but, of course, we had seen, on radar and otherwise, all the ships coming in. And we had access to the tide tables and knew that it was a very difficult thing to do. I've forgotten the tidal range, but I think the tides in that area are something like 20 feet.

Q: It's very dramatic.

Admiral Lee: Very dramatic changes from low tide to high tide. So that the landing had to be very precisely timed. We, of course, had no part in that. Our part was close air support. But we were following this, because we got all the messages having to do with it. And I think one of the things that was probably good for me professionally during this period is that during the whole period of the Korean War, when all of this action took place in the first nine months, I had a ringside seat. I read the messages, heard the admirals, generals, and other senior officers talk. So it was a very educational period. I even met Senator Claude Pepper, Democrat from Florida.

We were in the Inchon area for the landings and for perhaps a week after that--providing fighter cover, close air support for our troops, and bombing behind fleeing

North Koreans. As you might remember, during the Inchon landings we had put together also a sizable force in the Pusan perimeter. And the day before the Inchon landings, the Pusan perimeter forces mounted an attack. It was a two-pronged affair. The North Koreans just collapsed in a matter of two weeks. Their army had become nothing, because we'd cut them off from the north with the Inchon landings. And within about two weeks' time, we had all of South Korea to ourselves and had captured thousands and thousands of North Korean troops. Absolutely amazing. The Inchon landing was certainly a stroke of genius by MacArthur.

Q: Was the operational pace for these two carriers as demanding as it had been around Pusan?

Admiral Lee: About the same. We operated seven days a week--first light of day to dusk, sending out F4Us loaded with ordnance. And the pace was about the same.

Q: Did the makeup of the staff change since you got into a completely different mission from ASW?

Admiral Lee: None whatsoever. Colonel Neefus, of course, was liaison with Marine squadrons. We had six aviators on the staff. Plus we had a destroyer commander by the name of Shupper, who later made rear admiral, and a submarine commander. We had enough staff. And it was a good staff for this purpose. We had no problems in meeting our obligations.

Q: What do you recall of Admiral Ruble as an operational commander?

Admiral Lee: I thought Admiral Ruble was an adequate operational commander. I wouldn't say that he was the best operational commander I've seen, because he didn't take a great interest in the airplanes, the weapons, and the missions. He wasn't all that well versed in those things. He had a very good overall view of what we were doing in the war and what we were supposed to do, but he didn't really get into the nuts and bolts of it. And I don't think he'd ever flown a combat plane like the F4U, like some other operational commanders.

Since those days, I've seen lots of operational commanders. I would say that Admiral Ruble was a very intelligent man. But I've seen better operational commanders. I had a very good personal relationship with him, and it was a very good tour from that point of view. For instance, one time when we went into Sasebo, we had a helicopter on the <u>Badoeng Strait</u>, one of the first helicopters on aircraft carriers. It was sent to us for search and rescue missions.

Q: Was this an HO3S, Sikorsky?

Admiral Lee: Yes

One time Admiral Ruble and I got the helicopter and flew over to Nagasaki. He wanted to see where the atom bomb had hit. We flew all around the city at low altitude and looked at the site of the second bomb hit.*

Nagasaki is not very far from Sasebo--about 50 miles. It's a seaport town on the west coast of the island of Kyushu From the helicopter we could see the devastation caused by the second atomic bomb, which I believe was an implosion-type weapon, the first one being the gun type, if I remember correctly.

After the Inchon Landings, we then moved back around to the east coast of Korea. And at the same time, during October and early November, MacArthur was pushing the United Nations troops to the north. And I, of course, wasn't aware of what was going on in the United States and the differences between General Marshall, who was then Secretary of the Defense, President Truman, and General

---

*Nagasaki, Japan, was the target of the second U.S. atomic bomb, which was dropped by an Army Air Forces B-29 bomber on 9 August 1945, three days after the bomb on Hiroshima.

MacArthur.*

As we moved around to the east coast, we resumed doing the same thing we had before, providing close air support for the troops as they moved north. We moved quite far north in the Sea of Japan. And it was getting cold. But we still didn't have too many problems on Badoeng Strait and Sicily. We were replenished at sea: food, ammunition, and fuel. And we might have gone through Sasebo on the way back north. I don't remember that.

Q: I'd be interested in your recollections of operating that kind of a carrier and air group in wartime compared with what you'd known in the Essex in World War II.

Admiral Lee: Well, on Badoeng Strait we had one catapult, and I've forgotten the number, but about 20 F4Us--might have been 25--and the airplanes could not take a deck run. We had only one elevator to get them down to the hangar deck for maintenance work. So a great part of the work had to be done on the flight deck. And we could launch, at the most, only about eight aircraft per cycle. We would launch eight aircraft and send them over to the beach. And then in about an hour and a half perhaps another eight, and send

---

*George C. Marshall was Secretary of Defense, 1950-51. President Harry S Truman relieved General of the Army Douglas MacArthur as supreme commander in 1951 as a result of what he considered insubordination in his conduct of the war in Korea and in his public statements.

them over. And then recover the ones that we had earlier launched.

If I remember correctly, what we did was alternate launches. We would launch, normally, eight or ten aircraft, and wait about an hour and a half. Sicily would then launch eight or ten aircraft, and we would recover ours. And we would alternate like that all day long. Those carriers were very small, as you might remember, and were not the best rough-weather ships.

Q: They weren't really intended as attack carriers either.

Admiral Lee: No, they weren't intended as attack carriers, but I thought they performed very well. Limited in numbers, limited in size. We could launch an aircraft about once a minute. Each ship had one hydraulic catapult, and I believe the load of the F4U was limited by the size of the catapult. But, even so, they did a remarkable job. Of course, we had all those Marines on board. We were servicing the airplanes, maintaining them, and handling all the ordnance. Typical Marine squadron.

Q: They were pretty experienced aviators, I think, too. A number had World War II service.

Admiral Lee: Most of them were captains and majors and the

like, and a great number had World War II experience. And they had a lot of time in the F4U. At first they were a little ragged around the carrier. But they got quite proficient because they were out there a long time.

Q: And they're very good at close air support because of their doctrine of working with ground troops.

Admiral Lee: Yes. It looked like the war would be over very quickly, and we'd all be home by Christmas. MacArthur had pushed his troops north of the 38th parallel, into North Korea, and headed up towards the Yalu River, Chinese territory. But in late November 1950, the Chinese came across the border in force. They caught our troops by surprise.

In November and December 1950, we again had a very difficult time in Korea. We had thousands of men trapped around the Chosin Reservoir. And some time in December, we evacuated from Hungnam thousands of troops.* And all during this Chosin Reservoir period and the evacuations, Sicily and the Badoeng Strait were up once again, providing close air support. And this time it was, perhaps, more important than ever before. We sent as many as we could up there every day. The weather was frequently not too good.

---

*For a first-person account, see Vice Admiral James H. Doyle, USN (Ret.), and Arthur J. Mayer, "December 1950 at Hungnam," U.S. Naval Institute Proceedings, April 1979, pages 44-55.

Q: Did that impose limitations?

Admiral Lee: Oh, yes. It imposed a lot of limitations. We had no all-weather capability on Badoeng Strait and Sicily. It had to be VFR.* And, of course, the flight to the beach was not too long, only 10 or 15 minutes, because we were up fairly close to the coast. Many times we could see the coast on radar, because Korea is a very mountainous country. But even so, it was just an amazing turnaround. First, we were being pushed out of Korea, down in the Pusan perimeter. And then for a period of two months, we were all-victorious. And then for the next two months, it looked as though we were going to lose it all, because our troops were being pushed down by the Chinese. An absolutely amazing turnaround.

Q: Did you have concern about enemy submarines operating that far north?

Admiral Lee: We were concerned about enemy submarines, but there wasn't a lot we could do about it. We had six destroyers with us.

By this time the Philippine Sea and the Valley Forge

---

*VFR—visual flight rules, as opposed to instrument flight rules (IFR).

were there. So in December 1950 we were giving a lot of close air support to our forces, mostly in North Korea, as they tried to fight their way south and escape from the Chinese. Sometime after the first of the year 1951, the line was roughly stabilized around the 38th parallel.

Now a few words about the chief of staff. When I joined the staff in early July, Captain Dennis Sullivan was chief of staff.* He was detached before we left San Diego. His relief, Captain Henry T. Dietrich, Naval Academy class of '26, joined us in Japan, just before we sailed in Badoeng Strait. His initial personal relations with Admiral Ruble were cordial, friendly, and correct. We lived in close quarters on Badoeng Strait. The flag quarters were tiny--bedroom, bath, cubbyhole of an office, and a small dining room.

Captain Dietrich and Admiral Ruble were very different men. Ruble had enjoyed the Naval Academy. Dietrich detested the place--a miserable four years. Dietrich didn't like the Navy's promotion and selection system. Ruble thought it was a very fair and equitable system. Ruble didn't always approve of Dietrich's operational planning. Dietrich resented any corrections by the admiral. And these two men had to eat together three times a day for months on end. Towards the end, there was almost no conversation between them. John Doherty, the admiral,

---

*Captain Dennis J. Sullivan, USN.

and I carried on a conversation at lunch and dinner; Dietrich sulked. It was grim; it was also a good lesson in personal relations.

Q: Makes it difficult to operate a staff.

Admiral Lee: Yes.

Q: Were you a go-between?

Admiral Lee: Yes, in a sense. I tried to stay out of the line of fire, but it wasn't always possible. I hadn't been involved in anything like that before. I can remember one time we were in Sasebo, when Admiral Ruble sent me over to ask Captain Dietrich if he'd like to go ashore and take a tour with him. And Captain Dietrich's answer was very short: "No thank you."

Q: What was the source of this friction?

Admiral Lee: I didn't know then. And I don't know to this date. For one thing, they were very different people.

One time Captain Dietrich sent out a message to a replenishment group, telling them to rendezvous with our force at a certain point on the west coast of Korea, when it should have been the east coast of Korea. And, of course, that embarrassed Admiral Ruble. My feeling is it was just a lot of little things. And we lived in such close quarters on those small ships that little things built up to big things. And the first thing you know the two men weren't talking. This happens aboard ship more often than people will have you know. These little things build up. It happened there, and I've noticed it many other times aboard ship. Department heads got so they wouldn't talk to each other at various times. These things happen on long cruises.

Q: How did it eventually resolve itself?

Admiral Lee: We got a new chief of staff. I don't know how this came about. But my guess is that Admiral Ruble requested a new chief of staff. And I can't now remember the name of the chief of staff, but, anyway, we got a new chief of staff. And Captain Dietrich went back to the Bureau of Aeronautics.

In addition to that, we were all relieved on this staff early in 1951. We got a new admiral, new chief of staff. The entire staff was relieved, one by one, as our reliefs came out and on board. I was relieved about the first of March 1951--about the time Admiral Ruble was relieved. He left perhaps a week before I did.

Lee #3 - 169

Q: Do you have any more to say about your personal relationship with him?

Admiral Lee: I had a very good personal relationship with Admiral Ruble. He was always a very kind man, very considerate. As a matter of fact, his orders from Carrier Division 15 were to be Commander Fleet Air Quonset Point.* He asked me to go with him to Quonset Point. I think he was a little bit upset when I said that when I got back to San Diego, I'd like to try to move over to a fleet squadron and get in some flying duty, since it was almost four years since I'd been in an operating squadron.

Q: He could probably understand that easily enough.

Admiral Lee: Well, he did. And I saw him when I got back to San Diego. He had left a week before we did. But I thought Admiral Ruble was a very able man. I thought he was very intelligent. He was fairly high in his Naval Academy class and had gone on to graduate school.** He had a master's degree in aeronautical engineering from MIT. He was a very bright man. But I don't think operations were his strong suit. I would put it that way.

---
*Quonset Point was the site of a naval air station near Newport, Rhode Island.
**Ruble stood 89th of the 412 graduates in the Naval Academy class of 1923.

Q: Any specific examples on shortcomings?

Admiral Lee: For instance, helicopters at that time were a new element, and we had a helicopter sent out to Badoeng Strait to act as search and rescue. The helicopter pilot wanted to be launched before aircraft were launched so he could be in the air if anybody went into the water. The admiral thought about this a while and decided that he wouldn't do that. He would keep the helicopter blades folded, and we'd run it out, and unfold the blades, and start it up, and then launch it if we had anybody go in the water, which I think was not the best way to use a helicopter. My impression was he didn't have a great interest in aircraft operations.

Q: Did the friction between him and the chief of staff rub off on the rest of the staff?

Admiral Lee: No, I don't think so. They were all professionals. They recognized what was going on and tried to be both supportive of Dietrich and to do their job.

I was rather new at the business, being a young lieutenant. I just tried to stay out of the line of fire. But the others were old hands. They'd all been to sea for a long time, and I think they took it in stride. It didn't affect our operations at all.

Q: Were there any differences you would observe in a carrier having a Marine air group, as opposed to a Navy one?

Admiral Lee: No, I don't think so. Marine squadrons are less disciplined than Navy squadrons. I guess that's because they're Marines. The maintenance of Marine airplanes has always been below par. They don't stress maintenance the way Navy squadrons do. But Marine squadrons are great performers. I thought these two squadrons did a great job. They flew long hours, day in and day out, supporting the troops in Korea for many long months.

Q: Do you have any recollections of the skipper of the Badoeng Strait?

Admiral Lee: Yes, the first skipper of the Badoeng Strait was Captain Arnold McKechnie, relieved early in the cruise by Captain John Alderman.* Both ran a good ship. I, of course, saw a fair amount of both, because whatever messages the admiral had, I usually took them to the captain--whether or not the admiral was going to the movies

---
*Captain Arnold W. McKechnie, USN; Captain John C. Alderman, USN.

if we were anchored--1,001 things. We had only about eight or ten enlisted men on the staff, and if any of them went to mast for one reason or another, the captain held mast on our staff people. They were technically assigned to the ship. That's the way the Navy works. I thought Captain Alderman was a very good captain for Badoeng Strait. I, of course, saw more of him and got to know him better.

Q: The captain of the Sicily, John Thach, was a famous aviator.* Any recollections of him?

Admiral Lee: Yes. Captain Thach was a very flamboyant type--a personality kid, very publicity-conscious. He made every effort to have newsmen come to Sicily. He made every effort to be interviewed by them. He sent out news releases almost daily. I don't think Captain Alderman ever sent out a news release. If he did, it was something that his people down in the ship prepared. Captain Thach on Sicily, I'm sure, helped work them up every day himself. And when the Marines were awarded medals, Admiral Ruble went over for the first batch, and I went with him, but Captain Thach very much wanted to present these medals to his Marine squadron.

---

*Captain John S. Thach, USN. Thach eventually became a four-star admiral; his oral history is in the Naval Institute collection. An excerpt dealing with his command of the Sicily in the Korean War was published as "'Right on the Button:' Marine Close Air Support in Korea," U.S. Naval Institute Proceedings, November 1975, pages 54-56.

But he ran a good ship. He had a very enthusiastic ship. And I think he did a great job with Sicily. But the contrast between the two captains was absolutely startling.

Q: Any comparison you would draw operationally?

Admiral Lee: Oh, operationally, I think Captain Thach was without a peer. He knew the F4U. He knew all the ordnance. He stayed up to the minute on everything that was going on. I think Captain Thach was one of the great operational commanders, certainly one of the best tactical aviators of World War II. And then later on, of course, one of the great tactical commanders.

Q: If you've got a great skipper like that, then it doesn't make so much difference on the admiral.

Admiral Lee: No. And, of course, our job in Badoeng Strait and Sicily was not directing the effort over in Korea. Our job was to supply as many airplanes as we could for close air support. Their targets were designated from Korea. Their patrol was in Korea. So that we had very little to do with them operationally.

Q: Just get them in the air and head them in the right direction.

Lee #3 - 174

Admiral Lee: Just get them in the air and headed in the right direction and loaded with the proper ordnance.

And we had a sort of a map room, a war room, where we kept track of everything that was going on in Korea--the front line, the attacks--because we got the messages all day. But even so, we were not running the war. We were supplying as many airplanes as we could every day, loaded with as much ordnance as we could hang on. We were not making any big decisions having to do with the war.

Q: There's some interesting background on Captain Thach's publicity efforts. He had come from working for Admiral Black Jack Reeves, Chief of Naval Air Training.* And it had been his mission, ordered by Reeves, to make publicity all over the country in the fight against the Air Force to save naval aviation. And he'd made numerous speeches, and had interviews with media people, and so this probably was a continuation of that effort.

Admiral Lee: He knew a lot of media people. He had them come out to <u>Sicily</u> and stay with him a few days. And he would give them the red-carpet treatment. He was the most

---

*Vice Admiral John W. Reeves, Jr., USN. Admiral Thach discusses this tour of duty in his oral history.

public relations-conscious officer I ever knew. And he was good at it.

Q: A very congenial personality.

Admiral Lee: Marvelous personality. Told great stories. Always had a big smile. A real personality kid but a very good operational man. In many ways he reminded me of Jerry Miller. Or, I should put that the other way. Jerry Miller reminded me of Captain, Admiral Thach. Both great personalities.

Q: You mentioned initially that you had some communications duties. And, of course, that's where the term flag lieutenant came from. What did that involve for you?

Admiral Lee: I was in charge of the flag bridge. We operated almost entirely with flag signals. At night, of course, we operated with what was then called TBS, which was tactical communications.* But in the daytime we operated with flags and flashing lights.

Q: What did you do at night since you were dawn to dusk as

---

*TBS was the voice radio; during World War II, the letters stood for "talk between ships."

far as flying operations?

Admiral Lee: Oh, at night we steamed around and got ready for our launch the next day. Because when night came on, of course, we had to secure flight operations. So at night we merely steamed in a formation and hoped a submarine didn't get us.

Q: Because of this heavy demand for your services, did you get much time in port?

Admiral Lee: Very little time in port. Sasebo was just around the corner. We went into Sasebo for several days at a time during this eight-month period--three or four times, I guess.

The first time we operated off Korea, we were out only a month. We came back so that Admiral Ruble could go up to Tokyo and learn about the Inchon landings. I don't think we got back into Sasebo until after the line had stabilized at the 38th parallel. So we were out there during that entire period. And I think we were out somewhere between 60 and 70 days. And after the line had been stabilized in Korea, generally along the 38th parallel, we did go back into Sasebo for an R&R period.* We had long periods at sea. I think those two little carriers and their two

------
*R&R--rest and recreation.

Marine squadrons played a big role in Korea, because we didn't have much else.

Q: Did you get involved in any combined operations with the big carriers?

Admiral Lee: None. We saw them once in a while, had some communication with them.

One time when we went into Sasebo, the Valley Forge was there. But we did no operating with them, because we had different speeds. The top speed of a jeep carrier was about 19 or 20 knots. And the big carriers routinely ran up to 30 knots, because they were operating jets at that time.

As I said earlier, around the first of March, we were each relieved individually from Badoeng Strait. And Badoeng Strait and Sicily stayed out there. I believe the Marine pilots were relieved individually also. But the squadron stayed; the ship stayed; and the staff officers were relieved and came back to the States. I returned to the San Diego area and was assigned temporarily to a new carrier division staff which was being formed, Carrier Division 17.

Q: Was that another of these ASW groups?

Lee #3 - 178

Admiral Lee: It was to be another ASW group. Some small carriers were being taken out of mothballs. But <u>Badoeng Strait</u> and <u>Sicily</u> were to stay out there. And I don't remember when they came home.

Q: Well, presumably, your experience out there would be quite valuable to these new ships that were working up.

Admiral Lee: Yes, I stayed on this Carrier Division 17 staff about three weeks to help them get organized and started. And then a new flag lieutenant came in and relieved me. I had arranged, in the meantime, to go to an attack squadron, VA-115, based at North Island.* While I was in Korea, I had a daughter born, Nancy, on November 5. We were off east Korea, and I learned about this by Navy message. So that when I got home in March 1951, I had a daughter four months old. My wife and I then moved into a new house, a little Palmer house, in Coronado.

My new squadron had just gotten back from a Korean tour on the <u>Philippine Sea</u> and was reforming. Our commanding officer was Charlie Carr.** The executive officer was Jack Sands, lieutenant commander.*** And I was the number three officer, the operations officer.

---
*VA-115--Attack Squadron 115. In March 1946, the Navy had dropped the designations VB and VT for bomber and torpedo aircraft squadrons, using instead VA for aircraft whose mission was attacking surface targets.
**Commander Charles A. Carr, USN.
***Lieutenant Commander Jack H. Sands, USN.

We had a routine retraining period from May to December 1951. This was my first experience with the AD.* I began to realize immediately what a marvelous airplane it was. I spent many years in naval aviation, and I learned there are very few great airplanes. Some airplanes have good engines; some airplanes have a good airframe; some have a good weapon delivery system; some maneuver very well, and so forth. It's a very rare airplane that puts all this together into one machine. The AD did this.

It had a marvelous engine--the R-3350 built by Wright--2,700 horsepower. It was a big airplane, had no bomb bay. Weighed about 10,000 pounds and would carry its weight in ordnance, carried 380 gallons of gasoline, I remember, which would give it an endurance of about four hours. It was the finest dive-bomber since the SBD, which was built by the same people. And you could maneuver this AD. It had a new form of speed brake--big boards off the fuselage, which later became the standard speed brakes for jet aircraft, whereas the earlier dive-bombers had split flaps, split to a 90-degree angle.

---

*The AD Skyraider, built by the Douglas Aircraft Company, had a Wright R-3350-26W engine. It had a wing span of 50 feet and empty weight of 10,546 pounds. The AD's maximum speed was 321 miles per hour at 18,300 feet and it had an initial climb rate of 2,800 feet per minute. It had two 20-mm. guns and a bomb capacity of up to 8,000 pounds.

Lee #3 - 180

Q: Off the wings.

Admiral Lee: Off the wings. But this AD was an absolutely great airplane in every way, and a very fine dive-bomber. You could maneuver it just about as well in a 70-degree dive as you could straight and level. And if you weren't on the target when you pushed over, you could maneuver onto it.

Q: That must have been a very satisfying tour of duty for you.

Admiral Lee: We had a very good tour. We retrained from May to December 1951 at North Island and El Centro.* And then moved aboard the Philippine Sea in January 1952 and headed for Korea.**

We got back to Korea in 1952. And I was looking at my log book last week; our first combat missions in Korea were flown in February 1952. By then the front had stabilized, and we were merely harassing the North Koreans. There was no movement back and forth.

This period, when I got out there in the AD squadron, we had a very fine air group, I guess two F4U squadrons,

---
*El Centro Naval Air Station, about 100 miles east of San Diego, just north of the Mexican border.
**The USS Philippine Sea (CV-47) was a slightly more modern version of the Essex-class carriers in which Lee had served previously, the Essex and Valley Forge.

one jet squadron, and then a big AD squadron.

Q: Were the jets the F9F?

Admiral Lee: The jet was the F9F-5, I guess.* It wasn't the best airplane, but it did fairly well.

During this period in Korea, from February to June, we went after targets of opportunity. By that I mean we went and looked for targets to hit. We attacked rail lines, trains if we saw them, tunnels--tried to block tunnels, attacked bridges, special targets like power plants. We roamed over most of North Korea. North Korea's a very desolate country, and we got there in the middle of the winter--very cold, mountainous. I saw very little flak.

In World War II, as I have mentioned earlier, the Japanese were very good gunners, and they put up a lot of flak. You could see these shells bursting everywhere. In Korea, I saw only a few bursts of flak. VA-115 lost only one pilot during the tour. And he no doubt was hit by small arms fire. Also, we had lots of forces out there then.

Instead of going into Sasebo, after about three weeks to a month on the line, we would go into Yokosuka, normally for about ten days. And, as you know, Yokosuka is a very

---

*The F9F-5 Panther was a straight-wing jet fighter built by Grumman; a later swept-wing version was the F9F-6/F9F-8, called the Cougar.

fine port with a shipyard attached. It's a Japanese shipyard which we had taken over. They did absolutely first-rate work. Yokosuka is just south of Tokyo, so we could take the train there. The shopping was marvelous.

I have one little story I'd like to tell about this time. We went into Yokosuka, I think the first time. I had a friend who was quite a ladies' man. After we had been in port three or four days, he met a very nice American girl--college graduate, daughter of a college professor, a very talented young lady. She was working for either the State Department or the Army, doing research in the Japanese records of World War II.

My friend thought he'd died and gone to heaven. He and this very attractive woman in her mid-20s had a great time for about the last five days we were in Japan. And, of course, he was the envy of the squadron. We were at sea for three or four days, and my friend came in one day with this terrible look on his face, as though the world was coming to an end. And this was the first thing in the morning. He didn't say anything, but he immediately went down to see the doctor. It turned out that he had gonorrhea.

Q: Did you do any night flying from that carrier?

Admiral Lee: No. We had an F4U-5N detachment in the air group.* They had four planes and six or seven pilots. And I can still remember the officer in charge of the detachment: Lieutenant Commander Slim Russell.** And he had an ensign by the name of Fred Dunning straight out of flight training.*** Those F4U-5Ns would be launched at night to wander over North Korea and come back and land.

It was always a great show watching them land. The F4U-5N was a big, clumsy airplane. During the course of the cruise--I'm not sure, but I believe they banged up three of their four airplanes in night landings. They would either prang them up on landing, or run them into the barrier. Night landing was very difficult on those straight-deck carriers.**** The rest of us did no night flying, although all of us had night qualified earlier. We had night carrier bounce landings on a field, and then had qualified on the Philippine Sea in December of 1951 in night landings. But we did not operate at night, only day flying.

---
*The F4U-5N model of the Vought Corsair had a radar pod at the leading edge of the starboard wing to enable it to operate at night.
**Lieutenant Commander Allard G. Russell, USN, officer in charge, Unit Charlie, Composite Squadron Three.
***Ensign Freder S. Dunning, Jr., USN.
****Within a few years, angled-deck carriers began joining the fleet. Thus, if a plane missed one of the arresting wires with its tailhook, it could add power, go off the angled deck, and approach the ship again--rather than crashing into planes farther forward on the straight deck.

Q: Did you have any concern about enemy fighters when you were over Korea?

Admiral Lee: I never saw a Korean airplane. We thought with the AD, we could handle almost anything over there, because we were very confident of our airplane. But I personally didn't see a North Korean fighter or a Russian fighter. And I don't think anybody in our squadron saw one.

Q: Combining that with not very effective antiaircraft, you were relatively safe.

Admiral Lee: It seemed that way. As I said earlier, VA-115 lost only one pilot. I just happened to remember his name, Ensign Wolf, and I think he was hit by small arms fire and crashed while making a bombing run, our only loss during the entire cruise.* So that we had a very--I would call it almost a dull tour--milk runs over North Korea, looking for targets.

Q: Could you, please, describe a typical mission?

Admiral Lee: A typical mission would be launched with four

---
*Ensign Jerry D. Wolf, USNR.

Lee #3 - 185

ADs, say. We would be sent to reconnoiter a route. I remember one of the routes was "Cindy." We had very good maps of North Korea. And we would drop down to 500 or 1,000 feet and follow Route Cindy from one end to the other. A route might be a railroad track; it might be a road. And we were to look for any rolling stock, trucks, and the like. At the end of the run, if we had not found a target, we had other targets designated on which we were to unload our ammunition, and our ordnance, such as a bridge, a power plant, an airfield, or what we believed to be some type of military installation--communication center. We had designated targets where we'd drop our ordnance if we didn't otherwise get rid of it.

Also, North Korea is filled with tunnels, and the trains all go through tunnels. And we might be given the task of closing up a tunnel. We would dive in towards a tunnel and release our bombs. We always tried to cut the rail lines. If our route for a particular day was a rail line, we would try to find any rolling stock, knock it out, and then make cuts in the rail line so their resupply problem would be made difficult.

Q: The rolling stock would be an interesting diversion in the midst of these relatively dull missions.

Admiral Lee: Rolling stock would have been a great

diversion. I ran across only two or three pieces of rolling stock. Because, as you can understand, the North Koreans put their trains in tunnels during the day. Also, all their trucks, so that we just ranged far and wide over North Korea over a period of months--and bombed them and strafed them, and shot rockets at them at will, while the negotiators were trying to reach some agreement at Panmunjom.*

Q: It was really a stalemate for about two years.

Admiral Lee: It was called the stalemate war. Anyway, it was a far cry from the first eight or nine months of the war. During the course of this particular year, I had applied once again for graduate school. And sometime in the spring, I was notified that I would be going to Monterey, because in that particular winter, the graduate school for the Navy, which had been based at the Naval Academy for many years, had been moved to Monterey. I was notified that I would be going to Monterey in July, and would begin graduate school in nuclear engineering effects, which wasn't my first choice, but it so happened that I was too senior to go into aeronautical engineering. But I was eligible for this particular course, so I applied for it.

---
*In October 1951, negotiations between the warring powers were moved to Panmunjom, a village on the 38th parallel. The wrangling there went on until the armistice agreement was finally concluded in July 1953.

So in June of 1952, I was detached from VA-115 while we were in Yokosuka. The squadron went out for one last tour on the line, but I flew home. By that time I'd been in the squadron for 15 months and had almost completed a Korean tour. I thought I had very little more to learn by being in a squadron. And I also wanted to go back to school.

Q: Especially if you were doing the same thing over and over again.

Admiral Lee: Yes. Although, as I say, the AD was a marvelous airplane--easily maintained.

Q: How did she handle around the ship?

Admiral Lee: Great. Everything about the AD was absolutely first rate--catapulting, deck launching, landings on the ship. I don't think we ever got a barrier with the AD. Beautiful carrier plane, absolutely the finest airplane I ever flew. Now we have airplanes that are very much more maneuverable, much higher performance. But I don't think I ever had anything to do with an airplane that was the equal of the AD, all around, for its day. It's just too bad we didn't have it during World War II.

Q: Especially instead of the SB2C.

Admiral Lee: Yes, which was the all-time worst airplane.

Q: From there you went to Monterey and an encounter with quantum mechanics.

Admiral Lee: I learned about the Peter Principle.* It really was not an engineering course, as such. The school offered successful candidates who attained a B average a master of science degree in physics. And it was mostly mathematics, physics, and chemistry. Graduate school was a little different from the university I attended.

PG school's academic year comprised four ten-week quarters per year. Most colleges and universities are on a two 15- or two 16-week semester basis, or a three ten-week quarter basis. The PG school at Monterey got an extra quarter out of its students each year, which I suppose was fair enough since we were being paid 12 months a year. And in our particular case for the summer we went to Sandia Base down at Albuquerque, and took a weapons employment course, which lasted about seven weeks.

---

*In 1968, Laurence J. Peter, a Canadian born educator enunciated his whimsical principle--in a hierarchy every employee tends to rise to the level of his incompetence. That is, the individual is promoted one step beyond that which he is capable of handling.

In my class were 14 students--six Navy, one Air Force, one Coast Guard, and six Army. I ended up about in the middle of the class. We had two absolutely brilliant students--one Coast Guard who went to Stanford and got a Ph.D. in physics, and one Navy who went from Monterey down to Oak Ridge's nuclear power school.

Q: Do you recall their names?

Admiral Lee: Yes. The Coast Guard officer who went to Stanford was a Lieutenant Chambers.* He later headed the physics department at the Coast Guard Academy. Lieutenant Joseph Skoog went to Oak Ridge, then went into nuclear submarines, and took the Skate to the North Pole.** We had another one who went to Oak Ridge, and his name was Don Hathway.*** He later taught physics as a civilian at the Naval Academy.

I found it was a tough two years--lots of hours and no easy courses. As an example, about the third quarter of the second year, I took a course called quantum mechanics from a Professor Watanabe.**** Quantum mechanics is about what you'd expect. It's about 98% math and 2% physics. It

---
*Lieutenant Edward E. Chambers, USCG. As a lieutenant commander, Chambers taught at the Coast Guard Academy in the early 1960s.
**Lieutenant Joseph L. Skoog, USN.
***Lieutenant Donald L. Hathway, USN.
****Dr. Michael Watanabe.

is a mathematical description of the atom and what goes on in the atomic structure when electrons emit energy or absorb energy. I thought we worked very hard in the quantum mechanics course, then came the day of the final exam, and Professor Watanabe wrote one problem on the board. Absolutely nothing rang a bell. And I was not alone when I looked at this problem. It wasn't anything we'd been studying for ten weeks.

Q: How do you know you weren't alone?

Admiral Lee: I talked to the other students afterwards. All of them had the same feeling: "Where in heaven's name did Professor Watanabe get this problem? It's not related to anything we studied." Anyway, I struggled through this particular problem. Never got an answer that was satisfactory to me.

I think that was the turning point for me in physics. I decided that I had reached the Peter Principle level--in other words, the level of my incompetence--and I really was not all that interested in physics beyond the particular level that I had studied. As I said a moment ago, most advanced physics is mathematics, certainly 90% mathematics and 10% physics. I also had seen some real talent in our class. Two people in my class went down to Oak Ridge, and two went to Stanford to get Ph.D's.

Q: What was the Navy's objective in sending officers through that particular discipline?

Admiral Lee: The idea was that we should have naval officers who were experts in the effects of nuclear weapons. We studied such things as heat transfer and the effects of atomic explosions, both heat and shock, and so forth, on all types of structures. It was a joint course sponsored by the AEC.* There were Army, Air Force, Navy, Coast Guard officers in the class. All the services were to have people knowledgeable in the physics, chemistry, mathematics, and the effects of atomic weapons.

But, anyway, we were there for two years, and they were tough years, busy years. I ended up with about a B average, working about as hard as I could work. So I decided after those two years of graduate school that I had about enough school. I ended up with a master's degree in physics. Later I did go to a tough school for another year, but it wasn't by choice.**

Q: Did the Navy have a specific requirement for a payback tour for that postgraduate education?

---
*AEC--Atomic Energy Commission.
**As a commander in the early 1960s, Lee went through the Navy's nuclear power training program.

Admiral Lee: At that particular time, for each year of graduate education, we had to pay back two years. So I was obligated for four years of service after graduation.

Q: But did it have to be something specifically related to that?

Admiral Lee: No, this was obligated service. Payback was whatever the Navy elected. And I did pay back a couple of tours later, as you will find out.

Also, while I was in graduate school, I was promoted to lieutenant commander. Then on graduation in June of 1954, I again applied for duty in an operating squadron. I didn't exactly get that, but I was ordered to Air Development Squadron Three in Atlantic City, New Jersey.

I don't really have anything else to say about PG school. Unless you have some questions.

Q: You said it was a tough grind. I'm wondering if you had any time for leisure activities or socializing with some of the other students.

Admiral Lee: We did a reasonable amount of socializing. We played squash. They had some squash courts nearby. And we had picnics and small parties. But it was one

Lee #3 - 193

continuous grind for two years.

Q: Much more so than Columbia had been, I take it.

Admiral Lee: I thought Columbia was a holiday compared to graduate school. Columbia was very different. You sort of set your own pace. At Columbia I always took some tough courses, but I always had a couple of courses that weren't so tough. I think the contrast between the two might be interesting. I thought on balance that the professors at the Navy's PG school stood up very well. They had some very fine professors there. I can still remember several of them. We had a Professor Fry, who was head of the physics department, and I thought the equal of any I had at Columbia.* I thought we had some very fine professors in mathematics, also as good as the Columbia types.

I was very impressed with the caliber of instruction at PG school. And everything was--with one or two minor exceptions--I thought, very good. Certainly better than the Line School and in every sense on the level of the instruction I had at Columbia.

Q: What did you do during that time to keep up with the naval profession, such as carrier developments and what have you?

------
*Dr. Austin R. Fry, physics department chairman.

Admiral Lee: Well, you don't. But I didn't find that unusual, because at Columbia I was intent on getting a liberal arts education, and I had no contact with the Navy and really didn't attempt to keep up. The same thing was true at PG school. I made no attempt whatsoever. There wasn't time. If you take 16, 20 hours a week, and they're all technical courses, and all tough courses--the likes of quantum mechanics--you don't have time for much else.

Q: That places a real burden on the rest of the family to really have you there, but doing without you.

Admiral Lee: That's right. I thought my wife was going to leave me. (Laughter) I think it was worthwhile. I would do it again. Probably as much as anything else, it was a turning point in my career, because it gave me the confidence that I needed. And I felt that I was, perhaps, as academically qualified as just about anybody around, having had Line School for a year, and Columbia, and then graduate school. And I knew the physics, and chemistry, and math pretty well by then.

It's hard to look back and say, but having a master's degree, it seems to me doesn't hurt along the way. I'm sure that's why Rickover brought me into the nuclear power program.* So I rather think that PG school was very important for my later career. But you really pay a price during the course, though, because the Navy works you much harder than civilian colleges and universities, and maybe for a good reason because they're paying you a year-round salary. There's really no summer break, four ten-week quarters a year and a summer school at Sandia, whereas Columbia was not like that at all.**

But, anyway, it was a good tour. We made some friends that we still have today. For example, a couple we visited in Seattle, Washington, just last week was a PG school classmate, a submariner by the name of Skoog. So we had a nice little group there. But it was one tough grind.

After graduation, we headed for Atlantic City, New Jersey, where I joined VX-3, Air Development Squadron Three. VX-3 was formed to develop tactics for the Navy's new carrier airplanes. It was my introduction to jet aircraft, which I thought at the time was very important, because this was 1954, and the Navy was moving very rapidly to all jet carrier aircraft. And I, as yet, had not gotten into jet aircraft because I had spent so much time in school. I had spent five of the last seven years in school, which was a lot of time to be away.

---
*Vice Admiral Hyman G. Rickover, USN (Ret.). Even though he reached statutory retirement age in 1962, Admiral Rickover remained on active duty, as head of the Navy's nuclear power program, until 1982.
**Sandia, New Mexico, was a site of nuclear weapons training.

Q: What was your job in the squadron?

Admiral Lee: When I first joined the squadron, I was put into the development office. The development office handled all projects. But they didn't really have enough projects for all of us there. The captain at the time, Hawley Russell, was unhappy with his maintenance department, so he asked me if I'd like to try that.* I said yes. So I went down and was the logistics officer, in charge of aircraft maintenance, support, and modifications. I ran the logistics department for about the first year I was there. I was in the development office for about three months, then maintenance/logistics for about a year or a little more. Then I was administrative officer of the squadron for about the last nine months I was there under a new captain. But it was a very rewarding tour in a lot of ways, because I was able to get checked out in and fly the F9F-8, swept-wing airplane called the Cougar.** I also flew the AD once again as well as the F7U and the FJ.***

---
*Captain Hawley Russell, USN.
**The F9F-8 had a Pratt & Whitney J48-P-8A turbojet, wing span of 34 feet, gross weight of 20,600 pounds, maximum speed of 705 miles per hour at sea level, and an initial climb rate of 8.5 minutes to reach 40,000 feet.
***The Vought F7U Cutlass had two Westinghouse J46-WE-8A turbojets, wing span of 39 feet, gross weight of 31,642 pounds, maximum speed of 680 miles per hour at 10,000 feet, and an initial climb rate of 13,000 feet per minute. The North American FJ-2 Fury had a Wright J65-W-2 turbojet, its wing span was 37 feet, gross weight 18,790 pounds, maximum speed 676 miles per hour at sea level, and initial climb rate of 7,230 feet per minute.

Q: I'd like to hear your reactions to those various planes, in light of what you've said about the propeller types.

Admiral Lee: Well, the F9F-8 was the first jet that I flew. And it was a typical "Grumman Iron Works" airplane-- stoutly built, strongly built, but grossly underpowered. It was not an afterburner aircraft. It had an engine in it with about 7,000 pounds of thrust. It was not a great performer. It was a nice plane to fly and a good carrier plane. But not something you'd want to take into combat.

The F7U Cutlass, built by Chance Vought, was perhaps the worst airplane the Navy ever bought. The engines were equally as bad as the airframe. And for political reasons, the Navy bought 300, 350 of these airplanes and deployed only one or two squadrons. It was so bad they off-loaded them in the Med.*

It was an impossible aircraft to maintain. It was underpowered, and the engines were also very difficult to maintain. They were J46 engines built by Westinghouse. Westinghouse built some of the finest jet engines made early on, such as J34 that went into the Banshee, the F2H, which was a fine airplane.** Then they got contracts to

---
*Med--Mediterranean Sea.
**The McDonnell F2H Banshee fighter had two Westinghouse J34-WE-34 turbojets.

build two additional engines: the J46, which went into the F7U, and the J40, which went into the F3H, and both of them were failures.* That put Westinghouse out of the jet engine business. They were disasters. And the F7U was also a disaster, although we did our best with it in VX-3.

The other jet I flew up there was the FJ. The FJ was the Navy's version of the F-86, built by North American. A very fine plane, very maneuverable. The only problem with the FJ was the engine. Our version of the F-86 had the J65 engine, which was an engine built by Wright based on a British design, the Nene engine. It wasn't the best engine, but the airplane was a very good airplane, the FJ.

Q: The F-86 had done very well in Korea for the Air Force.

Admiral Lee: Yes. The F-86 was a good airplane. The F-86 in Korea had a different engine than our FJ but the same airplane basically. We had made it carrier capable.

As a matter of fact, an odd thing happened there. We developed the F-86 plane, originally called the NA-134 and then decided not to use it. The Air Force took it up, and continued the development, and made it into the F-86. They had such success with it that we went back to it and called

---

*The McDonnell F3H-1 Demon fighter had the Westinghouse J40-WE-22 turbojet engine, which did not provide enough power. As a result, the F3H-2 model was equipped with the Allison J71-A-2E turbojet. In addition, 29 of the original F3H-1's got the Allison engine during refits.

it the FJ.

Among the things we did at VX-3 was the initial calibration of the airplane for low-level flying. We worked out group instrument approaches to carriers. We had the tacan project--the tacan was the first navigational aid which gave you both azimuth and distance. And now all aircraft carriers, and almost all land stations are equipped with tacan. We got the first one in Atlantic City and evaluated it. The Sidewinder--we were given the Sidewinder missile to evaluate, which at that time had just come out of NOTS China Lake and was one of the great inventions of the Fifties.* The Sidewinder missile we're still building--improved versions of it.**

We had one of the first mirror landing systems at Atlantic City. And we did the first qualification landings on USS Bennington, which had a mirror landing system and angled decks in 1955, which was very interesting. I landed both the F9F-8 on the angled deck, mirror landing system, and the AD-5N. We had not planned to land the AD-5N on the Bennington, but the jet landings with the various types we had out there went so well that Captain Dosé asked me if I would fly the AD-5N on the mirror on the Bennington, which I did.*** We made about five, eight landings in the AD.

---
*NOTS--Naval Ordnance Test Station, China Lake, California.
**The AIM-9 Sidewinder, which first became operational in 1956, is a short-range air-to-air missile. It was used a good deal in the Vietnam War.
***Commander Robert G. Dosé, USN.

Q: Was Dosé the skipper of the squadron?

Admiral Lee: The skipper of the squadron for the first year I was there was a very colorful ex-aviation cadet by the name of Monk Russell--very well known, very popular man, very popular with the troops. The captain for the second year was a man by the name of Robert Dosé, one of the finer aviators I've run across.

Q: Why do you say he was one of the finer aviators? What would make him that in your mind?

Admiral Lee: You know, there are some people who are just born aviators, natural aviators. They just can seem to do no wrong in an airplane. They fly beautiful carrier landings and approaches. In gunnery runs, in bombing runs, everything they do is done smoothly and properly. Some people just seem to have that knack--like a basketball player. A natural athlete makes all the right moves. I've known a few aviators like that. One of them was Bob Dosé, the skipper here. Another one in VX-3 was Donald Engen, one of the best aviators I ever ran across.* He later became head of the FAA.**

---

*Lieutenant Commander Donald D. Engen, USN, who eventually became a vice admiral.
**FAA--Federal Aviation Administration.

Q: Recently retired from that.

Admiral Lee: Yes. But I suppose in my naval career, I ran across ten or a dozen aviators like that.

Q: Any others whose names come to your mind?

Admiral Lee: Yes, Edward L. Feightner and Marlar Stewart.*

Q: Would you put McCampbell in that group?

Admiral Lee: No, I wouldn't really. I'd say McCampbell's strong feature was his competitiveness. I'm not sure that I was that much of a judge of McCampbell, because when I knew him, I was a brand-new ensign and all eyes and ears on a new aircraft carrier. But my guess about McCampbell is that he was a very competent aviator, but I wouldn't put him in the class of Dosé and Engen. But he had something that, I think, all great leaders must have. McCampbell was a great competitor and a great leader--great combat leader--which is, in the final analysis, I suppose, for our business, the bottom line. But he was certainly a

---
*Commander Edward L. Feightner, USN, about whom Admiral Lee talks later in the oral history; Lieutenant Commander Marlar E. Stewart, USN.

competent aviator.

Q: Were there any specific incidents involving either Dosé or Engen that you recall from that period?

Admiral Lee: Yes, as a matter of fact, We were out having carrier qualifications on one of the carriers, not <u>Bennington</u>. Engen came in a little fast on one of his landings; the hook parted and he went into the barrier. I was the senior member of the accident investigation board. There really wasn't much to say about it. We unwrapped the wires and pulled the airplane out of the barrier. About the only thing you can say is that he was a little fast, the hook parted, and he got a barrier.

Bob Dosé was a top-notch aviator in every sense. I went out on a number of flights with him. I remember one time we went out over the Atlantic and fired Sidewinder missiles at a drone airplane. And as I say, everything Bob Dosé did in an airplane was just the way you'd like to do it. He was one of those guys--all the right moves.

Q: I gather this squadron was a lot like what the Operational Development Force did for shipboard-type weapons.

Admiral Lee: Yes, VX-3 was a part of the Operational Development Force.

Q: I see.

Admiral Lee: Since that time, VX-3's been decommissioned, VX-4 now does what we were doing in VX-3. VX-4 is out at China Lake, I believe. But we were a part of the Operational Development Force. I've only listed half a dozen projects here--the more interesting ones. We had a number of others less interesting, but it was a tactical development squadron. And all the aviators, with one or two exceptions, had fleet tours or were graduates of test pilot schools, and so forth. So it was a highly qualified group of pilots in VX-3.

Q: Did you have any interchange work with the test pilot group at Patuxent River?*

Admiral Lee: No, although we were in contact with them on various things. We did have a Royal Navy test pilot school graduate assigned to the squadron. We had interaction with them, and anything that they learned from the Royal Navy or Royal Air Force, why, we would learn about. And our people--many of our pilots were test pilot school

---
*Naval Air Test Center, Patuxent River, Maryland.

graduates, and we had close liaison with Patuxent.

Q: For example, the mirror landing system that you mentioned was a British innovation.

Admiral Lee: Angled deck too. Steam catapult too. We seem to get most of our good things from the British.

Q: Could you elaborate, please, on that low-altitude flying that you were talking about?

Admiral Lee: When I joined VX-3 in 1954 after graduation from PG school, they had a project involving developing low-level flying and tactics for the AD aircraft. We had a project officer, and we had about a dozen ADs. I was merely a pilot in it. If I remember correctly, the scope of the project was to develop the tactics the AD should use for low-level flying, such as speed, range, fuel tanks, engine settings, and then come up with how many pounds of fuel you would use per mile, and so forth. This was put together in a book that Commander Operational Development Force published and eventually sent to all the AD squadrons. The same thing was later done for the A4D and other types of airplanes.* These low-level runs were

---

*The Douglas A4D Skyhawk attack plane was introduced to the fleet in the mid-1950s. As a commander, Lee later commanded an A4D squadron.

made by VX-3 and other squadrons.

Q: You also want to avoid detection too.

Admiral Lee: Avoid detection--that kind of a project. I probably flew 15 or 20 of those flights.

Q: So that book you developed was the fleet doctrine on that subject.

Admiral Lee: It would have been. It was also tied in with some work that VX-4, I guess, was doing in the delivery technique. At the end of the run pilots make one of those, toss deliveries; that's how they were delivered.* We didn't do that part of it. That part of it was done by VX-4 at an instrumented range. But it was all tied together by OpDevFor in this tactical publication that was put out for fleet squadrons.

That was about the size of it at VX-3

Q: What do you remember about the F8U?

Admiral Lee: I did fly the F8U, but I didn't fly it in
___
*The loft method was developed to protect the plane and pilot from the effects of the nuclear weapon it dropped. The idea was to approach a target at low level to avoid enemy radar detection. The plane then began climbing, released the weapon, and continued on over onto its back to return to the carrier from which it was launched.

VX-3.* I'd be happy to talk about it; this might be a good time.

The F8U was a fighter plane built by Chance Vought. It was sent to VX-3 about the time I was leaving. Later on, in about 1962, when I had an air group in Enterprise, we had an F8U squadron. I went through the F8U RAG, replacement air group, and qualified in the F8U aboard a carrier. So I had a fair amount of F8U time. The F8U had a very good engine in it, the J57 built by Pratt & Whitney, a great engine. And the F8U itself was very maneuverable, a very fine airplane. It had one problem which I thought made it unacceptable for the Navy.

The problem with the F8U was that it was unstable on the glide slope. That is, it wouldn't maintain a constant speed. Pilots had to pump the throttle back and forth to keep it on speed. It was a very difficult plane for carrier landings, because it was longitudinally unstable, speed unstable. Most planes, like the AD or the F-4, were very stable on the glide slope, very stable.** You'd get your speed and altitude set up and coast right on in. The F8U would not do that. There was no way you could get it

---
*The Vought F8U Crusader was equipped with the Pratt & Whitney J57 turbojet engine; in its eventual configuration as the F-8E, it had a wing span of 35 feet, gross weight of 34,000 pounds, maximum speed of 1,120 miles per hour at 40,000 feet, and took 6.5 minutes to climb to 57,000 feet.
**The McDonnell Douglas F-4 Phantom II was the principal Navy carrier fighter during the Vietnam War. It was also a long-lived aircraft, operating in fleet squadrons from the early 1960s to the mid-1980s.

set for a carrier landing. You had to pump your throttle back and forth.

As a matter of fact, it was so bad that after a while, say, after about ten years, the Navy put an automatic throttle in the F8U, keyed to the angle of attack indicator, and this thing was pumping all the time, keeping the airplane on speed. The airplane should not have been accepted by the Navy. It was dangerous. As a result, we had many carrier landing accidents in the F8U.

I think in terms of performance, it was a good. It was the best performer we had at the time.

Q: And it was still small enough to fit in the Essex-class carriers.

Admiral Lee: Still small enough for Essex-class carriers, which was important, because we still had a lot of Essex-class carriers, and the F-4 was too big for the Essex-class carriers. But it was a very difficult plane to fly aboard a ship.

Q: The F7U had a strange tail arrangement. Did that make it unusual to fly because of that?

Admiral Lee: No, I thought the F7U handled fairly well. The major problem with the F7U was a lousy set of engines.

It was a very unreliable airplane, very difficult to maintain. It also was a very poor performer. But in terms of flying, landing, and taking off, it handled very well.

Q: Certainly looked unusual.

Admiral Lee: It was unusual. It was another plane we should not have bought.

The F8U's successor, in a sense, the A-7--also built by Chance Vought, was almost a dead ringer for the F8U--had a different wing on it, a set of flaps, and so forth, and a different engine.* But it was very difficult to tell them apart, if you looked at them. The A-7 really was a very fine carrier airplane, oddly enough.

I think my tour in VX-3 was a very good tour. I learned about jet aviation and got caught up to date on naval aviation. We were working with all these new pieces of equipment, such as tacan, and the mirror landing system, and angled decks, which would be a part of naval aviation for a long time to come. And, of course, in VX-3, with the typical pilots we had there, the only conversation morning, noon, and night was aviation. The hangar flying went on 24 hours a day.

---

*The A-7 Corsair II attack plane had an Allison TF41-A-2 turbofan engine, wing span of 39 feet, maximum takeoff weight of 42,000 pounds, and maximum speed of 698 miles per hour at sea level.

Q: How does a squadron like that compare with a carrier squadron in terms of cohesiveness and working together, and that sort of thing? Is there as much unity?

Admiral Lee: No, there isn't as much unity, because in a squadron like VX-3, you have a lot of senior people. We must have had a dozen lieutenant commanders, a captain, and three or four commanders. And then we were divided into groups working on various projects.

Q: So you've got little cluster within a big group.

Admiral Lee: Little clusters, yes, within a big group. But even so, it was quite a cohesive squadron. I think it worked very well. Whereas, in a fleet carrier squadron, with a commanding officer, executive officer--and we're all doing the same thing--you have a team spirit, which you don't have in a VX-3. A carrier squadron is like a football team. You know, the old college spirit type of thing. I'd say 80% of the young pilots in a fleet squadron are ensigns or lieutenants (junior grade), first fleet squadron. And they're gung ho and ready to go. They believe anything that a lieutenant tells them.

Q: Was there a sense of being part of an elite in that developmental squadron?

Admiral Lee: I think that was one of the objectionable features. Some pilots who had been through test pilot school, gone to VX-3, and so forth, sort of looked on themselves as super aviators. That was the part I liked least about it, because they thought we were an elite group, special people. They thought they knew about all there was to know about aviation and naval aviation. There were a few like that. But it wasn't all that bad.

Q: You've probably read Tom Wolfe's book, <u>The Right Stuff</u> and his pyramid.* Do you go along with his theory on that?

Admiral Lee: Yes. You know how he writes. Everything is exaggerated about two orders of magnitude.

Q: In an entertaining way.

Admiral Lee: In an entertaining way, yes. I like his stuff. I think it's great. I thought <u>The Right Stuff</u> had it about right, if you take into account that in order to

---

*Tom Wolfe, <u>The Right Stuff</u> (New York: Farrar, Strauss, and Giroux, 1979). Wolfe's book is about the early U.S. astronauts and includes considerable material on military test pilots.

make it entertaining, he had to exaggerate a bit. That's about the way VX-3 was. If a pilot pitched in off the end of the runway in an F7U, the reaction was, "Well, he did something wrong."

Q: Well, that's the point that Wolfe kept making repeatedly, that an individual would say, "Well, that's not going to happen to me, because I won't screw up."

Admiral Lee: Yes. Yes, I found The Right Stuff presented a pretty good picture.

Q: It also talked about the burden from an emotional standpoint that that puts on wives. How did your wife react to your being in naval aviation?

Admiral Lee: I think she reacted very well. My wife is one of the most stable women I've known. I think her role throughout my naval career was to provide support to other wives who were having problems. Whatever troubles my wife had, she never brought them to me. She's a very stable woman.

Q: That helps.

Admiral Lee: Yes. I knew and observed many wives who had a very difficult time with naval aviation. Even so far as to getting their husbands out of naval aviation. This happened in a number of cases. But I never had that problem with my wife. It was not something we talked about. But I'm sure that if I had that problem, I would have gotten out--well, I don't know. Who knows?

Q: But it makes it easier for you, from a mental standpoint, not to have to cope with that additional problem.

Admiral Lee: Yes. My wife never gave me any indication that, as they used to say, "she was nervous in the service." As a matter of fact, she was always giving support, which was a very good thing.

Q: What was Atlantic City like as a place to be based and living?

Admiral Lee: Atlantic City is on a reef, an island. And there's a bay between Atlantic City itself and the mainland. The naval air station is on the mainland. We had to drive roughly 15 miles to get to Atlantic City. Atlantic City was very closed up and barren in the wintertime, before the days of gambling casinos. And in the summertime, it was a resort. We lived down on Summers Point in a development about ten miles south of the naval air station, on the mainland, opposite Margate. We had a very quiet development, and really didn't get involved in the vacation resort bit over at Atlantic City.

Q: Were you able to take advantage of it from time to time?

Admiral Lee: Oh, yes, although we rarely went to Atlantic City. There was a causeway down our way, and we could go over to the Margate beaches, which is the beach south of Atlantic City. The only way I can describe is that in the summertime it was a typical beach resort. There were lots of honky tonks, lots of sun, and sand, and hotels all open, vacationers all around--very open city. And, no, we did very little in Atlantic City.

Q: Did you have more children by then?

Admiral Lee: In New Jersey we had a daughter, number two daughter, Barbara. She was born in 1955 in Summers Point Hospital.

But if I were to sum up my VX-3 time, I'd say it was very worthwhile. My introduction to jet aviation was the most important part of it. I got a good understanding of jet aviation and flew several types. And at that particular point in my career, it was very important to get started in jet aviation, because in a very few years the props were gone.

Q: Admiral Matthews said one of the biggest impacts was the shorter cycle times compared with the propeller planes operating from carriers.*

Admiral Lee: A jet could travel at 400 miles an hour, get over the beach, hit its target, and be back in an hour. A propeller plane, operating from the same distance offshore, would take about three hours to get over and back, and do the same thing. So the carriers had to adjust to a shorter cycle time, which we did very well. And what we did was put the ADs on a three-hour cycle, and they'd come back every other cycle, and the jets would have about an hour and a half cycle. There was another side to it. The jets didn't have enough fuel to stay up three hours. But they could travel about as far as the props, get there and back in about half the time.

When I left VX-3 in spring/summer 1956, I hoped to go to a fleet squadron as executive officer. Many of my lieutenant commander friends were going to fleet squadrons.

---

*Rear Admiral Herbert Spencer Matthews, USN, who has been interviewed as part of the Naval Institute's oral history program.

The detailer at that time in Washington was a fellow by the name of Commander Richard H. Mills. It just so happens that he was the flight officer of VB-15 on Essex in 1944. Dick Mills told me in no uncertain terms that I wasn't going to a fleet squadron, I was going to the Navy special weapons school in Norfolk, Virginia, to pay back some of my Navy PG training.

Q: You wondered what kind of a friend he was.

Admiral Lee: And I wondered what kind of a friend he was. As a matter of fact, I accused him of not being a friend at all. But he said, "Well, that's fine, but you're going down to the special weapons school." So I was very disappointed to be going to the special weapons school at Norfolk, which was a part of the fleet training center.

In June of 1956 I headed to Norfolk and reported in to Fleet Training Center, Navy Special Weapons School, as an instructor, as I watched all of my friends from VX-3 going out to fleet squadrons as executive officers. I was one very disappointed young lieutenant commander. And I probably had a very long face when I reported in down at the special weapons school.

The Navy had a special weapons school on each coast. We had a seven-week weapons employment course. Every carrier division staff--and most other big operational staffs--had one or two graduates on it. About that time all carrier attack airplanes were equipped to deliver atomic weapons. It was the big thing then. In order to get in the budget, the services had to be able to have an atomic weapons capability. So we gave the atomic weapons capability to ADs and A4Ds, and we bought the A3Ds.* We went into the business 100%.

Q: Were the AJs phasing out by that time?

Admiral Lee: Yes. The AJs were first.** They were being phased out, and about that time the A3Ds were coming in. We taught a seven-week course in atomic weapons, much like the course that I had taken down at Albuquerque in the summer of '53.

We also taught a one-week orientation course 30 times a year for naval officers and senior civilians from the Department of the Navy. Taught them all about atomic weapons. We also taught a one-week weapons planning course for senior officers--let them play games for a week with atomic weapons.

But one of the things I did accomplish at the special

---

*The Douglas A3D Skywarrior had two Pratt & Whitney J57-P-10 turbojets, wing span of 72 feet, gross weight of 82,000 pounds, maximum speed of 610 miles per hour at 10,000 feet.
**The North American AJ Savage was powered by two propeller driven engines with a turbojet in the tail. It had a wing span of 75 feet, gross weight of 52,862 pounds, and maximum speed of 471 miles per hour.

weapons school was to learn public speaking, which I had never done. And I will never forget my first effort. Classroom teaching was no problem, but for the one-week courses--the orientation course and the one-week course for senior officers--we gave what were in effect 50-minute presentations. We used slides and other training aids.

My first time out I started off all right. I got about halfway through the thing, and then forgot everything I was supposed to tell them. And there was no way I could get it back. But somehow or other I stumbled to the end of the damn thing, and it was over. It was an absolute disaster.

I've since read descriptions about this happening to other people in maybe their first or second public speaking try. You know, it all just came apart, and their minds became blank. And that happened to me. The officer in charge of the school was a very fine 1100, one of the best bosses I ever had, Charlie Jenkins, Naval Academy, 1939.* Very good man. But, anyway, he stroked me a little bit. I went back and worked again, and after a little more practice, I got pretty good at it. At the end of two years, I was a very polished public speaker. I did very well.

Q: Do you remember any famous students you had in any of

---
*Commander Charles W. Jenkins, USN.

those courses?

Admiral Lee: No, although we had everybody through there. All kinds of admirals, but I never got to know them. They just came and sat. We had everybody. We had a lot of two-stars and a passel of captains and commanders.

Q: Was this mostly the thrust of it on tactical use of nuclear weapons?

Admiral Lee: The seven-week course taught them about nuclear weapons: what's available and so on. And we taught them the mathematics of atomic explosions--how to calculate the damage from 24-kiloton weapons from pressure; how to calculate the damage from heat, or the thermal part of it; how to calculate the damage from the nuclear part of it, radiation.

Then their job was to plan strikes and estimate the damage. It was a good course. Seven weeks, a long time, every day. We took them through the whole thing--the whole gamut of weapons, the delivery systems, so that they could do their jobs when they got out there. In the one-week orientation course, we started right off with basic physics for the senior officers. Then we'd give them how the thing worked, a look at the weapons, and the delivery vehicles. Then we would go into some weapons effects: the shock

Lee #3 - 219

wave--what it would do; what ships had to worry about. Then we'd go into the temperature and so forth. And then at the last we would maybe work a weapons employment problem for them in the orientation course.

Q: How tight was the security for this course?

Admiral Lee: Very tight. The students had to have top secret clearance to take it.

Q: You undoubtedly became a better teacher as you went along.

Admiral Lee: Yes. But, anyway, my job was to teach the physics. After teaching the same course over and over, one gets bored and wants to teach something else. But we had a good crew. It was a good little school, and I suppose for its time--I was there from '56 to '58--it was very worthwhile.

Q: Were the students virtually all aviators in these courses?

Admiral Lee: Oh, no. They were everybody. We had Supply Corps officers, and doctors, and 1100s, and aviators. It was a LantFlt activity.* And we got an awful lot of people from Washington.

Q: This was when the Polaris program was building up.** Did you get submariners?

Admiral Lee: Yes, we had submariners, lots of submariners. We had lots of everything. Because we could handle about 50 people in this orientation course. And we had it about 30 weeks a year, downstairs in an amphitheater. Upstairs we had classrooms for the seven-week course. And we ran a continuous seven-week course. You know, we'd teach one for seven weeks, and then have a week break, and then start another.

Q: Did the curriculum evolve at all while you were there?

Admiral Lee: Not a great deal. We tried to keep our presentations up to date. For instance, when we were talking about delivery systems, we tried to keep up to date on the various airplanes, what they could do. We tried to keep up to date on the various missiles such as Polaris, what its capabilities were. And we tried to keep up to date on all the weapons by maintaining liaison with Atomic

---
*LantFlt--Atlantic Fleet.
**In the late 1950s the Navy was in the process of developing the Polaris missile for launching by nuclear submarines.

Energy Commission.

Q: Was there anything about defense against atomic weapons in the course?

Admiral Lee: Yes. We had, obviously, a section on defense. And we described the various defensive measures that ships had available, such as a washdown system. Another was closing the ship up tight for a period of time after an explosion goes off to keep nuclear particles from getting in until you could get out of the area of the bomb burst.

Q: Presumably you'd turn away from the blast to avoid that pressure effect.

Admiral Lee: Yes. But we had a section on defensive measures, for ships primarily, since this was a Navy course, and what the Navy had done to protect its ships.

But I think they were good courses. And I think they were very useful for that time and period. It was fairly new when I joined. It hadn't been in operation too long. The services set up the initial schools for atomic weapons at Albuquerque. I went to that initial school in 1953, and I think it had been in operation then for several years. I think the Navy decided to set up similar schools on the East Coast and West Coast--one for each fleet--in the early Fifties. They were patterned on the Albuquerque school, which was run by a joint command down there and was the senior school of this type.

But we had a very happy tour in Norfolk. And I enjoyed teaching. We also had a third daughter, Marion, born in Norfolk in April 1958, and that completed our family.

In the last year I was there, I was selected for promotion to commander. And I also learned that the Navy had begun a selection process for command of squadrons. Up until this time, the detailers had decided who would have squadrons and sent them out. Well, Arleigh Burke in 1957 decided that there were so many people competing for squadron commands, that we should have some sort of a formal selection system.*

So he set up in 1957 a formal selection system in the Bureau of Naval Personnel for picking people for squadron commands. He set up a selection board which looked through the year groups and picked people who would get command because no more than, say, a third to a half of the commanders who were naval aviators were going to get squadron commands at this particular time. So you can imagine my joy in the spring of 1958 when I was told that I

---
*Burke was then Chief of Naval Operations.

was on the command list, and I would be going to command of a squadron later on that year--not XO, but command.

Q: It was especially good not to have to be an exec.

Admiral Lee: Yes. So in late May or early June 1958, I was detached from the special weapons school and ordered to Jacksonville, where I was to assume command of VA-46. I first had to go through what was then just the beginnings of the RAG. There I checked out in the A4D. I also had to go through instrument school. So I had about six or seven weeks of training before I could join VA-46. This could all be done in Jacksonville. I went through instrument training, and then to the A4D RAG.

In August 1958 I reported to VA-46 and relieved Commander Ray Hawkins as commanding officer.* VA-46 had been stationed at Cecil Field for about 18 months, flying F9F-8s. They were transitioning to A4Ds also and had had three accidents. Shortly after I took command, we had two more. Things weren't looking good.

But, anyway, another of the embarrassing events in my naval career I'll now talk about. I was still a lieutenant commander, hadn't made my number yet, when I assumed command of the squadron. I thought I was really king of

---

*Commander Arthur Ray Hawkins, USN, had commanded Attack Squadron 46 since March 1957. He has been interviewed as part of the Naval Institute's oral history program.

the hill. I had read lots of books about leadership and command. I thought the thing to do when you go in and take command is to gather all the troops around and tell them how it's going to be--Hollywood style! After I'd been there a few days, maybe a week, I got all the officers together in a ready room. I had written out everything I was going to say. So I told them, "This is how we're going to do it. This is how it's going to be." And even today, when I think about that, I'm embarrassed. I learned a good lesson.

There was a saying in the old Navy that, "You don't change the sails for the first half hour of your watch." The watch officer before you might have known what he was doing. And if you've got something that's working, don't fiddle with it. Over the next few weeks and months I found out that it wasn't going to be that way. After you've had a little experience, you learn to take one problem at a time. And there's no correct answer for most problems. You know, you can solve most problems several different ways. And you solve them in the best interests of the individual and the squadron, in the circumstances.

Q: What had been the tenor of your remarks, that you were going to change things right away?

Admiral Lee: Yes, we were going to do it A, B, C. You

know, they say Lee puts everything in columns. I was going to do it: A, B, C: "Now we're going to do everything this way."

Q: Do you remember any of the specifics?

Admiral Lee: I can't remember them now. I'm too embarrassed. I threw it all away. But, anyway, that got me off to a great start. And, as I say, even today when I think about that probably half hour pitch I gave these guys--really feeling my oats, I'm embarrassed. But it was a very good lesson.

Q: Did you have a turnover period with Commander Hawkins in which he briefed you on the squadron?

Admiral Lee: Not much. A little bit. Ray Hawkins was a former Blue Angel.* I never really knew him as an aviator, but he must have been a pretty fine aviator.

Q: Also a World War II ace.**

---
*Hawkins was assigned to the Navy's flight demonstration team, the Blue Angels, from 1948 to 1954, with the exception of a period in 1950-51, when he was executive officer of Fighter Squadron 191. Hawkins commanded the Blue Angels from August 1951 to April 1954.
**Hawkins was credited with shooting down 14 Japanese aircraft in World War II.

Admiral Lee: World War II ace and so forth. But my idea of running a squadron was the way Mini ran VB-15. And I had a feeling that Ray Hawkins had been running a very loose squadron. Maybe sometimes a loose squadron is okay. I don't know. It worked for Ray.

Q: Well, Mini had a different situation too. He was starting from scratch and had to teach things.

Admiral Lee: Yes. Anyway, shortly after I assumed command, we headed for Guantánamo on Franklin D. Roosevelt.* And not too long after I took over command, we had two more accidents. That meant the squadron had had five accidents in maybe six months. I started delving into that area. I found that we really didn't have much of a safety program. And we really went to work in that area. The whole schmear--maintenance, pilots, checklists, training briefings. After those two additional accidents, we really concentrated on safety. That squadron went for three or four years without an accident--A4D squadron, VA-46. It's a remarkable record.

The message is you've really got to work at safety. And it's the whole bag from maintenance right down on the

---

*The USS Franklin D. Roosevelt (CVA-42) was one of three ships in the Midway class. She had been commissioned in 1945 and modernized, 1954-56, with the addition of an angled deck, hurricane bow, and steam catapults. She displaced 62,674 tons at full load and could make 33 knots.

hangar deck or flight deck, right up to the briefing for flights. For instance, I came into the ready room one time, to observe a briefing. I had said, "When the water temperature is below 60 degrees, we all wear exposure suits--standard procedure." We had a number of pilots in VA-46 who thought the rules didn't apply to them. The executive officer was briefing this flight. None of them were in exposure suits. I had that sort of a problem. Well, we straightened them out pretty soon. The message was you follow the rules. And then you know, "If you have an engine failure, and you land in the water, we can get you back okay."

Q: "The rules are for your benefit."

Admiral Lee: Yes. That's difficult sometimes to put across. And I had a real problem in this squadron in that regard. But, even so, I think we had a pretty good squadron. We went down to Guantánamo for a shakedown cruise with <u>Roosevelt</u>, and I guess we were down there three months or so. We also made a weapons training trip to the Guantánamo area. All the squadrons at that time did weapons training at Guantánamo on an instrumented range down there.

One of the problems I had as a commanding officer was that Ray Hawkins was a very personable guy. And he went from VA-46 to become air officer of the Franklin D. Roosevelt. These young pilots had been with him a year, 18 months down at Cecil; they thought the sun rose and set on Ray Hawkins. And here's this nobody, Kent Lee, coming in here and giving them a bad time. It was a difficult time.

Q: They still thought he was the skipper.

Admiral Lee: Yes, so that was a little bit of a problem.

Q: Did they go around you on occasion?

Admiral Lee: If they did, they didn't do it twice. I didn't make vice admiral by being a nice guy. As I say, they didn't do it twice. But I had a very difficult time in this squadron. I was a very unpopular CO, my guess is. Maybe a third of the squadron thought I was a pretty good guy. The rest of them, I think, thought I was a real horse's ass. Be that as it may, we were with Roosevelt until Christmas. Roosevelt had three A4D squadrons and Intrepid had only one. So the Navy decided that VA-46 would go to the Med on Intrepid rather than Roosevelt, which was a great break for me.*

---

*The USS Intrepid (CVA-11) had been commissioned in 1943, mothballed after World War II, and then recommissioned in 1954 after a modernization that included an angled deck and hurricane bow. She had a full-load displacement of approximately 41,000 tons and top speed of 33 knots.

We made the move in January. We had one of the greatest teams I've ever run across on <u>Intrepid</u>. Paul Masterton, who later made vice admiral, was the captain.* Chris Cagle was the executive officer.** The group commander was Jack James.*** I was quite happy to get out from under <u>Roosevelt</u> and Ray Hawkins, and get on to some new ground with VA-46.

I had another problem. Since Ray Hawkins was an ex-Blue Angel, VA-46 had a flight demonstration team. They went out and put on air shows which is very dangerous business. And if you're doing that in a fleet squadron, you're not doing required training. So I put a stop to air shows. No flight demonstration team. That didn't go over too well. But they had been sitting at Jacksonville for 18 months, and Ray Hawkins had been the leader of the Blue Angels, you know. A very charming man, big, good-looking. I don't know if you've ever met him or not.

Q: Yes, I've interviewed him.

Admiral Lee: In January of 1959 we departed Norfolk for a Mediterranean cruise. <u>Roosevelt</u> was also going to the Med. We were going over together.

Before we got to the Med, I gathered all my 18, 19,

---
*Captain Paul Masterton, USN.
**Commander Malcolm W. Cagle, USN.
***Commander Jack M. James, USN.

and 20 year olds in the ready room. I gave them a facts-of-life talk. I explained to them what life was like in the seaports that we would visit. I explained the situations that they would encounter ashore. For instance, most wouldn't plan on having anything to do with local women. But after one beer local women looked pretty good, and after two beers, they'd look much better; then after three beers, they would be absolutely irresistible. I told them there was about a 75% chance that they couldn't resist the physical charms of these ladies after three beers. If they went to bed with one of these dollies, chances are they'd come home with VD. We went through that in great detail.

The squadron had some welfare and recreation money. We got a share of the profits from the ship's store. I took some of this welfare money and bought several cases of rubbers, condoms. We had them in the ready room. After I'd gone over the facts of seaport life and exactly what the situation was, I told them that I wanted them to come by and get a package of rubbers. Whether or not they intended to go to bed with one of these dollies when they got ashore, it would be good insurance. You only have to look at the records to see what happens. And so we passed out the rubbers to the liberty parties.

We went in the first port, came out. My squadron had practically no VD. About 20% of the people in the other squadrons had VD, which was sort of standard. And then the Catholic chaplain heard about what I'd done. He was livid. He went to see Captain Masterton and put me on the report. He said that I was corrupting the morals of these young men.

Q: Condoning sin.

Admiral Lee: Condoning sin. And the Protestant chaplain, who was a Southern Baptist, wasn't very far behind him. They were very upset. The captain called me up. I told him exactly what I'd done, and I asked him to look at our VD records. I said, "It's paying off."

He chuckled a little. All he said to me was, "Well, don't use welfare money. That really is illegal."

Q: Well, it is for recreation in a sense.

Admiral Lee: Yes, it's for recreation. I was afraid to use that. But that is a very good example of how shortsighted some of our people were. Now, as it turned out, in about five, six years after that, everybody does what I was trying to do then--the lecture, the rubbers, the pro stations, and all of that. If you really work at it, you can keep your VD rate down. I had 150 men and maybe I had three or four VD cases. Another 150-man squadron would have 25-30 VD cases after a trip into Naples or Barcelona.

The other thing that I would like to talk about during the course of this cruise, in addition to my rocky start as a commanding officer, was night flying in the A4D. And I haven't really talked about the Skyhawk yet. The A4D was another Ed Heinemann machine. In many ways a very fine little airplane, very light weight, very good performer. The engine was that Wright J65 early on. Later we shifted to a Pratt & Whitney J52, a much better engine.* But, all in all, a pretty good little airplane. It filled a void in the Navy attack community for many years.

It had one very bad feature. It was unstable on the glide slope in landing configuration. Pilots had to fly the A4D every minute of the time when they were coming aboard ship, or any other time for that matter. It wasn't an airplane you could turn loose, which you can the F-18 or the F-4. The A4D wouldn't do that. It wasn't as bad as the F8U, which was very unstable in speed. But if you turned the A4D loose, it would go off to the right, or go off to the left, climb a little bit, or glide a little bit. So that, for daytime operations from the carrier, it was very good. No real problem. Very good performer--

---

*The first production models of the A4D-1 in 1956 had either the Wright J65-W-4 or J65-W-4B turbojet engine. The A4D-2 had the Wright J65-W-16A. In 1957 the Navy ordered ten copies of the A4D-3 with the Pratt & Whitney J52-P-2 turbojet. The first flight of the A4D-5 with the J52-P-6A engine was in 1961. The new engine substantially reduced fuel consumption. The A4D-5 was redesignated A-4E in 1962.

catapults, takeoffs, and daytime carrier landings.

For night operations, the A4D was very tough. It wasn't designed for night flying and night operations. Commanding officers of A4D squadrons, and the senior officers, had been day aviators their entire careers. I'd never done any night flying from a carrier to speak of, only to qualify in the AD, and maybe another airplane--SB2C, night quals. We had not operated at night. Almost overnight the Navy went to all-weather operations. We had had some night squadrons such as the F3H. They had been flying nights for the last six or eight years, and doing very well, and getting better at it. The airplanes were pretty good instrument platforms. The A4D, the F8U, and the F11F were really not suitable for night carrier operations in my view.* But we went at it anyway. And we lost a lot of people.

I had two very good friends--contemporaries of mine, both commanding officers of squadrons--who were killed in night carrier operations in A4Ds. And I think the real reason is that they had no experience in night operations. You know, the commanders getting command of these squadrons today have been night flying from carriers since day one. Back in those days, I was a commander and commanding

---
*The Grumman F11F Tiger was a refinement of the F9F. It had a Wright J65-W-18 turbojet, wing span of 32 feet, gross eight of 22,160 pounds, top speed of 750 miles per hour at sea level, and initial climb rate of 5,130 feet per minute. It first joined a fleet squadron in 1957 and began phasing out of front-line use in 1959.

officer of an A4D squadron, and this was my first carrier night flying. The A4D was, in my view, an unsatisfactory night carrier airplane. But we flew, and it was very difficult. It was probably the most difficult thing I ever did. But, you know, later on I became an air group commander. I decided I'd go back and try AD night flying, just to see what that was like after flying jets at night, because we had an AD squadron in the group. And, you know, it was a piece of cake, amazing. Very, very easy; the AD was a very stable airplane. And you could just sit there and drive yourself in.

Q: How was it for handling otherwise--once in the air, maneuverability?

Admiral Lee: Fine. It was a nice airplane, good airplane. Good weapons platform, very maneuverable. It was maintainable. But for night carrier operations, what we needed were a number of things. We needed the proper night instruments. And during the course of our Med cruise, we did get a new gyro. The first gyros we had were these bar types. They would jump up and down going down the catapult. Then we got a spherical type, which was very good. And all the instrument systems in the A4D were improved over the next two or three years. And it also got an automatic pilot, which was pretty good and helped a lot. But we lost a lot of good aviators in those years. And a lot of them were senior aviators. As I say, I had two very good friends who were lost, A4D skippers in night carrier flying.

Q: Who were they? Do you recall their names?

Admiral Lee: Yes. One was John Shuff, graduate of Georgia Tech, aviation cadet, graduate school in aeronautical engineering.* And the other was Bill McNeill.** He was a Naval Academy graduate, class of '43. And his father was the McNeill who was the Assistant Secretary of Defense, controller. He was killed on <u>Intrepid</u>. He was the skipper of the other A4D squadron, VA-66. John Shuff was killed in another squadron. But those are just two examples.

I believe <u>Intrepid</u> was about as happy a ship as I've ever been aboard. We had a very fine Mediterranean cruise. The VF-74 skipper, William Shawcross, made admiral, and I made admiral.*** But we had a very fine group, and a good cruise. I think those <u>Essex</u>-class carriers, the way they were designed, put together, the way they ran, were conducive to a happy ship. Great ships.

---

*Commander John W. Shuff, USN.
**Commander Wilfred J. McNeill, Jr. USN, killed in the Mediterranean 27 May 1959.
***Commander William H. Shawcross, USN.

Q: How would you explain that? What was it about their design that made for happy ships?

Admiral Lee: I think they had a good wardroom, good location, good facilities. I think they had good facilities for the officers, good ready rooms for the pilots. It was a comfortable ship. I think they had good quarters for the enlisted men. It was a marvelous design as ships go, I think. Everything about it.

Q: Do you have any more specifics about Masterton and Cagle?

Admiral Lee: Masterton was a very good operator and sort of a fatherly type. He was not the spit-and-polish type. And he was a very gentlemanly, kind man and ran a good ship. Typical example: my condom and VD bit; you know, some captains would have been very upset. All he did was chuckle a little bit. That sort of gives you a description of the man; he thought it was very amusing, a good idea, "But don't use welfare funds."

Chris Cagle was a very talented man, has written a number of books--Naval Aviator's Guide--and written a number of articles.*

---

*Captain Malcolm W. Cagle, USN, The Naval Aviator's Guide (Annapolis: U.S. Naval Institute, 1963). Cagle retired as a vice admiral.

Q: Wrote one on the Korean War, coauthor.*

Admiral Lee: Yes. He was executive officer. And, as I say, Jack James was the air group commander, also a good man. But we had a very happy cruise.

Q: What are the highlights that you remember from being in the Mediterranean?

Admiral Lee: I suppose the highlights in the Mediterranean were, first the operations we had. Flying in the Mediterranean is like flying in no other place I've been. It's like flying in a soup bowl, especially in the time of year when we were there. The Mediterranean air is not crystal clear, such as you see here. There's a haze that looks like sand off the Sahara, or smoke. And the higher you get, the thicker it is. It's like flying around in a soup bowl. And this was especially difficult at night.

We had some very good flight operations, took part in all the Sixth Fleet operations, day and night. And I think one of the best things that happened to us in VA-46 was that we had no accidents. And we brought back every pilot that left Cecil Field with us. As a matter of fact, we

---

*Cagle and Frank Manson wrote <u>The Sea War in Korea</u> (Annapolis: U.S. Naval Institute, 1957).

brought back all the same planes and all the same pilots--no losses. And by the time we got back, we had a first-class safety program.

Q: What do you recall about the relationship with the enlisted men in your squadron?

Admiral Lee: I think, as a naval officer, one of my strongest points was my relations through the years with enlisted men. I sometimes had rocky relations with officers, such as in VA-46. But all through the years, I made it a practice to--whether I was a division officer in one of the early squadrons I was in--say, maintenance officer, operations officer, or later commanding officer of VA-46, or commanding officer of Alamo or Enterprise, I always made it a practice to wander around the ship as much as possible, and have a cup of coffee with the leading petty officers--always. And I tried every day to have a cup of coffee with one or more of these leading petty officers, just to pass the time of day, and find out how they were doing, and what their problems were, and if they had any suggestions for doing things better on the ship. That sort of thing.

If I got a good suggestion, of course, it wouldn't look proper to immediately charge off on it, but after a week or two--and after consulting with the executive officer--we would put it into effect. This type of communication sounds simple, but it paid tremendous dividends. In that way I think I learned more about what was going on in the squadrons and in the ships than all the reports put together which were coming up to me. I tried always to be very circumspect in making changes based on these thoughts and ideas or recommendations. But I think in the long run it paid very fine dividends.

Q: You've got to be careful that the enlisted men don't try to use this as a means of circumventing the chain of command.

Admiral Lee: Yes. It could be deadly in that sense. And that's why when I got a suggestion that I thought was worthwhile, or a report on how somebody was doing, and so forth, I always ran it back through the executive officer, maybe two or three weeks later.

Q: On the other hand, it's great for morale for the troops to know that you're receptive and interested in what they're doing.

Admiral Lee: Yes. Typical example: In VX-3, when I was logistics officer. Every day I'd spend some time on the hangar deck. I'd walk over to some second class or third class who'd be working on an airplane, and I would go through what he was doing so that I would understand it and could ask some intelligent questions. And they loved it.

Q: Especially since you'd been a mechanic yourself.

Admiral Lee: Yes.

Q: How large a group of enlisted men did you have in VA-46?

Admiral Lee: About 150.

Q: Were they mostly maintenance personnel?

Admiral Lee: We had about a dozen office personnel and storekeepers, 100 maintenance personnel, perhaps 30 ordnance people, and then odds and ends other than that. So the great bulk of our people in VA-46 were maintenance people.

In World War II the squadrons had no maintenance people. Shortly after World War II, we went back to the old system, so that in VA-115 and in VA-46, we had our own maintenance people. We were responsible for maintaining the 12 airplanes we had with these 150 people.

Q: Did you have a setup for seeing that family problems were taken care of while the ship was on a deployment?

Admiral Lee: Yes, that's one of the difficult things to do. I think the very best solution is to make sure that you have this set up before you go. And my wife was a great help in that regard, because she always got along well with the officers' wives and made contact with the senior enlisted wives, and did whatever she could, or let us know what ought to be done.

Once you're in the Mediterranean, it's very difficult to do much in Jacksonville. But I think, by and large, the Navy support system is pretty good, especially in aviation. We had worked together and lived together before going to sea. And we knew most of the problems, and most of the wives, and most of the children. And, as I say, they were very close knit. And the squadrons are always losing pilots and people, and they're organized for this sort of thing. So I think the very nature of the beast, we had a pretty good support organization. In the various units I was a part of, the ships and so forth, I don't ever remember that we had a real problem that we couldn't handle. We never had anything hit the newspapers that I know about.

Q: Are there any specific operations that especially stand

Lee #3 - 242

out from that time in the Mediterranean?

Admiral Lee: None really. We had no wars; we had no action of any type. We merely took part in routine exercises in the Sixth Fleet, such as with the British. And I don't think at that time we took part in any operations with the French. But none that were memorable, none that were unique. I think it was a standard Mediterranean cruise, from Naples to Piraeus, to Barcelona, to Majorca, two or three times, and then home. We came back to the States after six or seven months in the Mediterranean. I think we left in January and got back on August 31, 1959. And, as I said earlier, we came back with all planes we went with and all the pilots. We didn't lose any, which, believe me, for those days wasn't bad.

Q: Well, that reflects your efforts then to build up safety.

Admiral Lee: Safety--a good safety program which includes good maintenance. Because if those planes weren't right and ready to go, we didn't fly them. That's part of the safety program, insisting on that. But a good safety program, as the Navy has learned, really pays off. And a good safety program has to have very tough discipline. The pilot who violates the rules doesn't fly. And you just can't be a nice guy when you're running that kind of a program. But it really pays off.

We got back to Cecil Field on August 31, 1959. Before we got back I had a set of orders to the Office of Naval Research in Washington, D.C. I was going up there to be a physicist and to pay back some more of my PG school training. I was relieved of command by Al Hall, who was a friend of mine--he and I were at Columbia together.* He relieved me in mid-September 1959, and had the squadron for a year also without an accident.

We moved to Washington, bought a house, and I had my first experience with bureaucracy and with the civil service. My wife and children were very happy in Washington. It was a very pleasant place to live. We lived in Aurora Hills, which is very close in. It's right across from Army-Navy Country Club.

I reported to the Office of Naval Research and was given a project--direct conversion of heat to electricity. And you might say that we do that all the time, but we really don't. We convert heat to electricity by steam and turning turbines. But there are ways to convert heat to electricity directly. For instance in thermo-electronics, and in big vacuum tubes. But, anyway, that was my area. I had $300,000 to $500,000 I was to put out on small research contracts--college professor-types and company scientists

---
*Commander Alfred J. Hall, Jr., USN.

Lee #3 - 244

who wanted to work in this area, build a gadget and improve direct conversion of heat to electricity. We were thinking of the space age.

Q: Were you thinking in terms of specific applications yet, or was this basic research?

Admiral Lee: Basic research, but there are many specific applications--a refrigerator, for instance. There are refrigerators built on this principle. You merely heat them, direct conversion of heat to electricity. Or the obverse, conversion of electricity to heat. But I must confess I realized all over again after I got to the Office of Naval Research and had been there several months that the world of physics and Ph.D's was not for me. The Office of Naval Research has a good reputation for funding college research, but it's staffed by civil servants. And there are Ph.D's by the dozen in chemistry, physics, and other disciplines in the Office of Naval Research.

For academic people and scientific types, a day of hard work for them is a day of talk. I suppose I had two hours of work a week. The rest of it was meetings, and reviews, and talk, talk, talk. And there were people there who had done this for years and years. We had one man who had been at the Office of Naval Research for at least 25 years, and his specialty was batteries. He knew everything there was to know about batteries. That's all he did. And he did 20 or 30 minutes work a week, ran $300,000 worth of research a year. But I suppose he was worth his money because of his knowledge of batteries. I decided after I'd been there, say, a year, that the Office of Naval Research--and scientists, in particular--was really not my cup of tea. I wanted more action.

The Office of Naval Research funds projects in all scientific areas. However, they don't have a lot of money, maybe $300,000-$500,000 per area. They would fund a $50,000 project here and a $50,000 project there. And that $50,000 would finance a professor and maybe two graduate students. Very worthwhile. But for the people at ONR, there wasn't much work once the paperwork of letting out a $50,000 research contract was completed. We kept track of it. And it's done a lot of good, I think, in the scientific world and in the college community. Thousands and thousands of graduate students have gotten through graduate school on this money. But it's not a very demanding job in the Office of Naval Research. That was the part that was a little bit difficult for me, inasmuch as I'd just come from a very active 15 months or so as commanding officer of a squadron.

Q: Did anything fruitful come out of your projects on heat and electricity?

Admiral Lee: No and yes. At that particular time there were great hopes for direct conversion of heat to electricity. There were scientists who would come in and tell me that ten years from now, two-thirds of our electricity would come this way, pushing their projects. I was skeptical, but I wasn't well versed enough to really fully understand the field. But, in short, no, nothing really big has ever come of it.

I later worked for the assistant secretary for research and development, a man by the name of Robert Frosch, who himself had run a laboratory.* He was a graduate of Columbia, theoretical physics Ph.D. He was a Jewish intellectual and a guy with his feet on the ground. He said to me one day, which sort of startled me at the time, but I know he was 100% correct--that 98% of the research that's done is junk. It comes to nothing, repeating things that have been done already. And only 2% of it, he said, is really good stuff and worthwhile. But it's sometimes very hard to separate that 2%. But I'm sure he was right. But anyway I got a good exposure to this, and we certainly enjoyed Washington.

---

*Dr. Robert A. Frosch, Assistant Secretary of the Navy (Research and Development), 1966-73. Frosch was director of Hudson Laboratories, Columbia University, 1956-63. He got his bachelor's degree from Columbia in 1947 and master's degree in 1949. He was thus a student at the university at the same time Lee was.

And then right out of the blue I got a set of orders sending me to Omaha, Nebraska, of all places. The President had decided that instead of letting each unified and specified commander have his own war plan, that we would have a joint war plan, which made good sense. And I hadn't realized at the time that CinCLantFlt had his plan, CinCEur had his plan.* And there was absolutely no coordination in the atomic weapons area. With the coming of the Polaris systems, the President decided something had to be done about war plans. So he decided that the services would have a joint plan. It would be put together in Omaha, SAC headquarters.** In effect, he said, "You services get together and work this out. Everybody's weapons will be in one plan."

Q: We're going to run out of tape. So I hope we can save that one for the next time.

Admiral Lee: All right.

---

*CinCLantFlt--Commander in Chief Atlantic Fleet, a Navy command; CinCEur--Commander in Chief Europe, a joint-service command.
**SAC--Strategic Air Command.

Lee #4 - 248

Interview Number 4 with Vice Admiral Kent L. Lee,
U.S. Navy (Retired)

Place: Logon Farm, Admiral Lee's home near Gordonsville, Virginia

Date: Monday, 16 November 1987

Interviewer: Paul Stillwell

Q: Admiral, in Jerry Miller's oral history he indicated he was sort of shanghaied by Admiral Burke to go out to Omaha on short notice to beef up the Navy representation on the Joint Strategic Target Planning Staff. Did you have a similar experience with hurried orders?

Admiral Lee: I think everybody who went to Omaha had a similar experience. I think a little background might be appropriate. Up until the Joint Strategic Target Planning Staff was formed in Omaha, the various unified and specified commanders had their own plans. Each commander, such as CinCLant, CinCPac, SACEur, had some nuclear forces.* They wrote their own plans, picked their own targets. Since the Strategic Air Command had the great bulk of the strategic forces, that was all right.

But with the coming of the Polaris system, it was decided that we could do better than that, that the then-

---

*CinCLant--Commander in Chief Atlantic, a U.S. joint-service commander; CinCPac--Commander in Chief Pacific, a U.S. joint-service commander; SACEur--Supreme Allied Commander Europe, a U.S. officer serving as commander of NATO forces.

current system of having each unified and specified commander write his own plan was not satisfactory, because there should be some coordination. The Air Force, in the persons of General Tommy Power, who was CinCSAC, and General LeMay, who was Chief of Staff of the Air Force, proposed a Strategic Command.* Their idea was that the Air Force would be in charge of the Strategic Command and that Polaris would just be a part of the command. Well, that, of course, sent the Navy right up the walls.

Q: Specifically Admiral Burke.

Admiral Lee: Specifically Admiral Burke. Burke fought that tooth and nail. President Eisenhower then eventually got into it, and he decided we would have a joint staff.** In the fall of 1960 Joint Strategic Target Planning Staff, or JSTPS, was set up in Omaha, Nebraska. General Power would be the director, and the Navy would send a vice admiral out to be the deputy director. However, initially, General Power said that he could do it alone. He didn't really need any help from the other services. He had all the tools to do it, a computer and trained people. Admiral

---
*General Curtis E. LeMay, USAF, commanded the Strategic Air Command from 1948 to 1957 and went on to become Vice Chief of Staff of the Air Force, 1957-61, and Chief of Staff, 1961-65. General Thomas S. Power, USAF, commanded SAC from 1957 to 1964.
**Dwight D. Eisenhower, President of the United States from January 1953 to January 1961.

Burke, it's my understanding, said, "Oh, we've got some good people. We'll have them out there next week to help you."

Well, next week is about what it was, because there was no Navy out there before that. It was the Strategic Air Command, strictly an Air Force operation. Admiral Burke rounded up through his agent, the Chief of Naval Personnel, what I always considered one of the most talented group of naval officers, small group, that I've run across. We had Admiral Parker, the vice admiral and deputy director, and we had two other young admirals: Johnny Hyland, who was representing the Atlantic command, and Paul Masterton, who was my commanding officer on Intrepid, representing Pacific Command.* We also had Jerry Miller, who was sort of Admiral Parker's right-hand man, several aviators such as Miller, Fraser, Fretwell, Talley, Lee, and two or three line officers, one of whom later made admiral, Leslie Sell.**

This experience was my first taste of inter-service rivalry; I had just gotten a little exposure to Washington in the Office of Naval Research. Then this thing came up

---

*Vice Admiral Edward N. Parker, USN; Parker has been interviewed as part of the Naval Institute's oral history program. Rear Admiral John J. Hyland, Jr., USN; Hyland eventually reached the rank of four-star admiral. His oral history is in the Naval Institute collection.
**Commander LeRoy B. Fraser, USN; Commander Uncas Fretwell, USN; Commander George C. Talley, USN; Commander Leslie H. Sell, USN.

overnight, and I was sent to Omaha, probably for the same reason that others were sent. I'd had an A4D squadron, which was an atomic weapons delivery squadron. You'll recall I also taught at special weapons school and had a degree in physics. So they probably looked through the records and picked all these people with the qualifications they wanted. They ended up with a very fine group.

The issues were, of course, how to put together this Joint Strategic Target Planning Staff, first, and then, second, how to put together this so-called SIOP, single integrated operational plan. As it turned out, General Power didn't let too many arguments take place there. The SIOP was nothing, more or less, than an extension of SAC's plan. He just took SAC's plan, included the Polaris and the forces of all the other unified commanders, and called it SIOP-1. That's what it amounted to. But the big issues, which were fought tooth and nail, were the values such as survivability to be accorded the Navy and Air Force tactical and Army forces, especially the Navy. In other words, the ultimate worth of these systems to the SIOP.

Q: And that was tough, because there was no background of experience for Polaris yet.

Admiral Lee: No. There were very few arguments about the SAC forces, because they'd been doing it for a long time,

Lee #4 - 252

and they wouldn't hear of any arguments against the numbers they were using. The numbers they used for SAC forces--and for ours, for that matter--were questionable. I'll give you an example. Being a little bit of a mathematician, I'm familiar with what scientists and mathematicians call "to the significant number." For instance, if you know a number to one whole number, such as 90, you know that this number is 90 and not 91 and not 89. That's to one significant number, to 90. Then if you multiply it by some other number with the same, you know, 90 times another one, say, which is 80, you don't take it past the decimal point because it's not a significant number.

Well, we took all these systems and assigned them values for everything, values for the weapon doing damage--values for the circular error probable, or CEP, values for survivability, values for this, that, and the other, multiplied them all together. We came up with the resultant damage expectancy on the target, out to the second, and third, and fourth decimal points, which to a mathematician or a purist was improper. But that's the way it was done.

Q: Since they were guesses at best.

Admiral Lee: Guesses at best, and taking guesses out to the third decimal point. That's what happened.

Well, anyway, my first job out there was to be on a study chaired by an Air Force lieutenant colonel, and the title of the study was "The Survivability of Aircraft Carriers." We studied away for about six weeks or so. When the study was finished, the lieutenant colonel had to present it to General Power and staff. We had some good Navy help on that study; I was the senior Navy guy. The aircraft carrier came out of the study looking quite good. Of course, since it was chaired by General Power's own lieutenant colonel, Power had a difficult time not accepting it, and he was livid. As a matter of fact, the lieutenant colonel was finished. He never, to my knowledge, served on another study. I think General Power thought that he'd been flummoxed by us Navy types on this study.

There were some things that I didn't like about the SIOP, although overall I thought it was good. My major misgiving was no reserves. That was the part that I thought was incomprehensible. We had more forces than we could ever use profitably--several bombs on every worthwhile target, but no reserves. Everything in one shot. SAC didn't believe in reserves. The simple reason they didn't believe in reserves is because they didn't have any reserves that were not vulnerable. Their airplanes were all vulnerable to a counterattack. Their missile sites were all vulnerable to a counterattack. So since SAC had no decent reserves, the SIOP had no reserves. Nor were we allowed to put even one Polaris submarine in reserve. No reserves--everything went in one big blast.

The aircraft carrier would have made a great system to have in reserve. It could be steaming around the ocean, not targetable. We had no reserves for SIOP-1. That, to me, was the big fault. I just cannot imagine firing everything you have at the signal "Fire." It's not logical--wasn't then and it isn't today. SAC's idea of having reserves was that whatever wasn't launched in the first launch, such as an aircraft with a mechanical problem, would be in the reserves, as would missiles that had not fired properly. The reserves were whatever was left over, the duds. What we'd do is repair them and have our reserves. That was their philosophy--whatever was left over.

Another area which was of great interest to SAC was submarine survivability. At General Power's direction, we had another great study on submarine survivability, Polaris survivability. Jerry Miller wrote an article and asked me and others who took part in it--Lew Neeb and Peter Fullinwider, who were all in Omaha together--to review, make corrections, edit, and make additions and deletions, as we saw fit.* This article, "The Battle for Polaris Survival," was published in the April 1986 edition of

---
*As of 1961, they were Commander Lewis H. Neeb, USN, and Lieutenant Commander Peter L. Fullinwider, USN.

Submarine Review.* It's a very good story of the Polaris survivability study. Since I had a little more technical training than most, it was my job to put together the model for a war game which would stand the light of day mathematically or scientifically. Jerry Miller ran it, with lots of help from SAC types.

Q: He said in his oral history that he was the umpire.

Admiral Lee: Yes. There were a lot of people looking over his shoulder.

I think my most lasting memories of Omaha have to do with the most remarkable Navy group there. We had a great time. We had skating parties; we had lots of athletics; badminton; volleyball; squash; golf; tennis; there's a wonderful country club. The Navy group there got along very well together. It was like being in a fraternity.

For instance, they had a little league at Offutt, and I went down with a friend of mine by the name of Fretwell.** I'd read a lot about little league, and I went down to the organization meeting just to observe. Lo and behold, I came out with a team of 18 youngsters. I have three daughters. Jerry Miller and Fretwell also had

---

*Submarine Review is a quarterly publication of the Naval Submarine League. The article appeared on pages 5-14.
**The Strategic Air Command headquarters were at Offutt Air Force Base, outside Omaha.

teams. There were seven teams in the league. We had a great time playing little league baseball all summer. Jerry Miller's team and Fretwell's team ended up the year playing for the championship.

Q: What was it like as a place to rear your own daughters?

Admiral Lee: Oh, marvelous place. The winters and summers were horrendous in Omaha. In the winters the winds blow. It's cold, there's snow and ice. It's been said that the only thing between Omaha and the North Pole is barbwire, and I can believe it. The summers were hot; the winds blow; there'd be dust and sand in the wind. So those people who grew up in that general part of the West had to be hearty souls or they didn't survive. But in terms of the people, I think they're the friendliest, most remarkable, most self-reliant people in all of the United States. Most of them are only two or three generations removed from their pioneer ancestors, and they're absolutely the greatest people I've run across in these United States, in almost every respect.

There's one other thing that I should say about that place, and maybe Jerry Miller has stated it. The JSTPS was to be a joint staff, staffed by Air Force, Army, Navy, Marines. Well, it turns out that wasn't exactly the way it was done. There were the two divisions--the intelligence division, which had, you might say, a sprinkling of Navy, Army, Marines, and tactical Air Force in it, but the great majority was staffed by SAC types, and they were single-hatted. At least a half of dozen of them were single-hatted--and I'll define that term in a minute.

In the other division, which was the important division, the SIOP division which put the plan together, every man in the SIOP division from the Air Force was double-hatted. They had their regular job with SAC. They were the people who had put the plan together beforehand, and they were just double-hatted to JSTPS. We were sort of slipped in there with them. It was an out-and-out SAC division we were a part of. There was no such thing as a really separate JSTPS staff. These people with their SAC hats, if they had a disagreement with the Navy, went straight to General Power. Admiral Parker would hear about it when General Power had made a decision. Power was a very articulate and a very intelligent man.

I'd say most naval officers and enlisted men and chiefs and the like that I had worked with through the years were men of intelligence and men of integrity, very reasonable people. When I got to SAC, I ran across for the first time what we call "SAC fanatics." Most naval officers had been moved around. Most naval officers were college graduates, and a fair number of them had graduate school. A fair number also had been to one or more of the war colleges.

In the Strategic Air Command, under first LeMay and then Power, about 95% of the people in this command and on these staffs had been in SAC since graduation from flight training. They were not allowed to go to college; they were not allowed to go to war college; they had spent their entire Air Force careers in the Strategic Air Command. It had become a religion to them. If they ever left SAC for a period of time, chances are they were never allowed back in. They got preferential promotions in SAC, so they had a tremendous number of what I would call high school graduate fanatics in the Strategic Air Command. Now, fortunately, that changed several years later. But it was a frightening thing.

In the early 1960s, as a young commander, I thought with organizations like that we could have "Seven Days in May."* So the Strategic Air Command and the organization that LeMay and Power put together, though efficient--although they were never all that well tested in battle after World War II--I don't think it's the kind of a military organization that we ought to nourish in our country. I thought it was very bad.

---

*The novel Seven Days in May, by Fletcher Knebel and Charles W. Bailey II, was published by Harper & Row in 1962. The plot was set in the year 1974; in the story, high-ranking U.S. military officers tried to overthrow the government at a time when the President's prestige was low as a result of an unpopular disarmament treaty with the Soviet Union.

Q: What memories do you have of General Power?

Admiral Lee: General Power was a man of medium height, about five-eight or five-nine. He considered himself a very macho type, because he went down and played around with the martial arts people and got himself a black belt and that sort of thing. But, aside from that, he was a very articulate man, very well spoken, and very intelligent. I don't know how well-read he was, because I never had occasion to talk to him personally. I observed him in many meetings. I had the feeling that he was in charge--no question about that--and that he was a very ruthless man. If some lieutenant colonel or colonel didn't toe the line, he was gone from SAC the next day. That was the way SAC operated, and that was the way General Power operated and LeMay before him. I think that Power was LeMay's right-hand man for a long time.

Q: How receptive an atmosphere did he create for you Navy officers that were just thrust upon him?

Admiral Lee: Not receptive at all. I think he resented us. I think he wanted us like he wanted a dose of clap, was my impression.

Lee #4 - 260

Q: Did it then depend on Admiral Parker to act as a buffer and diplomat on your behalf?

Admiral Lee: Admiral Parker was one of the great gentlemen I've known, and he did a great job. But General Power ran roughshod over Parker and everybody who got in his way. General Power made the decisions. I thought Admiral Parker gave it a college try. But the real power had to do with the unified and specified commanders. They supposedly had an equal voice in putting the plan together, and they had to approve or disapprove whatever numbers that we came up with. Admirals Hyland and Masterton were there representing the unified commanders, Lant and Pac, both also commanded by admirals. So that was the only brake on General Power, the fact that these two Navy people with equal commands had to approve or disapprove what he was doing. He had to come up with numbers that were satisfactory to them.

Q: There was another factor, too, in that he didn't have operational control over NATO assets.*

Admiral Lee: Well, he didn't have operational control over NATO assets, nor over Polaris, nor over Lant or Pac forces, and Lant and Pac forces both included some Air Force

---
*NATO--North Atlantic Treaty Organization.

assets. As a matter of fact, he didn't have operational control of anything other than SAC, which included maybe 3,000 B-52 and B-47, and B-58 bombers and all the Titan and Atlas, and a little later on, Minuteman missiles.* Those were the only things he had operational control over. But he wrote the plan for all the rest in the JSTPS.

Q: How did you go about the mechanics of putting together this plan after it became an integrated one, rather than just a SAC plan?

Admiral Lee: The SAC plan was fairly well set. The idea then was to start over again and use the SAC plan as the basis and integrate all the other forces. When you're doing targeting for a particular weapon, you have to pick one that's within range; you have to pick one that's within capabilities of that weapon and that system, whether it's an A4D from an aircraft carrier or a Polaris missile.

What you do is pick the targets that are suitable for each system. Then each system is assigned a launch time and a time over target. You keep a running record of the various bombs on the various targets so that you don't have 20 on this one and none on the other. You build up to a

---

*The Boeing B-52 Stratofortress is an eight-jet, swept-wing heavy bomber; the Boeing B-47 Stratojet was a six-jet, swept-wing medium bomber; the Convair B-58 Hustler was a four-jet supersonic delta-wing bomber. Titan, Atlas, and Minuteman were among the early Air Force intercontinental ballistic missiles.

point where you'd have a damage expectancy of, say, better than 90% on each one of the important targets.

Once you've done that, assigned all the weapons to targets, and you've got it approximately the way you want it, there was a computer program which sorted out conflicts. Each mission, whether it was a Polaris or an airplane, would be put on a card. On that card would be all the information on that particular sortie--the time of takeoff, time over target, size of weapon, and all that sort of thing, and the route. This would all be put in the computer.

If you had to resolve conflicts, if two weapons were arriving on a given target, same time or within a half an hour of each other, the red light would flash and you'd have to do some rescheduling. But this whole plan was put into a computer which was programmed to resolve conflicts, both en route conflicts and target conflicts. Once all of that was done and the re-targeting and rescheduling were done as necessary, it was all printed out. Then each unified and specified commander got a copy of the printout, and he then had to schedule his forces accordingly. That was the national war plan. That was what we had to follow.

Q: Who picked the targets?

Admiral Lee: The job of the intelligence division was to pick the targets. At Omaha the Air Force had what was called the strategic squadron. This strategic squadron, which was a SAC squadron, had all the photo interpreters in it, and they handled all the photography from the U-2 and the satellites.*

Q: Satellites being pretty primitive at that stage.

Admiral Lee: The satellites were primitive but did a good job. I looked at a lot of satellite photography, which I thought was very good in that period of time. These targets were put together by the intelligence division. Coordinates were used in word descriptions. Maybe some measure of its worth, like the most valuable one might be labelled a one. One not so valuable might be labelled a nine, some system of worth like that. Using other sources of intelligence plus U-2 photography, plus satellite photography, all of Russia was looked at.

The worthwhile targets were sent by the intelligence division, which worked on this all year round, over to the operational division, to be put in the SIOP to be targeted. For that matter, the unified and specified commanders were

---

*The Lockheed U-2 was a high-altitude reconnaissance plane. It had an 80-foot wing span, gross weight of 17,270 pounds with external fuel tanks, maximum speed at cruising height of 795 miles per hour, and service ceiling of 70,000 feet; powered with Pratt & Whitney J75-P-13 or J57C jet engine.

invited to submit their nominations for targets, CinCLant, CinCPac. Sometimes they submitted nominations for targets which were not held in our target base, but for one reason or another they wanted to have some of their forces on it, and those were put in.

Q: Did the Joint Chiefs of Staff have a role in the targeting decisions?

Admiral Lee: No. The Joint Chiefs of Staff played almost no role in JSTPS. The only role the Joint Chiefs played was, after the plan was put together the director of the Joint Strategic Target Planning Staff, in this case Power, would take it to Washington and brief the Joint Chiefs of Staff, the principals. He would brief them on the plan, and they would give it their stamp of approval, and that was it.

Q: Secretary Schlesinger raised the question some years later about counter-force versus counter-value, what kind of targets you give priority to.* Was that a discussion that came up during your time there?

---

*Secretary of Defense James R. Schlesinger. See "Arming to Disarm in the Age of Détente," Time, 11 February 1974, pages 15-20, 23-24.

Admiral Lee: Oh, yes.

Q: What were the pros and cons?

Admiral Lee: It was mostly words. We targeted both, and we had enough weapons in that time to target both. We targeted all the Soviet missile sites; we targeted all the Soviet airfields; we targeted communication centers; and we targeted all their steel mills, and Moscow, and all their cities. Besides that, of course, it's very difficult to hit an area like Moscow without doing some damage to the value, you might say.

So that after having helped put together the first SIOP, and then later going back to Omaha and being deputy director of the JSTPS and seeing it all over again, I came to the conclusion that this argument about counter-force and counter-value was just words; it didn't mean anything except to intellectuals. As a practical matter. you can't get one without the other. The way the targeting was done, they were given equal value, because we had forces to do it.

I daresay when I was out there the first time in 1960, we might have had 8,000 weapons to target. Let's say 8,000; that's probably plus or minus 10%. When I went back in 1972, which I'll talk about later on, we had maybe 12,000 or 13,000. You know, when you're targeting that many weapons, this business about counter-value and counter-force targets is not very meaningful. But for the people who really knew, who were in the business out there, it was never an issue. My feeling was that they sort of smiled a little bit at all these intellectual arguments about counter-force and counter-value, because it wasn't a very realistic argument.

Q: Well, especially if you had this launch-everything-at-once approach.

Admiral Lee: That was the approach.

Q: Did you get into communications and reliability of systems and that sort of thing?

Admiral Lee: Yes, that's what the arguments were all about. Reliability of the systems, reliability of the targets, chances of your system getting shot down en route, and then finally the CEP. The arguments went on for months on end about those things. That's why we had the survivability study for the aircraft carriers and the survivability study for the Polaris system, which Jerry Miller has previously described and which is described so well in the article.

Q: The novel <u>Fail-Safe</u> came out in that period.* What was your reaction to that?

Admiral Lee: I can't remember at the moment. I read the book.

Q: SAC sent out a bunch of bombers and then recalled them. But one plane had been hit by a missile so its communications were ineffective and the crew didn't get the recall message. Was this mostly just imaginative pipe-dreaming on the part of the author?

Admiral Lee: Yes, I think so. SAC supposedly has a fail-safe system such that they can launch their airplanes and recall them. This is one of the virtues they claim for their bombers; whereas once you launch a missile, you cannot recall it. That book was based on that SAC virtue, fail-safe, which didn't work. But I don't remember there was much discussion about fail-safe. Without a doubt, something like that could happen but, my Lord, in order for an airplane to get launched and to get far enough to be hit by a missile and have his communications out, you know, the Russians are attacking us by then. Wasn't very realistic in that sense. Because I don't think we're going to be able to get bombers to Russia and not have them come back

---
*Eugene Burdick and Harvey Wheeler, <u>Fail-Safe</u> (New York: McGraw-Hill, 1962).

at us.

Q: Did you have much time during that tour of duty for reflection--that here you're talking about possible destruction of the world?

Admiral Lee: Oh, yes, we debated all aspects of the SIOP, for hours on end, for days on end, every aspect. We had plenty of time to read, plenty of time to argue, plenty of time for debating. There were a lot of things about it that, to me, were incomprehensible. Item number one was no reserves. But SAC was so set in concrete that there was absolutely no changing any aspect of SIOP, none.

Of course, one of the items I haven't mentioned is that the Joint Chiefs of Staff gave us guidance. The guidance, very often, was written by SAC, and it was changed in Washington to fit the needs and ideas of the various members of the JCS. But my impression was the Strategic Air Command and the Air Force types in Washington got together and wrote the basic guidance. Then it had to be submitted to the JCS for approval. And, of course, at that time Admiral Burke and others had a shot at it.

Q: With this Navy enclave you had there, were you getting inputs from Washington on how to fight for the Navy position?

Admiral Lee: Every day.

Q: What examples do you recall?

Admiral Lee: Admiral Parker and Admirals Hyland and Masterton, of course, were in communication every day with their bosses. Admiral Parker was working for Admiral Burke. He kept Admiral Burke fully briefed on what was going on. Admiral Burke was a member of the JCS, so he kept things pretty much stirred up. I think all of these items were briefed to Admiral Burke, from the aircraft survivability study, to all the factors that were used, to the submarine survivability study. Admiral Burke was our greatest cheerleader. I think he thoroughly enjoyed every minute of it. He was a great fighter, anyway. I don't remember the specific guidance he gave Parker, because Admiral Parker, better known as Butch Parker, wasn't the type to mention it to us. But he made lots of trips to Washington, and so did Jerry Miller. Washington was very interested in what was going on.

The Navy's big concern was that we come up with an acceptable plan and acceptable organization like the JSTPS, so that that shadow of the Strategic Command would go away. The Navy could just see the end of the world with having a

Strategic Command and giving operational control of the Polaris system to the Strategic Air Command. Because we debated the future of bombers, and our guess was that the bomber fleet was going to go down, down, down. The SAC guys would turn purple when we would tell them this and that the missiles and other systems were going to take over this area.

Q: You've talked about how powerful General Power was at the top level. How were your working relations with Air Force counterparts at your level?

Admiral Lee: I'd say they were good. They recognized that we had a problem and they had a problem. I daresay, with the exception of a half a dozen colonels and lieutenant colonels, relations were acceptable. The people on the working level were wise enough not to get involved in the arguments which would have to be settled by the generals and admirals. We were wise enough in the Navy not to do that either, because we had to get the job done, I would say relations were pretty good.

Q: Can you speculate on what the result might have been if Admiral Burke hadn't sent your contingent there?

Admiral Lee: I think if Admiral Burke had not been on his

toes and sent the contingent there, that what would have evolved was a Strategic Command. I think Admiral Burke wanted to make sure that we fully understood the SIOP, the Navy forces got a fair shake, that it was a good plan acceptable to everybody. If he could bring off that, there wouldn't be a Strategic Command. I think his plan was to prevent a Strategic Command.

Q: Then he was successful.

Admiral Lee: He was successful. I don't think Admiral Burke made a great issue of the various factors that we fought so long and hard over--survivability, reliability, and all of that. Because in the long run, those little numbers are not all that important. It seemed to be a matter of life and death with SAC, but it really wasn't for us. Those numbers didn't mean that much. They never got out of the super secret area. Nobody ever saw them. They weren't useful in a political sense. So the numbers, as I say, that we fought for days, and months, and weeks about were really not that important, and I think Admiral Burke recognized that. What was important was to have an acceptable plan, something that would satisfy our political masters, and not have a Strategic Command. He was successful in that regard.

Q: He wanted to make sure the Navy would be a player at the table.

Admiral Lee: Yes.

Q: What was your personal contribution to this overall effort?

Admiral Lee: I sat on the various studies out there such as the aircraft survivability study; I was the senior Navy man. I had a hand in putting together the submarine war game study. Then, of course, we worked on the various Navy systems that were put into it, coming up with fuel factors and all the other factors for A4Ds. Also we served in a supporting role for Admirals Parker, Masterton, and Hyland. Because I don't think any commander or lieutenant colonel out there made much of a personal impact because every little number down to the fourth decimal point was scrutinized very carefully by three- and four-star generals and admirals. We were the Indians. I guess I was a fair Indian.

Q: Did the aircraft survivability study address both Navy and Air Force planes?

Admiral Lee: The aircraft survivability factors for SAC

were, you might say, fixed in concrete, because they'd been using them for some time. We, essentially, adapted those numbers to our airplanes. For instance, if a B-52 bomber was flown over an antiaircraft site, there was a 3% chance the bomber would be knocked down. They used random numbers in their computers to decide whether they got knocked down or not. The same thing was applied to our planes.

Q: Where did these numbers come from?

Admiral Lee: Oh, they dreamed them up. That's why I say they didn't know those numbers to plus or minus two digits. But yet we used them out to the fourth decimal.

Q: But after they'd been used for so long, they take on a certain legitimacy.

Admiral Lee: Yes, that's true, and they did there.

Q: What do you recall about the submarine war game itself?

Admiral Lee: I thought it was a very tense moment. What General Power wanted to do was to show that the Polaris submarine was vulnerable. We had given the Polaris submarine a survivability factor of one in the SIOP. General Power wanted to demonstrate that the Polaris submarine didn't have a survivability of one, and that was the purpose of the war game. My job in that war game with the Polaris submarine, as I say, was to put together the technical aspects.

Jerry Miller, I believe he told you, was an umpire. But we had a bunch of submariners out there who ran the Polaris side of it. Then we had some SAC types who ran the Russian side--they had half the Russian fleet concentrated over these submarines. He'll tell you about it. But we were very interested. At the end of it all, after General Power had been briefed on it, he ordered that it not be briefed anywhere, that it all be burned, as a matter of fact.

Q: That's exactly what Admiral Miller said. It had not turned out the way he wanted, so he didn't want anybody else to know about it.

Admiral Lee: We had a lot of fun in Omaha. I didn't think the SAC types out there were any match. They were not an intellectual match for the Navy types that Burke sent out.

Q: Again, that's a testimonial to his wisdom.

Admiral Lee: Also it was an education in inter-service rivalry.

And along about--let me see, I guess February or March of 1962--I got some good news. I think Admiral Parker and Captain Miller had a great deal to do with this. I think Admiral Parker and Captain Miller strongly recommended to Washington that I get an air group. I suppose the Navy looked at my record and decided that if Admiral Parker felt that strongly about it, they'd give me an air group.

Of course, an air group is the wish of every carrier aviator. A fairly high percentage of commanders get squadrons, maybe half. A carrier air group, that's a little more difficult. I considered myself very fortunate. I was detached in March of 1962 and went to Norfolk, where the air group was to be based, and went through the usual training.

The replacement air group training was well along. The RAG, so-called, had been started up in 1958. I went through the instrument training, had a refresher in the A-4, since I had been in an A4D squadron, so that wasn't any big problem. Went through the F-8 RAG and carrier qualified in the F-8 Crusader, checked out in the F-4 Phantom, and flew the A-1 again, propeller plane. I guess I had one flight in the A-5.*

---

*The North American A3J Vigilante heavy attack plane began entering the fleet in 1961; in 1962 it was redesignated A-5. It was powered with two General Electric J79-GE-2, J79-GE-4, or J79-GE-8 turbojets, had a wing span of 53 feet and maximum speed of 1,385 miles per hour at 40,000 feet.

Then, shortly after I got down to Norfolk, I learned that we would go aboard Enterprise. The Enterprise was a brand-new ship, just back from Guantánamo and we would be Enterprise's first air group.* (Air Group One had supplied aircraft and pilots for Enterprise's underway training in Guantánamo.) I relieved Commander James Holbrook, and I assumed command of Air Group Six in early July 1962.**

Q: Had this air group been based on another ship previously?

Admiral Lee: Yes. It'd been based on Intrepid. They had gotten back from Med cruise some few months before, and we had gotten a couple of new squadrons and an A-5 squadron, and it was to be assigned to Enterprise. The training was very good, very thorough.

I reported to Enterprise. Vince de Poix was the captain, Max Harnish the executive officer.*** Later on, John T. Hayward became the carrier division commander.**** I had had the group only about a month when we moved aboard Enterprise for some exercises and to head to the

---
*The USS Enterprise (CVAN-65) was commissioned 25 November 1961 as the Navy's first nuclear-powered aircraft carrier.
**Commander James L. Holbrook, USN.
***Captain Vincent P. De Poix, USN; Commander William Max Harnish, USN.
****Rear Admiral John T. Hayward, USN, was Commander Carrier Division Two from April 1962 to June 1963.

Mediterranean. And we spent August and September of 1962 in the Mediterranean. The idea was to show off Enterprise in the Mediterranean and J. T. Hayward, who had been a three-star admiral in the Pentagon, came down to two stars to take this carrier division command.* He wanted Enterprise.

Q: Did you get to know him?

Admiral Lee: Yes, I got to know him very well.

Q: What do you recall about Hayward?

Admiral Lee: John T. Hayward was a personality kid and a little bit of a maverick, a little bit of an iconoclast, with quite a sizable ego, but a very bright guy. He wanted to fly in the F-4, and I noted that he was very meticulous about keeping his own log books, which he had kept forever, logging every flight he'd ever taken. Of course, early on he had a squadron of AJs, the first twin-engine carrier-based atomic weapons aircraft.** But he was a very, very personable man.

Q: Are there any specific examples you might cite of your

---
*As a vice admiral, Hayward served as Deputy Chief of Naval Operations (Development) from April 1959 to April 1962.
**As a commander, Hayward was commanding officer Composite Squadron Five from December 1948 to June 1951.

encounters with him?

Admiral Lee: My encounters with Admiral Hayward were all favorable. He was a movie hound. He loves the movies, and he would have a movie every night. We made a little sign and put outside his flag cabin one night with a flashing light, and we called it "Hayward's movie emporium." He came out, saw that, and after a short time he was able to laugh about it.

Q: He did not have a lot of carrier experience really before that. He had been a bomber squadron commander in World War II and got his ticket punched with a short tour in the FDR as skipper.* But I think he was being groomed for flag for other reasons.

Admiral Lee: I didn't know that.

Q: What views of him did you have operationally?

Admiral Lee: At a later time, having seen some very fine operators, I was in a better position to judge Hayward. I would say that Hayward was more political than operational.

---

*During World War II, as a commander, Hayward commanded the shore-based Bombing Squadron 106, flying the PB4Y, the Navy version of the Army Air Forces B-24. As a captain, he commanded the aircraft carrier Franklin D. Roosevelt (CVA-42) from February 1956 to January 1957.

He was very much a political man, and I don't think he was all that talented as an operator. Now when I compare him to real operators, people with initiative, people with innovative ways of operating, and I think that two of the best operators I've ever known were Blackie Weinel and Jerry Miller.* If I were ever in a battle, I wouldn't want to meet one of those guys on the other side. Because they're so innovative if they don't get you one way, they will another. Hayward didn't have that.

Q: Well, on the other hand, you were showing off the ship and in that role, Hayward would be very good.

Admiral Lee: Hayward was very good. We toured the Med showing off the ship, having all the dignitaries come aboard. He was very good at that. But later on, he was aboard for our trip down to Cuba. Hayward himself I never considered as much of an operator--but he had a chief of staff, Captain Cook, who was very good, a very fine operator, and he ran the staff and the operation.** There was only one little problem. The chief of staff and Vince de Poix didn't get a long very well. Vince de Poix and Max

---

*John P. Weinel stood 533rd of the 581 graduates in the Naval Academy class of 1939. Operational commands included Fighting Squadron 22A, Carrier Air Group Five, USS Great Sitkin (AE-17), USS Ticonderoga (CVA-14), and Carrier Division Three. He retired as a four-star admiral in 1977.
**Captain Harry E. Cook, Jr., USN, chief of staff, Carrier Division Two, December 1961 to June 1963.

Harnish were two tough taskmasters. I wouldn't want to go back aboard ship with those two. They were tough hombrés.

Q: Any examples of that?

Admiral Lee: I tell you, I could give you a dozen examples of that, but maybe I would prefer not to because they're both friends of mine. Max is dead now, but Vince and Max were both martinets.* They wanted the ship spic and span all the time and didn't want to give you time to have people in dungarees to work on airplanes; it was that kind of a ship. It was really spit and polish, inspections every day. That's the kind of an organization they ran. It was very difficult to have airplanes up and ready to go without working on them and getting a little grease scattered around. But, anyway, they had a good ship.

Q: How did you get along with them personally?

Admiral Lee: Oh, I got along very well. I considered both Max and Vince very good friends afterwards, and I saw them in various jobs at various times. But they were very difficult to live with aboard ship, most difficult tour in that regard that I ever had.

---

*Harnish retired as a rear admiral; he died 19 September 1979.

Q: The usual pattern is to have one good guy and one bad guy in that combination.

Admiral Lee: These were two tough guys and two martinets. Made it a very difficult tour for the air group commander and the department heads.

But, anyway, we had a pretty good tour through the Mediterranean, and we made a lot of ports.

Q: Any highlights of the port visits that stand out in your mind?

Admiral Lee: None really, except that in every port we invited senior people, the mayors, the province governors, the naval commanders, aboard for a tour. It was just one tour after another in the Mediterranean. Those that didn't come aboard when we were in port, we would fly them aboard for tours of one type or another. It was showtime, showtime.

Q: Were there a lot of receptions?

Admiral Lee: Oh, yes. A number of receptions. There were receptions ashore for us. It was showtime. A new ship, the first nuclear-powered vessel in the Med in all of those ports. And it was a magnificent ship.

Q: What can you recall about the ship herself?

Admiral Lee: Oh, Enterprise was a great ship in every way. It had a unique bridge, because it had those phased-array antennas, big square bridge.* It was longer than any other carrier by 50 to 100 feet; it had more tonnage by 10,000 tons or so; had more flight deck space, more hangar deck space.** Everything was absolutely first-rate. There was never any grease on the hangar deck, and it was all spit and polish. So it was a magnificent show. We had a pretty good air group with some very good commanding officers. I thought we did very well by Enterprise.

Q: Were any of those squadron skippers well known?

Admiral Lee: Oh, yes. One of them, John Tierney, made rear admiral; and another made rear admiral, then vice admiral, James R. Sanderson.*** In VF-33, we had Richard

---
*The Enterprise was originally equipped with SPS-32 and SPS-33 radars with fixed, rather than rotating, antennas on the four faces of the island structure.
**The USS Enterprise (CVAN-65) was commissioned with an overall length of 1,123 feet, maximum width of 257 feet, standard displacement of 74,700 tons and full-load displacement of 86,000 tons. Comparable figures for the Kitty Hawk (CVA-63) class: 1,048 feet, 252 feet, 56,300 tons, and 78,000 tons.
***Commander John M. Tierney, USN, commanding officer, Attack Squadron 66; Commander James R. Sanderson, USN, commanding officer, Attack Squadron 76.

Truly, later an astronaut.* But out of that small group of squadron commanders, they all made captain, and two of them made rear admiral and one made vice admiral. Of course, I was the group commander. I'm going to talk a little bit later about some of these squadron commanders, because they play a role in a number of areas here which I think are interesting.

Q: Did you do much in the way of air operations during that Med cruise?

Admiral Lee: Yes, every time we went to sea we did operations, because we had visitors on board. We had to put on air show after air show. It was showtime. We had a new set of airplanes, F-4 Phantoms, first time in the Med. The F-8s had been in the Med before, but we had the A-5, supersonic bomber, first time in the Med. So we had lots of new things to show off. John T. Hayward was dedicated to showing them off. That was his big thing.

Q: Were you flying the A-4 as the group commander?

Admiral Lee: As the group commander I flew the A-4 and A-1

---

*Lieutenant (junior grade) Richard H. Truly, USN. Truly later became head of the space shuttle program; in 1989 he was appointed administrator of the National Aeronautics and Space Administration, the first astronaut to head NASA.

aboard the carrier.* I decided to fly the A-1, because the Skyraider boys needed a little boost in their spirits, and I decided I really didn't want to fly two or three different types of jets. Because some group commanders did, and I had checked out in the F-8, and the F-4, for that matter. But I decided to restrict myself to one jet and the A-1, and I had had tours in both of those.

Q: Was there any difficulty in going back and forth between two different types of planes like that, one propeller and one jet?

Admiral Lee: No, I didn't find any difficulty, because I knew them both so very well. But I thought it was a mistake for a lot of people to fly three or four different types of jet unless they were very highly experienced in each for another reason. Because one little hesitation, one little mistake--and jets are very unforgiving of these mistakes, and you just can't afford it. Now just mechanically flying, if everything goes well--almost any good carrier aviator, after a few flights, can fly any one of these aboard and off. But the problem comes with

---

*On 18 September 1962, Navy aircraft received new designations in order to conform to a uniform system within the Department of Defense. The A4D was redesignated A-4, and the AD was redesignated A-1. To avoid confusion, the new designations are used here throughout Admiral Lee's discussion of Carrier Air Group Six, even though he took command a few months before the aircraft were redesignated.

safety. It's pretty difficult to have reflex action for three different jets and you don't know which one you're flying that day. So that was kind of my philosophy. I restricted the people in my CAG staff to flying one airplane; that's it.* I flew the A-4 and the A-1 because I had squadron tours and deployments in both.

Q: Any specific operations that you especially remember?

Admiral Lee: Not in the Mediterranean. We took part in several operations, but having been to the Med before, they were just routine operations. Nothing spectacular.

Q: Were you keeping a special eye on the F-4 and the A-5 because they were so new?

Admiral Lee: Yes.

Q: What was your evaluation of each?

Admiral Lee: I thought the F-4 was one of the finest airplanes ever built.** I've talked about airplanes in

---
*CAG--carrier air group.
**The McDonnell Douglas F-4B Phantom II was the model that initially went to squadrons in the early 1960s. It had positions for a pilot and radar intercept officer in tandem. It had a General Electric J79-GE-8 turbojet with afterburner. The wing span was 38 feet, gross weight 56,000 pounds, maximum speed 1,485 miles per hour at 48,000 feet, and initial climb rate of 28,000 feet per minute. It could carry up to six Sparrow and four Sidewinder missiles.

previous sections. Of course, airplanes are a special love of mine and a special hobby. I have previously said that up to this point, I'd only flown what I considered one really great airplane. That was the A-1 and I described why. The F-4 was the next airplane, but instead of being a great airplane, I would say that it was near-great. It had a marvelous engine in it, the J79. It was a great airplane to fly; it had it all.

The one problem with the F-4 was reliability, primarily with the electronics. It was difficult to keep going, and it had a weapon system in it, the AWG-10, which was a good system when it worked. But we had reliability problems with it, and the maintenance man-hours per flight hour were perhaps 30 or 40 hours. Except for that one failing, it would have been a great airplane. But the F-4 was so good, there wasn't anything else in its class, nothing that would touch it in my view. For that reason, of course, the Air Force bought the F-4s by the hundreds, maybe a couple thousand. Because it was better than anything that they had on the drawing boards or were able to come up with. So the F-4 was the standard for fighters for about 20 years.

Q: It's just now been retired, as a matter of fact.

Admiral Lee: Yes. We took the first ones to the Med in

1962. But it was a great airplane in every way except reliability.

Q: And you certainly would not put the A-5 in the great category.

Admiral Lee: The A-5 was a political airplane. It was-- there was only one airplane that was worse than the A-5 in my opinion, and that was the F7U which was a disaster and also, in a sense, a political airplane.

Q: What do you mean by that term, political airplane?

Admiral Lee: I mean we really knew that the airplane wasn't very good. But because LTV was in Texas, it was very easy to get money for the F7U airplane.* Rather than turn it down, we accepted it. The same thing has been true through the years many times. The same thing happened for the A-7 and the Air Force. The Air Force really didn't want some of those planes, but always there was enough money to give the Air Force some A-7s. That's what I mean by a political airplane. The F7U was a political airplane.

The A-5 was a political airplane in another sense. The Navy wanted a supersonic atomic bomber for aircraft

---

*LTV Aerospace Corporation was a conglomerate that took over the old Vought company, LTV standing for Ling Temco Vought.

carriers for political reasons. So we built the A-5, and it was a real colossal dog. It had two good engines, but it wasn't a good carrier plane.

One of the most spectacular things I've ever seen in my life, one night in the Mediterranean on the second cruise, not the first cruise--I went to the Med again in January in Enterprise--we had an A-5 hit the ramp. Balls of fire and airplane came up the ramp and went over the side. Of course, we lost those two pilots. We had one or two pilots, including the executive officer in the squadron, who quit, turned in their wings after that. The A-5 was an unsatisfactory carrier airplane in my view. It came in at much too high a speed, and you had to be very precise to get it aboard a carrier.

Q: Was the size part of the problem, also?

Admiral Lee: The size wasn't such a problem. But it came in at such a high speed that there was very little margin for safety. Now we compounded this problem in the A-5 when we didn't really need it as an atomic bomber any longer. We converted it to the RA-5C, another colossal dog.*

---

*The A-5 was equipped with a side-looking airborne radar; vertical, oblique, and split image cameras; and active and passive electronic countermeasures equipment in converting it to the RA-5C unarmed reconnaissance plane. It was heavily used in the recon role in the Vietnam War.

That was a political airplane in the sense that the Navy had invested so much money in this program, they couldn't back away from it and admit they'd made a mistake. Admiral Pirie was the guy behind this, but it was a mistake.* We never should have bought the A-5, and we never should have converted it to the RA-5C. One of the worst airplanes we ever bought.

Anyway, we spent August and September in the Med, came home, were home about ten days, no more, when we were unceremoniously loaded back aboard Enterprise and headed south for Cuba. We just loaded our complete air group aboard with the exception of the A-5s. We left them ashore. We got some extra A-4s aboard, Marine squadron, so we had three A-4 squadrons aboard and one F-4, one F-8, and one A-1 squadron for the Cuban operation. We had an extra A-4 squadron instead of the A-5 squadron.

We, of course, went down to Cuba and were keeping track of what was going on down there. While down there, we got all the photography we needed and made plans to attack the missile sites in Cuba. We had lots of practice. We would usually practice at sea, loading weapons and dropping them on practice runs and attacks. We put together teams to attack these missile sites, first time we'd ever planned to attack missile sites. Now later on in

---

*Vice Admiral Robert B. Pirie, USN, was Deputy Chief of Naval Operations (Air) from 26 May 1958 to 1 November 1962. His oral history is in the Naval Institute collection.

Vietnam that became routine. But we studied those missile sites.

Q: What considerations went into your planning, since it had not been done before?

Admiral Lee: Survivability. We wanted to destroy the missile sites, but we did not have any guided standoff weapons in that time and period. So what we had to do was go in low. Our plan was to go in low, beneath the umbrella of the missiles, beneath their altitude capability, and attack the missile site and pull out. That was our basic plan, go in low.

Q: Just strictly using conventional weapons?

Admiral Lee: Strictly conventional weapons, non-nuclear and we had no guided ones.

Q: How much intelligence did you have on the Cuban antiaircraft capability?

Admiral Lee: We had very little. They painted a very grim picture for us pilots going in there. You always tend to make the enemy ten feet tall. But we had all the pictures of these surface-to-air missile sites that the Russians were putting in for them. We had all the pictures for the ballistic missile sites they were putting in. We made plans to attack all of those. We were just standing by on a day-to-day basis to go hit them.

Every day we would stream a sled behind the carrier as our target and practice our bombing. On the 26th of October I went flying in a VA-66 A-4. We were to make runs on the sled. After I'd been airborne maybe half an hour, one of my division pilots said that I was smoking and burning. And, sure enough, I was. So I came down to perhaps 10,000 feet and about 20 miles south of Enterprise. My red fire warning light came on, and I found it very difficult to leave that airplane. I'd been flying around in these airplanes for 20 years or so, never had a problem, and there it looked like I was going to have to leave this one. So that was the difficult part, making up my mind to leave.

I slowed the plane down to about 200 or 250 knots, somewhere in that range, and at 10,000 feet, I decided that I'd really better go when I could move the stick all around and there was no response. I knew the control lines had burned through, so I said to myself, "Here goes." I reached up and pulled the face curtain, and there was a tremendous thud. You have that face curtain over your face, which ignites the ejection seat and the first thing that--you just, you really don't know what's going on. You feel this tremendous thud and the world kind of blacks out for a minute, and you feel the parts flying every which way.

Just about the time that you become oriented, the parachute opens--it's all done automatically--and, once again, the jolt is such that you become disoriented. Then in a very few seconds, of course, you get oriented again. When I was fully oriented, there I was at about 9,500 feet or so, drifting down in a parachute to land in the water, south of Cuba.

So I then began to take stock of all my survival lessons, and I remembered there were two things that you do. Number one, you never release yourself from the parachute until your toes touch the water, because you have no depth perception over ocean. People have done that, thinking they were right at the water, and they released themselves and plunged 200 or 300 feet to their death. The other thing you do is the moment your toes hit the water, you release your parachute. Because if you don't, it will act like a sail and pull you through the water and drown you. So I didn't release the parachute until my feet hit the water, and then I had my hands on the releases for the parachute. You have to release them individually; there are two straps at your shoulders.

I released those, and you're pretty heavily weighted

when you hit the water, you know, with all that flight gear on and big shoes. You hit the water feet first and go down pretty far. It takes an eternity to bob to the surface. But I came up by and by and inflated my Mae West, and I also had a life raft with me.* Before I ejected, I had alerted my division mates, who had alerted Enterprise, so it wasn't long before they sent a helicopter after me, maybe a half an hour I was in the water before they got a helo there.

Q: What had become of the airplane?

Admiral Lee: After I ejected, the airplane was still burning fiercely. It just rolled over and plunged into the sea.

Q: I presume you had it on some kind of a safe heading.

Admiral Lee: I was about 20 miles south of the Enterprise, and there was nothing down there. I didn't want to get it up around the formation. It might hit a ship. After I landed in the water, I realized I was not injured, but I think every joint and every muscle in my body was sore. It's a wild ride, believe me.

---
*"Mae West" was the nickname for the inflatable rubber life belt used by the Navy, the name derived from that of a buxom movie star of the 1930s.

Q: Did you find that to be true--that your depth perception was not very good as you got close to the water? Were you surprised when you hit?

Admiral Lee: I thought it was pretty good, but I'm sure it wasn't as good as I thought. Because if I remember correctly, I thought I was going to hit the water quite a while before I did. If you have a lot of whitecaps, then your depth perception is not all that bad. If you have just a glassy surface, you have no depth perception.

Well, I was helicoptered back to the ship and piped aboard by Captain de Poix, "CAG returning" you know, BONG-BONG, BONG-BONG--and they made a big joke of it. But that was on 26 October, and we stayed down there through most of November. We were there through October and November, when the Cuban Missile Crisis was eventually settled. All that time we were down there with Hayward aboard as cardiv commander.

Q: How do you spend your time at this constant state of readiness without wearing too thin?

Admiral Lee: That's one of the problems with carrier aircraft duty. We tried to fly as much as possible. Get everybody in the air, keep our planes ready to go. We put out a sled every day. But it's very difficult to be in this state of readiness for two months, just operating south of Cuba, no ports. So what we did was do as much training as possible, do as much flying as possible, had movies every night. But it's not the easiest thing in the world to do.

Q: Especially when you face a potential danger that you know it's very likely you're going to lose some people. When did you realize that you were not going to have to attack Cuba?

Admiral Lee: We didn't realize that we were not going to have to attack Cuba until Kennedy had settled with Khrushchev.* We stayed down there a week or ten days to make sure that the Russians removed their missiles, which was part of the agreement. We had airplanes observing this.

In late November 1962, Enterprise once again headed for Norfolk after roughly two months in the Cuban area. I had a problem with one of the commanding officers during this period of time. He was commanding officer of VF-33, Commander Leavitt, who had been an aide to Admiral Russell,

---

*John F. Kennedy was President of the United States, 1961-63; Nikita S. Khrushchev was Premier of the Soviet Union, 1958-64. They were the two principal adversaries in the Cuban Missile Crisis in October 1962. In return for a U.S. guarantee not to invade Cuba, Khrushchev agreed to remove offensive missiles from the island.

who at that time was the four-star admiral in Naples, Italy.*

Leavitt was very popular, a very able squadron commander, very able aviator, very personable. But he would get drunk, and wouldn't be able to perform his duties as a commanding officer for three or four or five days at a time. I didn't realize this until we had gotten back to Norfolk from the Med cruise. And then I realized what had happened. He would supposedly be sick or down with a cold or something. Then it happened in Norfolk right after we got back from the Med, and it suddenly dawned on me what was going on. Leavitt was an alcoholic. Then I inquired around and found out it was true.

So I had a talk with Leavitt and told him that I wanted to help him in every way possible. I had just learned about all of this and I wanted it stopped. The next time he went on one of these binges and wasn't able to do his duty, we were going to court, and we'd let the powers that be decide his fate. Well, he understood that. He stayed on the wagon for some couple of months, I guess, then off he went again. Didn't show up for about a week.

I went over to see Commander Fleet Air Norfolk, Rear Admiral Forsyth Massey at the time, and reported all the facts to him. He held an informal hearing--admiral's

---

*Commander Eben Leavitt, Jr., USN; Admiral James S. Russell, USN, Commander in Chief Allied Forces Southern Europe. Admiral Russell's oral history is in the Naval Institute collection.

mast--and I was the principal witness. To make a long story short, Rear Admiral Massey recommended to the Chief of Naval Personnel that Commander Leavitt be relieved for cause of command of VF-33, and he was. You know, that's a very difficult thing to do. But you can't very well say, "I'm going to court if you do this again," and then he does it again and you don't go to court.

Well, anyway, about the same time, Rickover was looking for candidates to be XO of <u>Enterprise</u>, to relieve Max Harnish. He didn't have anybody in training. Max had been in the program for roughly two years, first in the building and now in operating. We had nominated an A-4 squadron commander on <u>Enterprise</u> by the name of Bob Bascom.* He'd gone up to Washington and Rickover said no he didn't want Bascom. Then we nominated a commander by the name of Jerry O'Rourke, who had an F-4 squadron on <u>Enterprise</u>.**

One day, right in the midst of these hearings on Leavitt, I got a call from the detailer, Commander Ted Dankworth.*** His question to me was, would I like to be interviewed by Rickover to be XO of <u>Enterprise</u>. I said, "Well, let me talk to my wife and I'll call you back

---

*Commander Wade Robert Bascom, USN, commanding officer of Attack Squadron 76.
**Commander Gerald G. O'Rourke, USN, commanding officer Fighter Squadron 102.
***Commander Theodore P. Dankworth, USN.

tonight." So I talked to my wife, and we decided I just didn't want to pay the price. I called Dankworth back in BuPers and said, "No, I certainly appreciate your asking but how about leaving me out. I'd really not like to pay the price. I don't want to go with Rickover for a year. I believe if I wanted to be XO of carrier, I could be XO of a carrier, but it's not one of the things I'm really wild about doing."*

Q: What was the price that you didn't want to pay?

Admiral Lee: A year with Rickover, primarily. I was scheduled to go to National War College the next summer. So I just didn't think it was something I wanted to do.

The next day I got called by Dankworth and his assistant, Commander Richardson, and they said to me that they had three candidates lined up to be interviewed by Rickover, and he was going to pick one of them. They had the guy all lined up that was to be picked, and as a personal favor to them, wouldn't I come up and make the threesome? So I inquired if they really were sure about this. They said, yes, they had it all set. O'Rourke and I were two of the candidates and the other one is a man whose name I've forgotten. Never saw him before, never saw him since. He was the guy wearing four-star aiguillettes. He

---
*BuPers--Bureau of Naval Personnel.

Lee #4 - 299

was somebody's aide in the Pentagon. O'Rourke and I drove up on a Thursday afternoon, because we had to be there for Friday interviews.

Admiral Lee: We reported in to Rickover's office bright and early on this Friday morning. All three of us were interviewed by the same three crown princes. Has anybody ever taken you through one of these interview sessions?

Q: I've heard some, but everybody's got his own fascinating story and I'd like to hear yours.

Admiral Lee: Well, anyway, we reported into Rickover's office. We reported with orders to the Atomic Energy Commission, and sometime during the course of the morning, I was interviewed by a fellow by the name of Rockwell, another one by the name of Panoff, and a Captain Crawford-- all very professional interviews, I thought.* I had no problems really with any of them, because I didn't want the job, and I was kind of relaxed about the whole thing. My view was that this would be a day of education. It's not often you get to go through this process, and I figured that those BuPers types knew what they were talking about. They had this all lined up with Captain Crawford, and I was just up there filling a spot, doing a favor to the

---
*Robert Panoff; Theodore Rockwell; Captain John W. Crawford, Jr., USN.

detailers in BuPers. You don't want to offend them too often.

Anyway, that afternoon I was told to go down and be interviewed by Rickover after having my three preliminary interviews. When I got down to Rickover's office, there was Jerry O'Rourke being thrown out of Rickover's office. Rickover was shouting at him, "Get out! Get out! You're lying to me." In adjacent offices Rickover had placed several telephone booth-like cubicle boxes. O'Rourke was led over to one of these so-called penalty boxes to cool off. I was then led into Rickover's office. He said to me, right off the bat, "How much of this program is for you, and how much is for the Navy?"

I said, "Oh, about 90 for me and 10 for the Navy."

He kind of relaxed about it, but he grumbled a little bit and said, "That's too high." But he didn't throw me out.

As it turns out, that's the first question he asked O'Rourke, and O'Rourke's answer was 50-50. Rickover had thrown him out. "You're lying." Didn't ask him another question. I got the same question and said 90-10 and he didn't throw me out. But he asked me lots of questions that I had difficulty answering. For instance, he asked me to define religion. How would you define religion?

Q: I'd say it's a set of beliefs, usually involving a

higher power, that one guides his life by.

Admiral Lee: Well, I said something like that, but he said to me, "You haven't said a sensible thing all day.

The next area of questions had to do with the number of officers in Enterprise. He asked me if I thought that the number could be reduced. I said, yes, I thought so.

After a little more of that and a few more remarks like, "You haven't said a sensible thing all day," he let me go. I went down then to get my orders from the administrative office which Captain Crawford ran. He was Rickover's right-hand man, and they told me just to sit tight for a while. So I was fidgeting back and forth; this was a Friday and I wanted to go home. O'Rourke and I had driven up together in my automobile and spent the night in a motel. Then I was told by Captain Crawford that I was to spend the night in Washington, and Rickover wanted me to write a paper on how to reduce officer numbers on Enterprise. O'Rourke was given his orders, and he could go home. I never saw the aiguillette guy again.

Q: Were you getting a little apprehensive at this point?

Admiral Lee: Yes. So I then took O'Rourke to the airport, to let him get a plane home. I found myself a motel room and started to write my paper. I had a couple of martinis to think about it, and then I began to get exasperated, at how ridiculous can you be and what a difficult chore. So I finally decided that with no rosters, no records, no numbers, no nothing, I couldn't write a decent paper that wouldn't be laughed out of court, so to speak. So I sat down and stated as much. I didn't have the numbers for people in first division, in second division, in engineering division, or any other division. I couldn't write a paper that'd stand the light of day sitting in a motel room with no reference material. I thought the numbers could be reduced, but I didn't have the resources to do it. I just wrote that on one sheet of paper.

The next morning I was there promptly at 8:00 o'clock and turned my piece of paper in to get it typed. I never saw it again. As the morning went on, I was getting madder, and madder, and madder, telling Captain Crawford that I'd had enough; I wanted to go. I didn't want any part of this in the first place. So then about 11:00 o'clock they gave me my orders and directed that I report to the Bureau of Naval Personnel. When I got there, I went to see the detailer who'd gotten me in this in the first place. He told me that I'd been selected, and I was going to kill him. Rear Admiral Duncan was in charge of this particular section or area.*

---
*Rear Admiral Charles K. Duncan, USN. Duncan eventually became a four-star admiral as Commander in Chief Atlantic Fleet in the early 1970s. His oral history is in the Naval Institute collection.

He took me to lunch, and we talked about this. He persuaded me that I should just count my blessings and go back to Norfolk, and they'd be in touch with me. Meantime, it had begun to snow and I got out of BuPers about 3:00 o'clock in the afternoon, and headed for Norfolk.

Well, anyway, I got back to Norfolk, and it was a fact. I was the candidate, and the plan was that I would go to the Mediterranean on Enterprise in January and would be relieved about the first of March in the Med.

Q: How were relations between you and Commander O'Rourke after you got picked and he didn't?

Admiral Lee: Very good. It wasn't something I wanted. It was common knowledge.

Q: Was it something he wanted?

Admiral Lee: Yes, he volunteered. So did Bascom. It was kind of a big joke in the air group and in the ship. Everybody had a good laugh that I'd been maneuvered into this. But I decided there wasn't much point in fighting.

Q: What was the tone of Admiral Rickover's approach when he was interviewing you? You said the others had been very professional. Was his less so?

Admiral Lee: At a later time, during my time with Rickover in his office, I observed many interviews. They were all the same. Everybody gets three preliminary interviews. If they're looking for one man and they have three candidates, they rate them--one-two-three. Each interviewer, such as Panoff, Crawford, and Rockwell, writes his description of you in one paragraph, about three inches long. He rates you--one-two-three in this group of three. All of this is put on one sheet of paper and sent down to Rickover.

Rickover has your service record, and his people have looked at your fitness reports. He knows what your grades were in college or where you stood at the Naval Academy. There's very little that they don't know about you. I'd been an officer for about 20 years, so all of that was available. There isn't really much that he doesn't know about you. His three people have these interviews, which take 30-40 minutes. Rickover reads this, and then he probes for a chink in your armor, a weakness. If some of his interviewers have noted a weakness, he probes there to see if he really wants to take you with that weakness.

Now I'll give you an example from a later time when I was acting as straight man. Somebody always goes in when Rickover interviews a candidate. There's always a third man, at least during my time there. I believe Captain

Crawford was the straight man when I was being interviewed, but I've forgotten. But, anyway, I did that a number of times. One time a man came into his office, and Rickover asked him what his hobby was, Rickover knowing full well what it was from these interviews. He said reading the Bible. "What other hobbies do you have?"

"That's it. When I'm not working, I read the Bible."

Rickover says, "That's all," and wrote a big "NO" across it. His comment to me afterwards was, "We don't need people like that in the nuclear program." Nothing wrong with reading your Bible, but we didn't want somebody that single-minded, and another way to look at it is unbalanced. Sometimes Rickover has axes to grind. He hates aides. He gave that aide a terrible time. The aide made a bad mistake of coming over there in uniform wearing his aiguillettes. But, by and large, he wants to put you under stress. He wants to see how you'll react, see if you come apart at the seams, see if you continue to give him reasonable answers when he's beating you about the head and shoulders. It's not an unreasonable approach.

Q: Was there some facet of your background that he was particularly probing?

Admiral Lee: No, he didn't. I'm sure he'd seen my grades at Columbia and graduate school. He was primarily interested in my opinions about _Enterprise_. I think he was trying to find out how much I read, how articulate I was. I didn't really get the blast of hot air and harsh words that a lot of people get.

Q: Was he demeaning to you in tone?

Admiral Lee: Yes, in a sense. He always is, he always is. For instance, he said to me, "You haven't given me a sensible answer all afternoon. You're an idiot like everybody else who comes in here." That's standard Rickover.

Q: But you weren't too bothered by this, since you hadn't invested much emotional capital in it.

Admiral Lee: Right. I didn't want the job. I wasn't looking for it. I was just doing a favor, and I thought it would be very interesting to go through this process with Rickover and his crown princes. I wasn't too worried about it. I thought if he threw me out, that's okay.

Q: Did he ask much about naval aviation?

Admiral Lee: No. In all my conversations with him, we never had a talk about naval aviation. I had lots of conversations, of course, through the years. We never talked about naval aviation.

Q: Was he interested in your physics background?

Admiral Lee: I'm sure he was. Rickover always made light of graduate school. "You're over-educated," he would say to people who'd been to graduate school. But if you take a look at the people he selected for his programs, about 90% of them had graduate school. He really liked people with the academic tickets. Some of them didn't turn out to be very good leaders, so he tossed them aside. But if you didn't have the academic tickets, he didn't want you to start with.

Well, anyway, I got back to Norfolk, Oceana, and began making plans to go to the Mediterranean. We left in early January, getting a new commanding officer for VF-33. Commander Jack Christiansen, came over to the Mediterranean and relieved me about the first of March 1963.* I came straight back to the States and went up to Rickover's office in Washington and reported in.

Q: How long might your tour have been otherwise?

Admiral Lee: Till July.

---
*Commander John S. Christiansen, USN.

Q: So it was not shortened all that much.

Admiral Lee: Not all that much. It would have been a year or a little more, because I was scheduled to go to National War College that July.

Q: Did you feel a sense of disappointment in getting cut short?

Admiral Lee: Yes, and I also wanted to go to National War College. That's the greatest job in the world, almost--being air group commander. Sort of the pinnacle in a career as a naval aviator, and it's the last flying job for a carrier aviator. But I figured I'd had a good run, so after I had accepted that it was my fate to join the nuclear power program, I didn't do much looking back. I decided, "So be it."

Rickover had a very difficult time picking aviators. Because he wanted people with good academic tickets and a good technical background, and they weren't all that easy to find. Now Vince de Poix was. He was a graduate school engineer, aeronautical engineering, went to MIT.* Max Harnish was a graduate engineer in ordnance engineering, and both of them were fairly high in their Naval Academy

---
*MIT--Massachusetts Institute of Technology, Cambridge, Massachusetts.

classes.* So was Michaelis, PG school-type in aeronautical engineering.** That's what Rickover wanted.

Forrest Petersen was typical of what Rickover wanted.*** Forrest Petersen went to the University of Nebraska for a couple of years; went to the Naval Academy; finished high in his class; went to Princeton with a graduate degree in aeronautical engineering after PG school.**** Then he went to test pilot school at Patuxent for a year, then went out to the X-15 program in the desert with the Air Force and NASA, and later got the Collier trophy.***** He was one of my classmates in the nuclear power program and supposedly the competitor. The two of us were to compete for the job. Now I don't know if you know Forrest Petersen.

Q: I've certainly met him.

Admiral Lee: Well, he's a very talented man. He looks

---

*De Poix stood 26th of the 581 graduates of the class of 1939; Harnish stood 26th of the 615 graduates in the class of 1943.
**Captain Frederick H. Michaelis, USN, relieved Captain de Poix on 20 July 1963 as commanding officer of the Enterprise.
***Commander Forrest S. Petersen, USN.
****Petersen stood 161st of the 914 graduates in the Naval Academy class of 1945.
*****In 1961, as a commander, Petersen was one of several recipients of the Collier Trophy, presented by the National Aeronautic Association, to the developers and test pilots of the X-15 rocket plane. Among the other recipients of the award that year was famed test pilot Scott Crossfield.

like and acts like a Nebraskan farmer. But don't let that deceive you, he's a very bright guy and very able.

But, anyway, I reported in in March to Rickover's office to begin this study. There were four of us to go through together: J. L. Holloway III, who was later to be CNO--and I think Holloway was an exception to the rule of how Rickover picked people.* Rickover was a great admirer of James L. Holloway, Jr., who was Chief of Naval Personnel and helped Rickover.**

Q: Another personality guy.

Admiral Lee: Another personality guy. He was one of the very few admirals that Rickover ever had any good words for was James L. Holloway, Jr. You never know about these things--but I rather think that's how J. L. Holloway III got into the program, because he wasn't high in his Naval Academy class; he was in the bottom half.*** He never went to graduate school. But he was selected.

I was in the class with Holloway, Petersen, and the prospective XO of Long Beach, Walter Schwartz. He was

---
*Admiral Holloway was Chief of Naval Operations, 1974-78.
**In the early 1950s, Captain Rickover was passed over by selection boards for rear admiral. Holloway, an admirer of Rickover, told Congress how to use the promotion laws to ensure that Rickover specifically would be selected. See Thomas B. Allen and Norman Polmar, Rickover: Controversy and Genius (New York: Simon and Schuster, 1982), pages 203-204.
***Holloway stood 339th of the 615 graduates in the class of 1943.

killed once he reported to Long Beach in an automobile accident.* But in all fairness to Holloway, he didn't have the technical background that we had before going there, but he did very well in the nuclear power program. He worked hard at it, and passed all the tests, both academic and at Arco. Holloway was a very talented guy and was a pretty good student. He had some tough competition, people with lots of technical background.

But, anyway, we reported into Rickover's office, and our schedule was to work from about 7:30 in the morning to 5:30 at night, five and a half days a week, get off at noon on Saturday. We really had individual or private study lectures and exams. We were examined on two or three things every week. The study involved math, and electricity, and all the physics texts having to do with nuclear power, and the chemistry involving nuclear power.

I had had all of this except the reactor physics part. There was some reactor engineering that I had not had. But all the rest of it, the math, the chemistry, the physics, I had had in graduate school. Petersen had a great deal of it except the physics and chemistry part. The only thing that was new to us, primarily, was the physics of a reactor and the engineering of a reactor. So I didn't find the

---
*Captain Walter W. Schwartz, USN, was a Naval Academy classmate of Petersen. He was killed in a four-car collision on U.S. 101 while en route from San Diego to Long Beach on 9 April 1966. He then executive officer of the cruiser Long Beach (CGN-9), based at Long Beach.

work academically difficult. It was very tedious. We covered a lot of material, and we were examined in great detail on everything.

The most tedious part was the three tours to Arco, Idaho, six weeks each, where we qualified on the A1W, which is a prototype for the Enterprise reactors.* Out there we were expected to work two eight-hour shifts each day, seven days a week. We had to qualify on every station and then finally qualify as a reactor operator. We took a final written examination and a final oral examination in order to qualify. I think we roughly spent three six-week periods in the desert near Arco under these conditions.

Q: Who were the instructors, both for the classroom phase and for the reactor phase?

Admiral Lee: In the Washington office, Rickover's civilian engineers: Murray Miles for chemistry; radiological warfare, radiological controls.** For each phase of reactor engineering or design, we had one of Rickover's engineers as an instructor. We would be given the books.

---
*Arco, Idaho, was the site of a Navy nuclear power training school. Two reactors, which would drive one shaft, were installed there as a training facility and prototype. Altogether, the Enterprise was equipped with eight A1W reactors. The A indicated the type of ship, and the 1W indicated it was the first reactor designed by Westinghouse for an aircraft carrier.
**Murray E. Miles was in the Naval Reactors organization of the Bureau of Ships; later he was chief of the nuclear technology branch of Naval Reactors.

Q: Were these people who really knew their business?

Admiral Lee: Oh, yes. They were very professional. Rickover had a very high quality staff. They didn't claim to be professors or teachers. But they knew their business about as well as anybody I've ever known. So that the quality of instruction was exceedingly high. If you had a problem or didn't understand something, they would help you. So the instruction was very fine indeed. I never had better, although I thought in graduate school we had some very fine professors. But these people were a different breed again. These were all engineers.

Q: It sounds like a very demanding regimen with two eight-hour shifts every day.

Admiral Lee: It was enough. That was at Arco, two eight-hour shifts a day, seven days a week. That was our work schedule. We weren't supposed to leave the site, although Holloway and I did get an automobile one time and go into Arco to have a few drinks and a haircut and a dinner.

Q: What assessment do you have of Holloway from being that close to him during that period?

Lee #4 - 314

Admiral Lee: As I said earlier, Holloway didn't have any great difficulty getting through the course. I thought he handled it rather well, since the only education he had was three years in the Naval Academy.

Q: Did he come to the others of you for help sometimes because you did have more background?

Admiral Lee: Yes, we helped him quite a bit in physics and chemistry, and other parts in math. We spent a fair amount of time with him helping him, but he did very well. But sometimes you need help in areas like this, and we, I thought, were very generous with our help.

Q: He was willing to work, it sounds like.

Admiral Lee: Yes, he was willing to work. Jim Holloway was a very politically oriented naval officer, much more so than any I ever knew. He was a very able naval officer, very good leader. He ran a good ship, did very well in this school, but very politically oriented. He would find out which way the wind was blowing, and that's the way he'd go, whether with Rickover or with a senator or anybody else. I understand his father, James L. Holloway, Jr., was the same way. Both of them had golden tongues, marvelous speakers. Jim Holloway III is one of the better speakers you'll ever hear, but very politically oriented. He tells you what you want to hear. But I think for a man to be successful in Washington, he has to have a certain amount of political sophistication. If he doesn't, he won't last long in Washington. Jim had more than his share.

Q: Well, he had it in the second generation; he had seen what had happened before.

Admiral Lee: We've got to have people who can understand politicians and talk to them in the Washington arena. He was very good at that. He was a very articulate man and wrote very well. He's one of the most articulate naval officers I've known. His father was too. Plus he wrote about as well as any naval officer you ran across.

Q: When I had an interview with Admiral Holloway III, it was almost like literature rolling off his tongue.

Admiral Lee: Very articulate man.

Q: Did a sense of camaraderie grow up among the fellow-students in that program?

Admiral Lee: Not really. Forrest Petersen and I became very good friends, and we've been good friends ever since. We had, I think, a little more in common. I introduced him to his second wife, as a matter of fact. I've been out to Nebraska to visit his farm, and Petersen settled down in South Carolina, near my old home. Holloway and I never became good friends, and I don't think he and Petersen ever became good friends. Holloway is not the type that has close friends; he has colleagues. Holloway keeps his distance.

Q: Was a spirit of competition fostered among the group?

Admiral Lee: No, no spirit of competition. We just wanted to survive. We helped each other to survive. I thought we did very well. Didn't have any problems. You never know how you do on the exams because they never tell you. But I never had to retake an exam. I don't think I ever failed an oral or a written exam, and I don't know if the others did, but I don't think so. But, Lord, we were examined in the course of a year several hundred times, one thing or another.

But one of the things that did happen to me while I was in the program was that I was selected for captain in, maybe, April of 1964, early selectee for captain, and so ended the competition with Petersen to go to <u>Enterprise</u>.

There was no competition as far as I was concerned. I was very delighted to see Petersen go to Enterprise.

Q: That selection knocked you out of the competition.

Admiral Lee: Yes. Petersen went to Enterprise when he finished the program, Holloway went to OpNav to await time to relieve Michaelis, and I was given command of an LSD, the USS Alamo, which suited me just fine.*

After leaving Rickover's office, I had about a month's leave before I had to head west. I used that learning about ship handling, because here I was going to be captain of an LSD, 12,000-ton ship, and I'd never been officially assigned to a ship. I'd been aboard ship many years' worth but always in the air groups. In order to prepare myself, I got out all these books on ship handling and rules of the road that I'd studied at Line School and got some additional books which I purchased.

I also went over to the Naval Academy and spent several days. The Naval Academy let me take out one of those twin-screw YPs, and practice with it, and drive out through the channel and back again, so I'd refresh myself on ship handling, rules of the road, and the various

---

*The dock landing ship Alamo (LSD-33) was built by Ingalls Shipbuilding of Pascagoula, Mississippi, and commissioned 24 August 1956. Length: 510 feet; beam, 84 feet; maximum draft, 19 feet; standard displacement, 6,880 tons; full-load displacement: 12,150 tons; maximum speed, 22.5 knots.

maritime markers, and marking systems for the channels.*
I had time to refresh myself on what I had studied at Line
School but had never really practiced. I thought that
being able to go down there and handle a YP was very
helpful. I had never really maneuvered a twin-screw ship--
I'd never maneuvered a ship before, for that matter. They
gave me all that I wanted down at the Naval Academy, and I
thought they were very generous with their time and help.
When I left for the West Coast, I felt that I was
reasonably well qualified to maneuver this ship.

Q: Did you do any boning up on amphibious warfare operations?

Admiral Lee: Not really. I looked around for some literature, but there isn't that much literature on amphibious operations except Admiral Barbey, I believe, wrote several books describing his amphibious operations in World War II.** But when I got out to Amphibious Force Pacific Fleet, I went through some schools which lasted maybe a total of two weeks, maybe three weeks, such as fire fighting school and the amphibious warfare schools.

But I think there's a lot of luck in a naval officer's

---

*The YP is a small patrol craft. A number of them are used for training Naval Academy midshipmen in ship handling.
**Vice Admiral Daniel E. Barbey, USN (Ret.), <u>MacArthur's Amphibious Navy</u> (Annapolis: U.S. Naval Institute, 1969).

career. Here is where I think I was very lucky. First off, I was sent to USS Alamo. The USS Alamo was a fairly new ship--twin-screw, landing ship dock, and a really fine ship, good design. Not only was the ship new, but it had an absolutely great crew. The ship was in great shape, had a good wardroom, and had won the E the previous year.* I was getting perhaps the absolute best deep draft in the Pacific Fleet, first-class ship. Some of my friends got sent out to real rust buckets, and that makes it very difficult, especially if you don't have all that much experience in the deep-draft Navy and the surface Navy.

Q: Well, it may be that you were considered one of the elite in this nuclear power program, so they would do well by you in BuPers.

Admiral Lee: However it came about, I was a very lucky man to be sent to the Alamo, because it was such a great ship. Not only was it a good design, as I said earlier, but it had a great crew, and a good wardroom, and I had a good executive officer.

Q: Who was he?

---
*The E for excellence is awarded to the ship in a particular organization, such as a squadron, that has the best performance either overall or an a specific area of shipboard operations during the year.

Admiral Lee: Joe Dordahl.* He was a USNR commander who had commanded one of these picket ships. He was a good man, a good executive officer, a good seaman, and a fine administrator.

Q: I wound up being in an LST squadron he commanded.**

Admiral Lee: Did he? Joe Dordahl? He was great for me as an exec. How was he?

Q: Well, I had little contact with him, because I wasn't in his flagship, but I remember seeing him coming across the brow.

Admiral Lee: He's a nice guy. Good man and I was delighted to see him get a good command. I did all I could to help bring it about. But he certainly did a lot for Alamo and for me personally.

But, anyway, I joined Amphibious Squadron Three, 12 ships: two LSDs, one APD, and all the rest were transports. I'd no sooner gotten aboard--and I think I relieved about the first of June 1964--when we headed for

---

*Commander Joseph P. Dordahl, USNR.
**In the late 1960s, Commander Dordahl was Commander Landing Ship Squadron Nine, a group of tank landing ships and rocket-equipped medium landing ships. The squadron was homeported in Yokosuka, Japan, and operated in support of the Vietnam War.

WestPac.*

Q: According to the record I saw, you took over on the first and departed San Diego on the 18th.

Admiral Lee: That'd be about right. We went first to Hawaii and took part in a little exercise off Hawaii, my first amphibious exercise. Then had some R&R in Hawaii, then on out to Buckner Bay, Okinawa, where we were joined by a rear admiral in charge of the amphibious forces out there. He was out of Subic, and his name was Squidge Lee.** He talked to us all in Buckner Bay. Then we went on down to Subic Bay. And very soon after getting to Subic Bay, we got all wrapped up in the Vietnam War. A Marine landing group was loaded aboard Alamo, and we set sail for the South China Sea. We were kind of a ready force in the South China Sea for what seemed like months on end.

Q: According to the record I saw, you departed Subic on the fifth of August, which was the day after the second Gulf of Tonkin incident.***

---

*WestPac--Western Pacific.
**Rear Admiral John M. Lee, USN, Commander Amphibious Group One.
***On 2 August, North Vietnamese motor torpedo boats attacked the destroyer USS Maddox (DD-731) in the Tonkin Gulf off Vietnam. On the night of 4 August, there were reports that the Maddox and destroyer Turner Joy (DD-951) were attacked by motor torpedo boats. No definitive proof has yet emerged on whether they were or were not, but at the time the incident led to the Gulf of Tonkin Resolution by Congress, authorizing conduct of war in Vietnam.

Admiral Lee: Wherever they needed assistance in Vietnam, we had the Marines and equipment aboard. We cruised up and down the South China Sea. On the <u>Alamo</u> I decided that all work and no play makes Marines very dull. So I cleared a space down on the well deck for a basketball court, and we had basketball competition every day. I would go down and play basketball with the troops. One of the things that caused a few laughs through the ship was one day I was down there playing basketball and got a black eye. But it was great fun. I used to go down there and just play with the troops, pickup basketball game. We had a lot of fun.

Another thing we did in the South China Sea, which I thought was just great fun at the time, was have swim call. We had swim call every other day for a while. I'd get permission to go off and do individual ship exercises. We'd go over the horizon and we would lower the stern gate--you know, those LSDs had a great big steel ramp, and we'd lower it down below the water line so the end of it was sticking in the water, and what we had was a steel beach. We could put two lines out with floats on them and put a boat in the water, our motor whaleboat.

I'd go swimming with all the troops, and we had a marvelous time. Until one day we were south of Saigon, having a swim call, and a sea snake came up right in our midst. The water is filled with sea snakes down there, and

I didn't know about it. That water was cleared in about three microseconds. Everybody was out of the water. Then I got information on sea snakes, all that I could find, and it turns out that there are just thousands of sea snakes in that part of the world, in the South China Sea. They're very poisonous. There was even a sea snake institute in Saigon.

Sea snakes are not aggressive. If you leave them alone, they'll leave you alone. But they're very poisonous. The reason that there was a sea snake institute in Saigon is that fishermen caught sea snakes in their nets, and in handling the fish, they'd pull in these sea snakes in these nets, there'd be sea snakes in there with fish. The snakes would get excited and bite the fishermen. After that, there was never any great enthusiasm for swim call, although we did have swim call a few times. But it helped relieve the tedium tooling up and down Vietnam.

Another interesting event. We were ordered into Subic and told to off-load our Marines and then were sent to Danang to pick up a torpedo boat. The CIA had given the Vietnamese these motor torpedo boats.* They would go up north and run raids against the North Vietnamese. I really never fully understood what they did with them, but they would rush around at great speed in these big motor torpedo boats. I could get one of them in the well deck of an LSD.

---

*CIA--Central Intelligence Agency.

It was kind of a windy day, and we went into Danang--
and you have to have fairly calm water to load in that well
deck. You flood it down until you get water deep enough to
float your boats or whatever you're bringing in. You bring
them in and chock them up and then pump the water out, and
the boat, whatever you brought in, sits on the chocks. But
it has to be fairly steady; the sea has to be relatively
calm to bring the boat in and get it all set. It was a
rough day. I despaired of ever getting a damn torpedo boat
into the well deck. I didn't want to spend the night in
Danang. Good way to get hurt.

Q: A hazard from sappers, for example.

Admiral Lee: Yes. So I decided, "Well, what the hell?"
Let's get under way. We tried every way we knew how by
using engines, and we'd anchor to get this motor torpedo
boat aboard. Tried everything we knew. Nothing worked.
So I suggested to our officers that, "We've tried
everything. Let's try something else. Let's pull in the
anchor and get under way at about three or four knots and
see what that'll do." And, you know, it was like magic.
We got under way at about minimum speed and heading out of
the harbor, and into the wind and waves, and that well deck
and aft of it, because we weren't going fast enough to
generate any wake, was like a millpond.

Q: You made a slick.

Admiral Lee: A slick is what it amounted to, because we had a flat bottom. We made a slick, and that torpedo boat came around as nicely as you please, and we were able to chock it up, pump out, all the while under way at just steerageway, and worked like a charm. I wrote that up and sent it in to the amphibious squadron commander, and he thought it was the greatest. But it got us out of Danang before nightfall, which is what I wanted to do.

We had a good tour out there. Had a little VD in Subic Bay and Olongapo the few times we were in there. But we spent a great part of our time out in the South China Sea. I believe we left in June, and I believe we got home in time for Christmas in 1964.

Q: What did you do to keep the Marines occupied during that long underway period?

Admiral Lee: Well, of course, the Marines really didn't belong to me. The Marines belonged to the Marine officers. We tried to make the Marines feel welcome. I said to them, "These ships were built for only one reason, for the Marines. The Navy has no use for them otherwise. Whatever we have aboard ship is yours. Whatever shortages we have, we share and share alike. Athletic facilities, we're going to do our best--swim call." The Marines themselves, their officers, worked out various things for them to do, calisthenics in the morning. But setting aside that space for a basketball court and moving things around helped a great deal, because that basketball court was going about 24 hours a day. Then, as I say, we tried to have swim call every few days. I thought that morale came along fairly well.

Q: Did they have any chance to practice amphibious landings?

Admiral Lee: No, except in the Subic area, but we were tooling back and forth in the South China Sea for the most part.

One of the things that I would like to comment on is the young Marine officers. I think that the finest young officers that I've seen in any of the services were the young Marine officers back in that period. They were a first-rate group of young people. Most of them weren't making a career of the Marines. They wanted to go through the Marine platoon training and have a tour in the Marines. They were as fine a set of young officers as I've ever seen, and I saw quite a few, because we had several groups aboard. All absolutely first-rate.

We did have some excitement on the way home. We came home by way of Yokosuka, the whole squadron. Back in those days, Honda motorcycles were the rage. I made a terrible mistake here. I allowed anybody who wanted to, to buy a motorcycle and bring it aboard ship. I even let them run them back and forth on the well deck on the way home. It probably was the worst mistake I made on Alamo. We got back to the States, and I think at least a third to a half of the people who brought motorcycles home ended up in hospital, in jail, or with traffic tickets. When we went back to Yokosuka later on, in March the next spring, also having to do with the Vietnam War, I said, "No motorcycles. I've had all those I can manage."

Q: You also had a visit to Hong Kong before that.

Admiral Lee: Yes.

Q: What do you recall about that?

Admiral Lee: Oh, we had a marvelous time in Hong Kong. Hong Kong is not very far from Subic, you know. And I think we took our Marines up to Hong Kong, and we had about a week there. I bought a lot of furniture; this furniture right here I bought in Hong Kong that trip. I bought lots of clothes; I bought that screen probably. We had a great shopping trip to Hong Kong, a great R&R trip. We all had a lot of fun and a lot of shopping. We had plenty of room on <u>Alamo</u>, and whatever people wanted to buy and bring home, they could. There were great bargains in Hong Kong in those days. I had some clothes made. So it was a good trip. Nothing spectacular happened. We didn't have any problems.

Q: Did you steam in company with the other ships of the squadron very often?

Admiral Lee: Only on the way out and on the way back. On the way out, three of us went out together for one reason or another. I've forgotten why now. On the way back all 12 came back together. Something very interesting happened there. You've heard various line officers tell you how good they are with a sextant, how good their navigating is, which I've never believed for a minute. So we decided we'd have a test on the way back from Yokosuka.

Every four hours every navigator in the formation would send his position, and he would merely state how he derived that position--DR, sun sight today, moon and stars last night--however he got it, he'd say.* Every four hours we'd send our position. What we really did was

___
*DR--dead reckoning, a method by which the ship's position is advanced by plotting course and speed from the last known position.

relate our position to the flagship and send in what, in effect, was the flagship's position. We'd take our own and then translate. We'd send the flagship's position every four hours, based on our position.

The idea was when we all got back to San Diego, we would take a look at this chart and just see how good we were as navigators. We worked hard at it, sent our positions in every four hours. But you wouldn't believe what the chart looked like when we got back to San Diego. Twelve people, 11--the flagship, of course, was always right.

Q: By definition.

Admiral Lee: By definition. But 11 of us were sending in positions every four hours, all the way from Yokosuka to San Diego. The spread you wouldn't believe.

Q: Hard to believe you were all traveling together.

Admiral Lee: Yes. The spread would be 20 and 30 miles. One man would be over here to the east of the flagship, and one man would be over here, the flagship's position always being right. Of course, he could have been way off too. But that was a good lesson, I think, for everybody that navigation is not as precise as a lot of people assumed it was.

Q: Who was the commodore?

Admiral Lee: Bobczynski.*

Q: What do you remember about him?

Admiral Lee: I remember he was professor of naval science at Notre Dame, a good Catholic, had a nice family, nice wife, very personable man, did not make admiral. But I thought he had a very good relationship with all those division commanders. Had no claims to being a great seaman or a great anything, very good man. He and I were good friends for some time after. I stopped into San Diego to see him when I had Enterprise down there. Some aviators had a tough experience with their tours in the line Navy. I never had that experience at all. I had a great time with my amphibious squadron, and I liked the squadron commander. We won the E for the 12-ship squadron, and also a Lancer Award, which was for an operation we had.

Q: How did your ship handling work out once you translated from the YPs to this much larger vessel?

---
*Captain Sigmund A. Bobczynski, USN.

Admiral Lee: Great. No problems. I think I became a pretty good ship handler. I did have a funny experience, though.

Before I get to that, one of the things I did on *Alamo* was build a library. We had no library. My philosophy is that any reading is better than no reading, especially for the youngsters we get in the Navy. If they'll read comic books, we'll stock comic books. But I built a library and got BuPers to send me a whole batch of books. We put together a very nice library for *Alamo*. A lot of good books in it, but a little bit of everything. That was fun, picking the books to go in this library.

Also every time our troops used to take exams for promotion, I would go down and give them a little talk before they started their exams and tell them how to take an exam. They had never taken one before, a lot of them. My advice was simple, but it was good advice. The idea was in taking an exam, "Never spend too much time on a given problem or question. Go right through the exam first time, answering those you know. Read and understand those you don't know, but don't spend all your time on them, because time will run out. After you've gone through the exam and you've read and understand all those that you didn't answer, then go back through it again and work those out. You'll find out that your subconscious has been working on some of those problems, and the second time through you'll know the answer. Then go through it again, and then the final thing is once you've done it twice, then spend your time working on the ones that you don't understand. Finally, make a guess." I'd go through that with them with the exams, and they did very well on promotions.

I didn't have any real problems with ship handling. I found that ship handling was like handling an airplane except much slower. I built a device to aid in going alongside tankers. It was based on simple trigonometry, knowing the height of the ship above water where I was going to hang this thing. If you want to be 120 feet when you get alongside or 90 feet when you get alongside, you just pick the bar out there that matches that and put that in the wake of the ship you're approaching, and, boy, you can be precisely 120 feet or 90 feet or whatever you want to be when you get alongside. It takes all the guesswork out. I had all the junior officers do this and use this machine. They understood it.

Now, of course, you can also go alongside, but I gave a test to many of our junior officers. "Okay, we won't use this and we'll let you see. You pick your distance." You know, it's surprising how great a difference there is. But, anyway, we were going alongside a ship one day, and one of the captain's acid comments was, on the other ship that, "If I couldn't calibrate my eyeball better than that, I'd quit." He wasn't impressed with our device for coming alongside.

Q: That's because he hadn't thought of it.

Admiral Lee: Well, it worked. It was great.

Q: Did you have any problems with the sail area on that ship?

Admiral Lee: Yes, as you know, it had a flat bottom and a big sail area.* It had a bad record of having collisions with other ships, the LSDs of that class. I learned never to get close in. Also, if you're going in and out of a harbor and you had a big cross wind, you wanted to be careful. You wanted to have enough way on, and you never wanted to get yourself in a position since the wind can blow you, because it would do it. Recognizing that, and knowing that, and having Joe Dordahl who had observed this sort of thing, we never had a problem. But you can get into real trouble, and some of the commanding officers did. They'd get too close to another ship with that flat bottom, and they didn't have any way to get out. It was like a sailboat without a keel. You had to be careful, but it was absolutely a great ship if you recognized these

---
*Sail area is the vertical hull area on which the wind exerts force. Thus the structure of the ship acts as a sail so that it can be affected by the force of the wind.

characteristics.

Q: You'd had command before of both a squadron and an air group. How did command of a ship differ from that?

Admiral Lee: That's an interesting question. I thought I had a very difficult squadron command. I needed a Joe Dordahl. I thought that I had a marvelous air group command. I thought CAG Six had some great commanding officers. We got a lot done; had a good air group, and so many people in that group became my friends for a career, such as John Tierney, O'Rourke, and Bascom, lots of them. Several made admiral, and they all did very well. They were a great group of people.

And when I got to Alamo, I got a great ship, but Burley was a submariner.*

Q: Your predecessor.

Admiral Lee: Yes, my predecessor. He was a small, short, baldheaded man, not much personality. He turned over to me an absolutely great ship. Alamo was a great ship before Burley got there. It had won the E a couple of years in a row, and they won it for Burley; then they went on and won it for me. So it was a great ship. But in Alamo, it was a

---
*Captain Thomas G. Burley, Jr., USN.

charmed year; I could do no wrong. The officers and men thought I could walk on water. And all the things we did--swim call, the basketball--I'd take on the wardroom in tennis, or squash, or badminton, and I'd beat them all. So we had a great time, I thought. We had a good wardroom.

The thing that is different about the 1100 Navy is the work. In *Alamo* normally, except for that Vietnam tour, we'd have an exercise about once a month or so, and you'd work very hard for three or four days, or a week on one of those exercises. Then life was fairly simple, and you didn't have a lot to do other than that. So I had a lot of free time. I could do a lot of studying, a lot of reading, and lots of other things.

On an aircraft carrier, it's very different. When you're at sea on an aircraft carrier, you're usually working 10 or 12 hours a day in a squadron or the captain of the ship much longer, because you have lots of flight operations. That's the name of the game, flight operations. That's an all-hands evolution and requires a lot of work from everybody from airplane mechanics on up. So the work load on an 1100 ship, such as an *Alamo*, versus the work on an aircraft carrier for the average officer, I would say on an aircraft carrier on a scale of one to ten, about nine and a half. On a ship like *Alamo*, maybe four. So it's a very easy life in comparison. But *Alamo* was one of the happiest tours in my naval career.

Q: Why do you say that?

Admiral Lee: I just enjoyed it. Had a good crew, we did a lot of things. For instance, we got back to San Diego in, I believe, in December 1964. Maybe you have the dates there.

Q: That sounds like it, yes.

Admiral Lee: Then we had an exercise about February, the Silver Lance exercise, great amphibious exercise.*

Q: That was in February and March of '65.

Admiral Lee: Yes, that was our big exercise.

Q: It was one of the biggest of the entire decade.

Admiral Lee: Rear Admiral Pratt was in charge.** The ship that performed best in the Silver Lance exercise was going to get the Lancer Award. And Alamo got the Lancer Award. There were several squadrons, and it was a big

---

*For details on Exercise Silver Lance see Lieutenant Colonel James B. Soper, USMC, "Observations: STEEL PIKE and SILVER LANCE," U.S. Naval Institute Proceedings, November 1965, pages 46-58.
**Rear Admiral Richard R. Pratt, USN, Commander Amphibious Group Three.

exercise. But good old <u>Alamo</u> and that crew--you know, we just led a charmed life. We could do no wrong.

Immediately after that exercise we were to off-load our Marines, head up to that Port Hueneme, and load on a Marine aircraft squadron, all their ground equipment, and all their men, trucks, vehicles, maintenance equipment, the whole works, everything except the aircraft, we were to load on the <u>Alamo</u> and take them to Yokosuka, Japan. They were going into Atsugi and then eventually to Vietnam. I made a great mistake in planning <u>Alamo</u>'s route to Japan. You know, if you look at the navigational charts, the way to go to Japan is via the great circle route. The great circle route goes up by Alaska and then Japan. But nobody ever goes that way.

Q: They go on a rhumb line.*

Admiral Lee: Yes. Why? Well, I decided we'd go the great circle route to Japan, shortest route. I tell you that's the damndest trip I've ever made: that flat bottom <u>Alamo</u> through that rough weather. We would go into one storm, have it for a day or two, come out into a clear area, right back into another, all the way to Japan. We didn't come

---

*A rhumb line is a course that intersects all meridians at the same angle; thus it is a straight line on a mercator projection of the earth. A great-circle course is an arc on a mercator projection, shorter in distance on the globe.

home that way. We came home via Hawaii, beautiful weather all the way. Then I understood why captains don't do the great circle route. I had asked for some routing. They had given me this other route, swinging down fairly close to Hawaii. But I decided to go the great circle route, and I learned the hard way.

Q: Was this in the nature of an emergency? Was it considered that, to get these people over there so quickly?

Admiral Lee: Yes. They wanted these F-4 airplanes out there, because they had an F-4 squadron at Atsugi, and I think it had been moved to Vietnam, so they wanted another one at Atsugi. I believe that was the case. We had to take the squadron to Japan.

Q: How did the airplanes get to Japan?

Admiral Lee: They either flew them out or took them on an aircraft carrier. I don't know how they took them out. We took, in our well deck and on our hangar deck and other places, all their mobile equipment--and they had a batch of it--and their men, and took them all to Yokosuka. Then all they had to do was bring pilots and airplanes somehow.

When I got back from Japan for the second time, I had a message directing me to report to Washington as soon as possible, to be interviewed by the Assistant Secretary of the Navy for Research and Development for the job as aide. As soon as we got organized after I got back, I flew to Washington and was interviewed by Dr. Robert Morse, who was then Assistant Secretary of the Navy for Research and Development.* I came back to San Diego--I was gone only three or four days--and very shortly thereafter was told I was to get the job. They wanted me back there very quickly. So I was relieved fairly soon. I didn't stay on Alamo a year either.

Q: You were relieved by Captain James T. Traylor, Jr.

Admiral Lee: Yes, that's the man. He relieved me on 7 May, so I had not quite a year on Alamo, 11 months. I was detached and back to Washington.

Q: Before you get there, I wish you could cover a little more on that Operation Silver Lance. What was involved in that, and what made the Alamo's performance so good?

Admiral Lee: It lasted for two or three weeks, if I remember correctly. We had several roles to play. We had two or three different loads of equipment to land at specific points and specific times, and Marines. It was a

---
*Robert W. Morse, Assistant Secretary of the Navy (Research and Development), 1964-66.

typical amphibious operation, where they had plans for air strikes. We landed on the different beaches, various Marines. We'd have our amphibious vehicles go in a wave to the beach.

Q: A lot depends on coordination and timing in one of those.

Admiral Lee: Yes. All of it depends on coordination and timing. <u>Alamo</u> was only one ship of many playing a role in this. I've forgotten how many ships were involved, but there must have been 25 or 30, anyway, plus lots of other ships. It was a First Fleet exercise.* The plan beforehand, which was advertised, was that the ship that scored the most points, so to speak, in all these various exercises, would get the Silver Lance award.

Q: Was there a grading system?

Admiral Lee: Without a doubt there was. When we were en route to Japan, we learned by message that the <u>Alamo</u> had won the Lancer award. Of course, that made the crew feel great. It was a marvelous crew, and they were great before I got there.

---

*The First Fleet, operating off the West Coast of the United States, was one of four numbered fleets in the U.S. Navy at the time; the others were the Second, Sixth, and Seventh.

Q: Did you have any special programs to communicate with the families of crew members while you were deployed?

Admiral Lee: We always sent newsletters to families of crew members. On leaving on a cruise, we had a sort of standard plan. We would tell them all about what to expect, how to get in touch with us and all the emergency information. Once a month we'd send a letter to all the families, telling them about the cruise and how we were doing. We did the same thing on Enterprise.

Q: Just to go back to that time off Vietnam, I remember being there in '68 and there was a lot of activity. The ships in the ready group were operating together. It sounds as if you had a much less demanding pace. Were you essentially left to your own devices?

Admiral Lee: Oh, no, we operated together all the time. The ships with a certain unit of equipment all operated together. There might be three or four ships carrying one Marine unit's equipment. They operated together. You had to. They all belonged to one Marine unit, brigade, or whatever it was, company. I never operated independently in the South China Sea. And what we would do is ask for individual ship exercises during the course of the day a couple times a week, two or three times a week. We were steaming around in circles, anyway, for all that time. We'd take individual ship exercises from, maybe 1200 to 1600 or something like that, and go off and have swim call and do a little seamanship practice or something, but that's the way we worked it. Never single ship--except going after that motor torpedo boat.

Q: Did you find any resentment on the part of your fellow skippers from having an aviator in their midst?

Admiral Lee: If so, I never detected any. In the 12-ship squadron we had three aviators. There was a man by the name of Frank Ault I'm going to talk about later, who was chief of staff of the cardiv for our Pueblo exercise.* He was a very able man who should have made admiral. The Navy's loss. Another one was a fellow by the name of Bill Donnelly, and he later went on to command the Ranger.** We had three aviators out of 12 in our squadron. I never detected any resentment whatsoever. There might have been some, but I thought the three aviators did very well. I've

---
*Captain Frank W. Ault, USN, commanding officer, USS Renville (APA-227). He later commanded the USS Coral Sea (CVA-43) and was chief of staff to Commander Carrier Division One during the seizure of the USS Pueblo (AGER-2) in January 1968.
**Captain William E. Donnelly, Jr., USN, commanding officer, USS Winston (AKA-94).

heard tell in other squadrons that aviators did join that there was a problem. But I think that would all depend on the squadron commander. Bobczynski wasn't that kind of a man.

Q: It would also depend on how well the aviators commanded their ships.

Admiral Lee: Yes. Yes. I don't know how Ault's ship turned out in the yearly competition nor Donnelly's, but I know they did well. <u>Alamo</u> won the E and the Lancer award, so you couldn't complain too much there.

Q: No.

Admiral Lee: The commodore was very pleased at our winning the Lancer award, because we were competing with ships from other squadrons. As a matter of fact, in my naval career, I worked for line officers, 1100s, many times. I never had any of those problems. I always found that they were some of the best people I ever worked for, some of the 1100s, as I've mentioned earlier. Never had any of that problem at all, certainly not in the amphibious squadron nor down in Norfolk, or at graduate school or line school, all 1100 officers.

Q: Well, in addition to the enjoyment, I'm sure there was a lot of satisfaction in having that kind of a tour also.

Admiral Lee: Yes, great. There was a lot of luck there.

There is another factor here. Some aviators wear their aviator wings on their damn shoulders. They're very conscious they're aviators--and they want everybody else to know. Some aviators like that--and I know quite a number of them--are kind of hard to take. People we had in our squadron, you never knew they were aviators. They were learning all they could about ships and amphibious forces and ship handling, which the 1100s were doing, too. I never heard any one of them mention flying, or do any hangar flying, so I think the aviators bring a lot of that on themselves--my impression.

Q: I think that's a good observation for the reason.

Admiral Lee: Because the people I worked for, the 1100s in my career, they weren't too interested in whether you were an aviator, or submariner, or an 1100. What they wanted was a good job done so that you wouldn't be a problem for them. But I think 90% of the aviators brought that on themselves, whatever problems they had in the 1100 Navy.

Q: Okay. On to Washington.

Admiral Lee: On to Washington.

Q: Do you have an idea what led you to be chosen for this job or picked as a candidate?

Admiral Lee: No, I don't. The Navy tries to put its best foot forward in choosing aides to the civilian secretaries and assistant secretaries, because aides can be very influential, and these civilian secretaries initially know little about the Navy. Robert Morse, who has a Ph.D. in physics, had been professor of physics and dean of the college at Brown University, was Assistant Secretary of the Navy.

He had an aide by the name of Captain Earl Yates, and Yates had been with Morse less than a year.* Morse became disenchanted with Yates for some reason that I never knew. Conflict of personality, I suppose. But, in any event, Morse wanted a new aide, and he communicated this, as I understand it, to the Vice Chief of Naval Operations, who usually handles this sort of thing. BuPers was asked to come up with nominations. It's my understanding they'll send over two or three jackets for the assistant secretary

---

*Captain Earl P. Yates, USN, was the first commanding officer when the USS John F. Kennedy (CVA-67) was commissioned on 7 September 1968.

to look at. He asked me to come back for an interview, and I did. I never discussed with him later why he chose me and not somebody else. All I do know is that he wanted a new aide.

But this was my first introduction to the Pentagon, and I had a front-row seat at how things were done in the Pentagon and decisions being made at high levels for almost two years. One of the things that immediately impressed me on reporting into Morse's office was the aides there. Nitze's aide was Zumwalt; Baldwin's aide was Dave Bagley; McDonald's aide was Ike Kidd; Rivero's aide was Jerry Miller.* We had an assistant secretary of the Navy for financial affairs by the name of Baird, whose aide was James Montgomery.** He also made rear admiral. It was a remarkable group of aides. The rumors around the Pentagon were that the aides were running the Navy, and there probably was a little truth in the matter, because Zumwalt was very influential with Nitze, and Zumwalt was a very smooth operator.

---

*Secretary of the Navy Paul H. Nitze; Captain Elmo R. Zumwalt, Jr., USN, who later became a four-star admiral; Under Secretary of the Navy Robert H. B. Baldwin; Captain David H. Bagley, USN, who later became a four-star admiral; Admiral David L. McDonald, USN, Chief of Naval Operations; Captain Isaac C. Kidd, Jr., USN, who later became a four-star admiral; Admiral Horacio Rivero, Jr., Vice Chief of Naval Operations; Captain Gerald E. Miller, USN, who later became a three-star admiral.
**Charles F. Baird, Assistant Secretary of the Navy (Financial Management), 1965-67; Under Secretary of the Navy, 1967-69. Captain James W. Montgomery, USN.

Q: Very aggressive too.

Admiral Lee: Very aggressive, and anything that Zumwalt did always came from the Secretary, according to Zumwalt. He handled the admirals coming in and out of Nitze's office with great finesse; he was a very smooth operator. Bagley with Baldwin was very good. Miller, of course, was a personality kid with Rivero. Ike Kidd, the number one horse's ass I've met in the Navy, was McDonald's aide.

Q: Why do you say that?

Admiral Lee: Well, he is. I'll describe him later.

But these were very aggressive people, all of them, and a very talented group. They had a fair amount to do with the decisions made in the secretariat during this period of time.

Now I also think this might be a good time to say a few words about the civilian secretaries. In 1965 I met, you might say, a set of these secretaries and assistant secretaries, and then I later came back to work once again in the secretariat, OPA.* The secretary at that time was Chafee. My impression of secretaries and assistant secretaries is that, by and large, we've gotten a very high

---
*OPA--Office of Program Appraisal. Admiral Lee covers this tour of duty in the second volume of his oral history.

quality man into these key jobs. A lot of them are like Bob Frosch, who is now vice president of General Motors; or Robert Morse, who's left the Navy to be president of Case Western Reserve; or Charles Baird, who was Assistant Secretary of the Navy for financial management, who later became president and chief executive officer of International Nickel. By and large, a remarkable group of men.

Over a period of about ten years, I knew most the secretaries and assistant secretaries in the Navy. In that time we had a few duds, but overall a talented group of men. We had a Secretary of the Navy when I was in NavAir by the name of Middendorf.* Middendorf is what I would call a dud. Middendorf was an incompetent Secretary of the Navy, in my view. But he was the exception in this particular area. By and large, I would give all of these men that I knew through the years very high marks. I think the Navy was lucky to have them. Most of them have gone on to do very well in other jobs and in other fields. For example, Baird's relief was a man by the name of Charles Bowsher, who is now the Comptroller General of the United States.**

Q: There was quite a difference between your Pentagon job

---

*J. William Middendorf II, Secretary of the Navy, 1974-77.
**Charles A. Bowsher, Assistant Secretary of the Navy (Financial Management), 1967-71.

and whether guys will or will not buy motorcycles in Japan.

Admiral Lee: Yes. But it was a very fine education for me over a period of two years, I worked for two good men, Morse and Frosch. They depended on my suggestions, and recommendations, and judgments in a lot of things where they had no experience.

Q: What are examples of those?

Admiral Lee: Such as how to handle this admiral; describe this admiral to him; they're looking for a new naval officer here; whether to pick this one or that one; what are the pluses and minuses; this aircraft program; is this really worthwhile for this R&D program? You have a chance to comment on just about everything that goes through the office, from people to the various programs.

Q: Was your experience in ONR useful in this tour of duty?

Admiral Lee: Not really. Not really. My experience in ONR wasn't really useful for anything I ever did later. But I learned most of the Navy programs here, and Morse and Frosch had about five or six assistants, technical assistants, one of whom was Ed Snyder, another Ted

Lonnquest, and all the others were civilians.*

Q: What do you remember about Ed Snyder?

Admiral Lee: Ed was the assistant for matters related to oceanography. Ed worked very hard at his oceanography job, and he knew everybody in the business in the oceanography area. He worked to keep them supported. If they called Ed in some particular area, he helped them. So Ed Snyder was highly respected in the oceanography community. He worked with and for all the people out there getting Navy money, which is what all of them were doing. He was very sympathetic to their needs. Ed Snyder was very popular.

Ed wasn't the world's greatest administrator. His desk would be a rat's nest. He would have 15 different books and reports on his desk, and that was standard Ed Snyder. You couldn't tell what was going on from looking at his desk. One day I made him clean up his desk, because I was the senior military officer in there, to give him a little discipline. But Ed did a good job there, was a good man. And, as I say, was really highly respected in that particular community.

Q: He was continued on active duty several years after

___
*Captain J. Edward Snyder, Jr., USN; Commander Theodore C. Lonnquest, Jr., USN. Snyder had a specialty in oceanography; Lonnquest was an aeronautical engineering duty officer.

retirement as Oceanographer of the Navy, so that was apparently quite a specialty with him.*

---
*As a rear admiral, Snyder served as oceanographer of the Navy from 1972 to 1979. He was placed on the retired list in 1975 and continued on active duty in a retired status.

Index to

Reminiscences of

Vice Admiral Kent L. Lee, USN (Ret.)

Volume I

A-1 Skyraider
  See AD/A-1 Skyraider

A3D Skywarrior
  Purchased by the Navy in the mid-1950s to be equipped with atomic weapon capability, 216

A-4 Skyhawk
  See A4D/A-4 Skyhawk

A4D/A-4 Skyhawk
  Used in tests studying low-altitude flying tactics in the 1950s, 204-205; given atomic weapon capability in the mid-1950s, 216; Lee took refresher training in this plane before assuming command of his first squadron in 1958, 223; flying characteristics and night flying capabilities, 232-235; Lee had refresher training in the Skyhawk prior to assuming command of Air Group Six in 1962, 275; Lee was forced to eject from an A-4 while deployed to Cuba in October 1962, 291-294

A-5 Vigilante
  Lee checked out in this plane before assuming command of Carrier Air Group Six in 1962, 275; shown off during Enterprise (CVAN-65) Mediterranean cruise in 1962, 283; Lee's assessment of this plane, 287-288; fiery crash on board the Enterprise during a 1963 Mediterranean deployment, 288
  See also RA-5C

A-7 Corsair II
  Lee's assessment of this jet aircraft as a fine carrier plane, 208

AD/A-1 Skyraider
  Lee feels this was the best plane he flew throughout his career in naval aviation, 53-54, 66, 179, 187, 206, 234, 286; AD-5N used to test the aircraft carrier mirror landing system and angled deck in 1955, 199; used for low-altitude flying tests in the mid-1950s, 204; as Commander Carrier Air Group Six in the early 1960s, Lee flew this aircraft to boost the morale of the A-1 pilots, 283-284

Accidents
  Lee damaged the nose of his SBD in a mishap while taxiing in 1943, 47; as a dive-bombing instructor in 1944, Lee survived a midair collision between two SBDs, 61-62; carrier landing accident by Lieutenant Commander Donald Engen in the mid-1950s, 202; crashes by Attack Squadron 46 pilots in the late 1950s, 223, 226; two squadron commanders killed during night operations in the 1950s,

233, 235; A-5 crash on the Enterprise (CVAN-65) in the Mediterranean in 1963, 288; Lee was forced to eject from an A-4 during a deployment to Cuba in October 1962, 291-294

Advancement of Enlisted Personnel
As practiced in the Navy in the early 1940s, 25-26; Lee's advice to crew members of the USS Alamo (LSD-33) in the mid-1960s on how to pass advancement exams, 331-332

Aerial Reconnaissance
Aerial photos were used to help Air Group Six plan for possible bombing strikes against Cuba in October 1962, 290-291

Air Development Squadron Three (VX-3)
Mission of testing new naval aviation developments in the mid-1950s, 195, 203, 209-210; planes tested, 196-199; calibrated planes for low-level flying, 199, 204-205; interaction with other test programs, 203

Air Force, U.S.
The Air Force's success in the Korean War with a plane originally developed and rejected by the Navy caused the latter to take a second look, resulting in the FJ, 198-199; the influence of the Strategic Air Command (SAC) pervaded the Single Integrated Operational Plan developed in the early 1960s, 248-253, 257, 261, 269-270; SAC didn't see the need to include reserve assets in strategic planning, 253-254, 268; discussion of typical SAC officer, 257-258; strategic squadron provided intelligence for target selection, 263; fail-safe ability to recall planes in the event of an emergency, 267; got stuck with the A-7, a "political plane," in the 1960s, 287

Air Group Six
Moved from the Intrepid (CVA-11) to the Enterprise (CVAN-65) in 1962, 276; discussion of squadron commanders in the early 1960s, 282-283; air operations during a Mediterranean cruise in the late summer of 1962, 283, 285; sent to Cuba in response to the October 1962 missile crisis, 289-295; squadron commander relieved for drinking in the early 1960s, 295-297

Air Group 15
Put off the Hornet (CV-12) in 1944 because the carrier's skipper was dissatisfied, 70; combat operations against the Japanese, 75-99; coordination between different squadrons, 78; relations between the air group and the Essex (CV-9) crew, 102

Air Group 17
   Trained at Fallon, Nevada, in 1945-46, 120; difficulty keeping maintenance personnel in the years immediately following World War II, 120-121

Aircraft Carriers
   Advanced flight students were required to make eight carrier landings on the Sable (IX-81) in the course of training during World War II, 47, 49-52; the escort carrier Breton (CVE-23) ferried replacement planes and pilots from Pearl Harbor to Pacific Fleet units in 1944, 68-69; the Hornet (CV-12) in 1944 replaced Air Group 15 because the ship's CO was dissatisfied with the air group's performance, 68, 70; in early 1944 the USS Essex (CV-9) took on Air Group 15 after its rejection by the Hornet, 70-71; combat operations by the Essex and her air group in 1944, 75-99; homing signal for guiding planes back to carriers, 90-92; the Essex weathered a typhoon in late 1944, 100-101; relations between the air group and the crew of the Essex, 102-103; role of ready rooms, 105-106; shipboard aviation mechanics in 1944, 110-111; logistic support of carrier-based aircraft was excellent in the Central Pacific in 1944, 113-114; the escort carriers Badoeng Strait (CVE-116) and Sicily (CVE-118) had Marine F4U squadrons embarked to provide close air support during the early stages of the Korean War in 1950-51, 150-151, 155-166, 171-177; different characteristics precluded CVs and CVEs from operating together off Korea, 177; the Philippine Sea (CV-47) attacked targets in North Korea during the Korean War, 165-166, 180-181, 184-186; night air qualifications held on board CV-47 in December 1951, 183; test of the mirror landing system and angled deck on the carrier Bennington (CVA-20) in 1955, 199; shakedown cruise to Guantánamo of the Franklin D. Roosevelt (CVA-42) in 1958, 226-228; the Intrepid (CVA-11) made a Mediterranean deployment in 1959 with VA-46 as one of the squadrons in the air group, 229-242; aircraft carrier survivability in nuclear war was studied in the early 1960s by JSTPS, 253; Air Group Six went aboard the new carrier Enterprise (CVAN-65) in 1962, made a Mediterranean deployment, and was on station for the Cuban Missile Crisis, 276-308

Alamo, USS (LSD-33)
   Lee boned up on ship handling at the Naval Academy before taking command in 1964, 317-318; ship described as a great design that was in excellent condition, 319, 334-335; deployed to the Western Pacific in mid-1964, 320-330, 341-342; recreation in the ship, 322-323, 325-326; Lee regretted allowing crew members to bring home motorcycles purchased during stop in Yokosuka, 327; port visits, 321, 325, 327-328; won the squadron E award, 330, 343; Lee compiled a library for the ship, 331; discussion of sail area, 333-334; work involved in running the Alamo versus an aircraft carrier, 335; won the Lancer Award for

performance in exercise Silver Lance in early 1965, 330, 336-337, 339-340; transported a Marine air squadron to Japan via the great circle route in the spring of 1965, 337-339

Alcohol
Officers on liberty at Ulithi Atoll in 1944 had to pay to join the club in order to be able to buy drinks, 111-112; a fighter squadron commander on board the Enterprise (CVAN-65) was relieved after several episodes with liquor in 1963, 295-297

Alderman, Captain John C., USN (USNA, 1928)
Lee's recollections of Alderman as commanding officer of the Badoeng Strait (CVE-116) in the early 1950s, 171-172

Amphibious Warfare
The dock landing ship Alamo (LSD-33) won the Lancer Award for top performance during Exercise Silver Lance off Southern California in early 1965, 336-337, 339-340

Amphibious Warfare Ships
The dock landing ship Alamo (LSD-33) was beginning a Western Pacific deployment when the Vietnam War broke out in the summer of 1964, later returned to the United States and won the Lancer Award, 317-343

Amphibious Squadron Three
Deployment to the Western Pacific in 1964, 321-322; navigation competition among units of this squadron on the trip from Yokosuka to San Diego in December 1964, 328-329; operations off Vietnam, 341; aviator skippers in the squadron, 342-343

Arco, Idaho
Students in the Navy's nuclear power training program in the mid-1960s made three trips to Arco to qualify on a prototype nuclear reactor, 311-313

Argentia (Newfoundland) Naval Air Station
Site of Navy cold-weather aircraft testing in late 1946, 125-129

Athletics
Physical training was an important factor for Navy preflight students at St. Mary's College, California, in 1942-43, 30-32

Atlantic City, New Jersey
Home of Air Development Squadron Three in the mid-1950s, 212-213

Atomic Weapons
See Nuclear Weapons

Atsugi (Japan) Naval Air Station
  Carrier Division 15 staff surveyed the airbase here in the summer of 1950 for potential value to the Korean War effort, 152, 154

Attack Squadron 5B (VA-5B)
  Given new designation in 1946 after being VB-17, 125; accompanied Valley Forge (CV-45) on shakedown cruise to Guantánamo in early 1947, 128-129
  See also Bombing Squadron 17

Attack Squadron 46 (VA-46)
  Lee took refresher training before assuming command of this A4D squadron in 1958, 223; casualties, 223, 226, 237-238, 243; Lee's difficulties as CO, 223-225, 227-228; shakedown cruise to Guantánamo in the Franklin D. Roosevelt (CVA-42), 226-228; Lee instituted a stringent safety program, 226-227, 237-238, 242-243; Mediterranean cruise in the Intrepid (CVA-11) in 1959, 228-238, 242; Lee disbanded the squadron's flight demonstration team, 229; enlisted personnel, 240

Attack Squadron 115 (VA-115)
  Retrained from May to December 1951 after Korean War deployment, 178-180; operations in Korea in 1952, 180-181, 183-186; casualties, 181, 184

Ault, Captain Frank W., USN (USNA, 1943)
  Characterized as a highly capable officer who should have made admiral, 342

Aviation Cadet Program
  Selection of Navy candidates for in the early 1940s, 27-28; preflight training at St. Mary's College, California, in 1942-43, 28-33; 40-41

Aviation Maintenance
  Poor quality of aviation machinist's mate training at Norfolk in 1940-41, 18-19; Lee feels that chief petty officers carried the maintenance load during World War II, 21-22; maintenance of planes at the Miami Naval Air Station in the early 1940s, 20, 22-23; a maintenance glitch in Lee's F6F prevented him from dropping a bomb during a sortie over Manila in 1944, 92-93; quality of maintenance in VF-15 on board the Essex (CV-9) in 1944-45, 110-111; logistic support of carrier-based aircraft was excellent in the Central Pacific in 1944, 113-114; Lee instituted a program to get pilots involved in maintaining planes during the personnel shortage immediately following World War II, 121; Marine squadrons demonstrated in the Korean War that they don't stress maintenance as much as Navy squadrons, 171

Aviation Safety
  Safety not a specific priority until well into World War II, 40-41; VB-15 skipper stressed safety during initial

training for new pilots in 1944, 73-74; after a high number of casualties in VA-46 in the late 1950s, Lee instituted a stringent safety program that paid off, 226-227, 237-238, 242-243

Aviation Training
V-5 program, 27-28, 30; preflight training at St. Mary's College, Moraga, California, in 1942-43, 28-33, 40-41; primary flight training at Los Alamitos Naval Air Station in 1943, 35-41; advanced training in Texas in 1943, 41-44; advanced training split between carrier and transport/patrol pilots, 44-45; operational training in dive-bombers in 1943, 46-52, 60-62; carrier landing practice, 47, 49-52; new arrivals to VB-15 in 1944 were given more than a week of excellent training, 73-75; new pilots were forced to do their own training in VF-15 in 1944, 83; VB-151 pilots trained in North Carolina in early 1945, 116-119

Badoeng Strait, USS (CVE-116)
Ordered to take on Marine squadrons in July 1950 for deployment to Korean waters, 150-151; operated as unit of Task Group 96.8 during the Korean War, 155-160; had one of the first carrier-based helicopters, 160-161, 170; close air support during Korean War, 162-166, 173-177; Captain John C. Alderman's performance as commanding officer during operations off Korea, 171-172

Bagley, Captain David H., USN (USNA, 1944)
Assessed as aide to under Secretary of the Navy Robert Baldwin in the mid-1960s, 346-347

Baird, Charles
This Assistant Secretary of the Navy is used as an example of the quality of the key Navy Department personnel in the mid-1960s, 348

Bascom, Commander Wade Robert, USN (USNA, 1945)
Suggested by the executive officer of the Enterprise (CVAN-65) in 1963 to be his replacement, but rejected by Vice Admiral Hyman Rickover, 297

Bennington, USS (CVA-20)
First qualification landings using a mirror landing system and angled decks held on this carrier in 1955, 199

Betty
Japanese bomber shot down by Lee's F6F near Formosa in October 1944, 85-86

Bobczynski, Captain Sigmund A., USN
Assessed as commodore of Amphibious Squadron Three in 1964, 330, 343

Bogan, Captain Gerald F., USN (USNA, 1916)
   Ran a first-rate naval air station at Miami in 1941, 20-21, 23

Bombing Squadron 15 (VB-15)
   Commanding officer in 1944 had difficulty making a carrier landing in a SB2C, 67-68; took on three replacement planes and pilots in June 1944, 71-72; personnel in 1944, 73; excellent training program for new pilots, 73-74; quality of squadron assessed, 75, 98-99; provided close air support to Guam and Tinian, 75-76

Bombing Squadron 17 (VB-17)
   Trained in Nevada and Maine in 1945-46, 120-121; Lee instituted a program to involve pilots in the maintenance of planes, 121; redesignated VA-5B in late 1946, 125
   See also Attack Squadron 5B

Bombing Squadron 100 (VB-100)
   Lee joined VB-100 temporarily at Barbers Point, Hawaii, in 1944 to get experience in SB2Cs, 63-64

Bombing Squadron 151 (VB-151)
   Formed and trained at a North Carolina auxiliary air station in early 1945, 116-117; personnel, 117-119

Bowdoin College, Brunswick, Maine
   Lee attended courses here in 1946, 122

Bowsher, Charles A.
   As Assistant Secretary of the Navy, 1967-71, used as an example of the quality of key personnel in the Navy Department during that period, 348

Breton, USS (CVE-23)
   Ferried replacement planes and pilots from Pearl Harbor to Pacific Fleet units in 1944, 68-69

Bridgers, Lieutenant John D., USNR
   Trained new pilots to VB-15 in 1944, 73-74

Bringle, Commander William F., USN (USNA, 1937)
   As Commander Air Group 17 in 1945-46, applauded Lee's program to get pilots involved in maintaining the aircraft, 120-121; assessed by Lee, 123-125

Browning, Captain Miles R., USN (USNA, 1918)
   As commanding officer of the Hornet (CV-12) in 1944, changed air groups because he was dissatisfied with performance, 68, 70

Bunker Hill, USS (CV-17)
   Air Group 15 returned to the United States in December 1944 in this carrier, 95

Bureau of Naval Personnel
   Established in 1957 a formal selection process for aviation squadron commanders, 222; role in picking candidates for the nuclear power program in the early 1960s, 297-300

Burke, Admiral Arleigh A., USN (USNA, 1923)
   CNO Burke regulated the selection process for aviation squadron commanders in 1957, 222; hurriedly sent certain naval officers to Omaha in 1960 to help the Navy get its fair share of strategic targeting responsibilities, 248, 268-272, 274; concerned about the Air Force's designs on Navy assets in target planning, 249-250

Burkett, Chief Gunner's Mate Ray C., USN
   As boot camp platoon commander at Norfolk Naval Training Station in 1940, 16-17, 28-29

Burley, Captain Thomas G., Jr., USN (USNA, 1941)
   Lee's assessment of his predecessor as skipper of the Alamo (LSD-33) in the mid-1960s, 334

Butts, Lieutenant Whitmore S., USN (USNA, 1929)
   As a division officer at the Miami Naval Air Station in 1941-42, 23, 25

Byrd, Rear Admiral Richard E., Jr., USN (Ret.) (USNA, 1912)
   Critical of Lee for going through clouds during primary flight training in 1943, before he had been trained in instrument flying, 38-39

Cagle, Commander Malcolm W., USN (USNA, 1941)
   Lee's recollections of Cagle as executive officer of the Intrepid (CVA-11) in the late 1950s, 229, 236-237

Callcott, Dr. Frank
   Columbia University professor's thoughts in the late 1940s on racial problems, 135

Carrier Division 15
   Makeup of staff in 1950, 149-150; duties, including supplying close air support, in the early days of the Korean War, 151-152, 162, 173-177; Lee's duties as aide and flag lieutenant, 156-157, 171-172, 175; provided close air support during September 1950 Inchon landings, 156-160

Central Intelligence Agency
   Provided motor torpedo boats to the Vietnamese for raids against North Vietnam in the mid-1960s, 323

Chafee, John H.
   Anecdote about Secretary of the Navy Chafee's reaction, years later, to his drill instructor from Marine Corps boot camp in 1942, 16

China, People's Republic of
    Entry of Chinese troops into the Korean War prolonged what had been viewed as a quick fight, 164

Civil War
    Residual bitterness toward the North in rural South Carolina in the 1920s and 1930s, 7-8

Close Air Support
    Provided by Marine Corps squadrons from the escort carriers Badoeng Strait (CVE-116) and Sicily (CVE-118) in 1950, during early part of the Korean War, 156-166

Cobb, Lieutenant Philip W., USNR
    As commanding officer of Bombing Squadron 151 in early 1945, perceived as not liking to fly, 117-118

Cold-Weather Operations
    Navy planes were cold-weather tested in Newfoundland in December 1946, 125-128

Columbia University, New York City
    Lee attended undergraduate courses in 1947-49, 130-132, 137, 193; Lee consciously avoided young instructors, 134-135, 141-142

Cook, Captain Harry E., Jr., USN (USNA, 1934)
    Favorable assessment as chief of staff to Commander Carrier Division Two in the early 1960s, 279; relations with the skipper of the flagship Enterprise (CVAN-65), 279-280

Corpus Christi (Texas) Naval Air Station
    Lee received training in Vultee SNVs and basic instrument training at Cabaniss Field in 1943, 41-42

Crawford, Captain John W., Jr., USN (USNA, 1942)
    As a member of Vice Admiral Hyman Rickover's staff in 1963, conducted part of Lee's interview to enter the nuclear program, 299, 301-305

Cuban Missile Crisis
    The Enterprise (CVAN-65), with Carrier Air Group Six embarked, was sent to Cuba in October 1962, 289-295

Dankworth, Commander Theodore P., USN (USNA, 1944)
    This detailer convinced Lee to interview with Vice Admiral Hyman Rickover in 1963 for a position he really didn't want, 297-300, 302-303

Demobilization
    Difficulty in keeping naval aviation squadrons going because of the loss of trained personnel right after World War II, 120-121

De Poix, Captain Vincent P., USN (USNA, 1939)
  Assessed as martinet-type skipper of the <u>Enterprise</u> (CVAN-65) in the early 1960s, 279-281; qualities for nuclear power program, 308

Dietrich, Captain Henry T., USN (USNA, 1926)
  As chief of staff to Commander Carrier Division 15 in the early 1950s, poor relations with his boss, Rear Admiral Richard Ruble, 166-168, 170

Dive-bombing
  Discussion of techniques for bombing land and ship targets, 54-59; capabilities of various Navy dive-bombers, 65-67, 179-180; bombing of targets in North Korea by carrier-based AD Skyraiders in 1952, 181, 184-186

Dordahl, Commander Joseph P., USNR
  Favorable assessment as executive officer of the <u>Alamo</u> (LSD-33) in the mid-1960s, 320, 333-334

Dosé, Commander Robert G., USN
  As skipper of VX-3 in 1955, asked Lee to test the AD-5N on the mirror landing system and angled deck of the carrier <u>Bennington</u> (CVA-20), 199; characterized as a brilliant natural aviator, 200-202

Education
  Rural public schools in South Carolina in the 1920s and 1930s, 5-8, 12; poor or no educational opportunities for blacks in rural South Carolina in the 1920s and 1930s, 5-7; Lee took two courses at Bowdoin College in 1946, 122; Lee took an undergraduate program at Columbia University, 1947-49, 129-143; Lee found his study of nuclear engineering effects at the Naval Postgraduate School from 1952 to 1954 much more demanding than expected, 186, 188-195

Eisenhower, Dwight D.
  President Eisenhower called for a unified war plan in the early 1960s, 247, 249

Electricity
  Lee was put in charge of overseeing research on converting heat directly to electricity in the late 1950s-early 1960s, 243-244, 246

Engen, Lieutenant Commander Donald D., USN
  Characterized as a brilliant natural aviator, 200-202

Eniwetok
  VF-15 pilots trained in the F6F at Eniwetok in August 1944, 79, 81-82; description of island facilities, 81-82

Enterprise, USS (CVAN-65)
   Embarked Carrier Air Group Six in 1962, 277; showcased during Mediterranean deployment in the late summer of 1962, 277, 279, 281-282; discussion of carrier's qualities, 282; sent to Cuba during the October 1962 missile crisis, 289-295; Lee was asked by Vice Admiral Hyman Rickover in 1963 to write a paper outlining how the officer complement of this carrier could be reduced, 301-302

Essex, USS (CV-9)
   Took on an air group in 1944 that had been rejected by another carrier skipper, 70-71; homing signal for guiding planes back to the ship, 90-92; weathered typhoon in December 1944, 100-101; relations between the air group and the ship's crew, 102; conditions on board in 1944, 103; role of the ready rooms, 105-106; quality of aviation mechanics in 1944, 110-111; mail call, 112
   See also Air Group 15

Essex-class Carriers
   Outstanding design of the Essex class, 99-100, 235-236; the size of these carriers was a factor in the acceptability of some jet aircraft in the 1950s, 207

F2H Banshee
   Favorable assessment of this plane by Lee, 197

F3F
   Maintenance of these Grumman biplane fighters at the Miami Naval Air Station in the early 1940s, 20, 22

F3H Demon
   One of the first Navy planes used for night flying in the 1950s, 233

F-4 Phantom II
   Lee's assessment of this jet aircraft, 206-207, 232, 285-287; shown off during Enterprise (CVAN-65) Mediterranean cruise in 1962, 283, 286

F4F Wildcat
   Early World War II fighter plane was inadequate to fight Japanese Zeros, 87

F4U Corsair
   Lee thinks the Corsair was the best fighter the Navy had during World War II, 88; heavily used by Marines during the Korean War, 155-156; operations from the Badoeng Strait (CVE-116), 162-163; F4U-5Ns used for night operations during the Korean War, 183

F6F Hellcat
   Lee trained in the F6Fs at Eniwetok in August 1944, 79-82; VF-15 pilot killed in his first combat mission in an F6F, 84; reliability of the .50-caliber machine guns in the F6F, 86; Lee's assessment of this fighter, 87-88; landing characteristics, 115; compared with the F8F, 125-126

F7U Cutlass
   Assessed as the worst airplane the Navy ever bought, 197-198, 207-208, 287

F-8 Crusader
   See F8U/F-8 Crusader

F8F Bearcat
   When flown in December 1946, demonstrated startling performance advantage when compared with the F6F, 125-126

F8U/F-8 Crusader
   The instability of this jet fighter should have made it unacceptable to the Navy, 206-207, 232-233; Lee checked out in the F-8 before assuming command of an air group in 1962, 275, 284; shown off by the Enterprise (CVAN-65) air group during a 1962 Mediterranean cruise, 283

F9F-5 Panther
   Flown by Marine pilots during the Korean War, 180-181

F9F-8 Cougar
   Lee's assessment of the first jet plane he flew, in the mid-1950s, 196-197; used to test the mirror landing system and angled decks in 1955, 199

F11F Tiger
   Characterized as not capable for night carrier operations in the mid-1950s, 233

FJ Fury
   Lee's assessment of this Navy plane that had been adapted from the Air Force F-86, 198

Families of Servicemen
   Support system for dependents in Jacksonville, Florida, when Attack Squadron 46 was deployed to the Mediterranean in 1959, 241; use of newsletters to keep the families of USS Alamo (LSD-33) crew members informed during 1964 deployment, 341

Feightner, Commander Edward L., USN
   Characterized as a brilliant natural aviator, 201

Fighter Squadron 33 (VF-33)
   Squadron commander removed in 1963 after several episodes with alcohol, 295-297

Fighting Squadron 15 (VF-15)
　　Personnel in 1944, 82-83; limited training for new pilots, 81-83; at Formosa in 1944, 84, 89-90, 95; during Leyte Gulf action, 93-95; in action in the Philippines in late 1944, 84-85, 92-93; compared unfavorably to VB-15, 98-99; routine on board the carrier, 105-106; logistic support, 113

Fleet Training Center, Norfolk, Virginia
　　Provided training on nuclear weapons effects in the late 1950s, 215-222

Ford Trimotor
　　Civilian aircraft in which Lee got his first plane ride in the late 1930s in South Carolina, 11-12

Formosa
　　VF-15 pilot killed near Formosa on first combat mission in an F6F in 1944, 84; VF-15 conducted fighter sweeps here, 88-90

Franklin D. Roosevelt, USS (CVA-42)
　　VA-46 embarked in this carrier on a cruise to Guantánamo in the late 1950s, 226-228

Frosch, Dr. Robert A.
　　Assistant Secretary of the Navy in the late 1960s-early 1970s who had a cynical but, unfortunately, accurate view of value of research grants funded by the Navy, 246, 348

Fry, Austin R., Ph.D.
　　Lee was impressed with Dr. Fry, who was head of the physics department at the Naval Postgraduate School in the early 1950s, 193

Fullinwider, Lieutenant Commander Peter L., USN (USNA, 1949)
　　Asked to review an article on submarine survivability while on the Joint Strategic Target Planning Staff in the early 1960s, 254

General Line School
　　Lee attended this training program for non-Naval Academy officers at Newport, Rhode Island, in 1949-50, 144-148

Guam
　　VB-15 provided close air support during invasion of Guam in the summer of 1944, 75-76

Guantánamo, Cuba
　　Navy squadrons conducted weapons training here in the late 1950s, 227; the Enterprise (CVAN-65) deployed here in the early 1960s, 276

HO3S
   The escort carrier Badoeng Strait (CVE-116) had one of the first carrier-based helicopters during the Korean War, 159-161, 170

Halsey, Admiral William F., Jr., USN (USNA, 1904)
   As Commander Third Fleet in October 1944, role in the Battle of Leyte Gulf, 94

Harnish, Commander William Max, USN (USNA, 1943)
   Assessed as martinet-type executive officer of the Enterprise (CVAN-65) in the early 1960s, 279-281; qualities for nuclear power program, 308-309

Hawkins, Commander Arthur Ray, USN
   Lee's predecessor as commanding officer of Attack Squadron 46 in the late 1950s, 223, 225-229

Hayward, Rear Admiral John T., USN (USNA, 1930)
   Assessed as a Commander Carrier Division Two on board the USS Enterprise (CVAN-65) in the early 1960s, 277-279, 283

Helicopters
   Lee felt his boss, Commander Carrier Division 15, didn't take full advantage of the benefits of having access to one of the first carrier-based helicopters in the early 1950s, 159-161, 170

Holloway, Vice Admiral James L., Jr., USN (USNA, 1919)
   Devised Holloway Plan shortly after World War II for the education and training of naval officers, 130, 144-147; one of the few flag officers that Vice Admiral Hyman Rickover admired, 310; assessed by Lee, 314-315

Holloway, Captain James L., III, USN (USNA, 1943)
   May have been accepted to the nuclear power program in 1943 on the basis of Vice Admiral Hyman Rickover's admiration for his father, 310-311; Lee's assessment of Holloway, 313-315

Holloway Plan
   Lee was sent to Columbia University for undergraduate courses in 1947 under the conditions of this plan, 130; General Line School established to train non-Naval Academy officers, 144-147

Hong Kong
   Great shopping bargains for Alamo (LSD-33) crew members during brief visit in 1964, 327

Hyland, Rear Admiral John J., Jr., USN (USNA, 1934)
   As member of the Joint Strategic Target Planning Staff in the early 1960s, 250, 260, 269, 272

Inchon, South Korea
   Tight security surrounded planning sessions in September 1950 in Tokyo for Inchon landings, 156-157; Carrier Division 15 provided close air support during landings, 157-160

Intelligence
   Aerial reconnaissance photos were used to help Air Group Six plan for possible bombing strikes against Cuba in October 1962, 290-291

Intrepid, USS (CVA-11)
   Made Mediterranean deployment in 1959 with VA-46 as one of the squadrons in the air group, 229-242; quality of top officers in 1959, 229; high morale in carrier, 235

Jacksonville (Florida) Naval Air Station
   Dive-bomber training at Cecil Field in 1943, 46-52; Lee kept on as an assistant instructor in 1943-44, 60-62; Lee's mishaps in SBDs, 47, 61-62; home base for Attack Squadron 46 in the late 1950s, 223-225

James, Commander Jack M., USN (USNA, 1942)
   As air group commander in the Intrepid (CVA-11) in the late 1950s, 229, 237

Japan
   Extremely cooperative with the U.S. Navy's efforts to establish bases in Japan during the Korean War, 154; Inchon landings planned at September 1950 meetings in Tokyo, 156-157; American naval personnel were given liberty during the Korean War in Sasebo, 160-161, 167, 176-177; liberty in Yokosuka during the Korean War, 181-182; when Alamo (LSD-33) skipper Lee regretted letting his crew bring home motorcycles purchased in Yokosuka in 1964, 327; the Alamo carried the ground equipment and personnel of a Marine air squadron to Yokosuka via the great circle route in 1965, 337-338

Jenkins, Commander Charles W., USN (USNA, 1939)
   As officer in charge of the weapons school at the Norfolk fleet training center in the mid-1950s, helped Lee gain his confidence as a public speaker, 217

Jet Aircraft
   Discussion of various jet engines, 197-198, 206, 286; quicker cycle of jet operations compared to propeller, 214

Jews
   Lee's first real exposure to Jews came while he was living in New York City in 1947-49, 133-134, 138-139

Joint Chiefs of Staff (JCS)
   Only role of the JCS in strategic target planning in the early 1960s was to be briefed about the final plan and give approval, 264, 268

Joint Strategic Target Planning Staff (JSTPS)
   Strategic target plans consolidated among the services in the early 1960s, 247-249; questionable estimates of survivability used by the Air Force, 251-252, 272-273; quality of naval officers on the staff, 250, 255; relations between mid-level officers of the various services, 270
   See also Single Integrated Operational Plan

Jorgensen, Lieutenant (junior grade) Carl, USNR
   Lee's recollections of Jorgensen as his platoon leader during preflight training in 1942-43, 32-33

Joy, Vice Admiral C. Turner, USN (USNA, 1916)
   As Commander U.S. Naval Forces Far East in the early 1950s, 151

Kidd, Captain Isaac C., Jr., USN (USNA, 1942)
   Lee's assessment of Kidd as aide to CNO Admiral David McDonald in the mid-1960s, 346-347

Kingsville (Texas) Naval Air Station
   Lee underwent advanced flight training here in 1943, 42-44

Korea, North
   Bombing of targets in North Korea by carrier-based attack planes in 1952, 181, 184-186

Korea, South
   U.S. escort carriers provided close air support to help stabilize the Pusan perimeter in 1950 in the early stages of the Korean War, 155-157, 165; Inchon landings in September 1950, 157-160

Korean War
   Two escort carriers loaded Marine squadrons for deployment to Korea in July 1950, 150-151; planning done by staff of Commander U.S. Naval Force Far East in Tokyo, 151-153, 156-157; U.S. Navy surveyed bases in Japan for support in war effort, 152, 154; Pusan perimeter, 155-157, 165; Inchon landings, 157-160; close air support of ground troops, 162-166; liberty in Japan, 160-161, 167, 176-177, 181-182; reversal of fortunes in late 1950, 164-166; night air operations, 183; lack of opposition from enemy aircraft, 184; example of routine bombing operation, 184-186

Kramer, Lieutenant Henry H., USNR
   VB-15 pilot drafted to switch to flying fighter planes in 1944, 81; killed at Peleliu on first combat mission in an F6F, 84

Lancer Award
   The <u>Alamo</u> (LSD-33) earned this distinction for top performance during exercise Silver Lance in early 1965, 330, 336-337, 339-340

Leadership
   World War II ace David McCampbell assessed as a leader, 97, 201; Lee came on too strong when he assumed command of his first squadron in 1958, 223-225; Lee made it a point in his various commands to keep in close touch with his leading petty officers, 238-240

Leavitt, Commander Eben, Jr., USN (USNA, 1945)
   Carrier Air Group commander Lee had this squadron commander relieved after several episodes with alcohol, 295-297

Lee, Vice Admiral Kent L., USN
   Parents and forebears, 1-5, 7-8, 13, 34; siblings, 3, 13; birth and early years in South Carolina, 3-13; children, 178, 213; Navy enlistment and boot training in 1940, 13-17; aviation machinist's mate school, 17-20; aviation machinist's mate at Miami Naval Air Station, 1941-42, 20-29; aviation cadet and flight training, 1942-43; 27-52; dive-bombing instructor, 1943-44, 60-62; training in Bombing Squadron 100 in 1944, 63-64; duty with Bombing Squadron 15 and Fighting Squadron 15 in 1944, 69-115; duty with Bombing Squadron 151 in 1945, 115-119; duty with Bombing Squadron 17, 1945-46, 120-129; studied at Columbia University, 1947-49, 129-143; General Line School at Newport, 1949-50, 144-148; staff, Commander Carrier Division 15, 1950-51, 148-177; operations officer, Attack Squadron 115, 1951-52, 178-187; student, Naval Postgraduate School, 1952-54, 186, 188-195; duty with Air Development Squadron Three, 1954-56, 195-214, 239-240; head, weapons section, Fleet Training Center, Norfolk, 1956-58, 215-222; commanding officer, Attack Squadron 46, 1958-59, 222-243, 334; technical aide nuclear physics, power branch, Material Sciences Division, Office of Naval Research, 1959-60, 243-246; operational planner, Joint Strategic Target Planning Staff, 1960-62, 247-274; commander Carrier Air Group Six, 1962-63, 276-308, 334; instruction in nuclear propulsion, 1963-64, 307-317; commanding officer of the <u>Alamo</u> (LSD-33), 1964-65, 317-344; executive assistant to the Assistant Secretary of the Navy (Research and Development), 1965-67, 246, 339, 345-351; director of the Office of Program Appraisal, 1970-72, 347-348; deputy director of the Joint Strategic Target Planning Staff, 1972-73, 265

Lee, Mary Edith Buckley
    Interest in genealogy, 1-2; met Lee in Oakland in December 1942, 33-34; dated Lee when he was stationed at Brunswick, Maine, in 1946, 122-123; trip along the East Coast with Lee in 1948, 136; married in 1948, 136; children, 178, 213; as aviator's wife, 211-212, 241

LeMay, General Curtis E., USAF
    As Air Force Chief of Staff in the early 1960s, wanted Air Force control over the unified war planning function, 249; method of running the Strategic Air Command, 258-259

Leyte Gulf, Battle of
    Lee made his first night carrier landing on the Essex (CV-9) in October 1944 during the aftermath of Leyte action, 93-95; Lieutenant Commander James Mini limped back to the Essex with his windshield covered with oil, 99

Liberty
    In Miami in the early 1940s, 27; in Eniwetok in 1944, 81-82; in Ulithi in 1944, 111-112; in Sasebo, Japan, during the Korean War, 160-161, 167, 176-177; liberty in Yokosuka, Japan, during the Korean War, 181-182; U.S. naval officer caught gonorrhea from an American woman while on liberty in Japan during the Korean War, 182; as commanding officer of Attack Squadron 46 during a Mediterranean deployment in 1959, Lee gave young squadron members a talk on VD that paid off with lower instances of disease, 230-232; a few Alamo (LSD-33) crew members contracted VD on liberty in the Philippines in the mid-1960s, 325

Liquor
    See Alcohol

Logistics
    Support of carrier-based aircraft was excellent in the Central Pacific in 1944, 113-114

Los Alamitos (California) Naval Air Station
    Site of primary flight training for Lee in 1943, 35-41

MacArthur, General Douglas, USA (USMA, 1903)
    As Supreme Commander Allied Powers Far East during the Korean War, 153-154, 161, 164; held top secret planning session in Tokyo in September 1950 for Inchon landings, 156-157

Mail
    Frequency of mail call on board the Essex (CV-9) in 1944, 112

Maintenance
    See Aviation Maintenance

Manila, Philippines
  Planes from Fighting Squadron 15 attacked a Japanese destroyer at Manila in late 1944, 92-93

Manteo (North Carolina) Naval Auxiliary Air Station
  Forming and retraining of Bombing Squadron 151 done here in early 1945, 116-119

Marianas Islands
  Bombing Squadron 15 provided close air support for Marines invading Guam and Tinian in mid-1944, 75-76

Marine Corps, U.S.
  Demanding drill instructor at Parris Island boot camp in 1942, 16; Marine squadrons transported to Korea in escort carriers in the summer of 1950, 151-152; Marine air operations during Korean War, 155, 163-164, 181; Marine air squadrons compared to Navy, 171; landing group embarked in the Alamo (LSD-33) for Vietnam duty in mid-1964, 321-323, 325-326; quality of Marine officers Lee dealt with in the mid-1960s, 326; the Alamo transported to Japan the ground equipment and personnel of a Marine air squadron that was on its way to Vietnam in 1965, 337-338

Massey, Rear Admiral Forsyth, USN (USNA, 1931)
  As Commander Fleet Air Norfolk in 1963, supported Lee's effort to have a squadron commander relieved for alcoholism, 296-297

Masterton, Rear Admiral Paul, USN (USNA, 1933)
  Lee's assessment of Masterton as commanding officer of the Intrepid (CVA-11) in the late 1950s, 229, 231, 236; as member of the Joint Strategic Target Planning Staff in the early 1960s, 250, 260, 269, 272

Matthews, Aviation Machinist's Mate Third Class Herbert S., USN
  Chosen to become an aviation cadet in 1942, 28

McCampbell, Commander David, USN (USNA, 1933)
  As Commander Air Group 15 in 1944, recollections of a bombing squadron commander's difficulties with carrier landings, 67; skill as a pilot, 70, 74, 89, 96-97, 118, 201-202; Lee saw him as a better pilot than administrator, 97; brought actor Wayne Morris to his air group, 104

McDonald, Commander David L., USN (USNA, 1928)
  As executive officer of the aircraft carrier Essex (CV-9) in 1944, 102-103

McNeill, Commander Wilfred J., Jr., USN (USNA, 1943)
  Squadron commander killed during a night flying operation from the Intrepid (CVA-11) in May 1959, 233, 235

Mediterranean Sea
　　Dangers for sailors of catching venereal disease in various Mediterranean ports in the late 1950s, 229-230; poor conditions in the Mediterranean for flight operations in the late 1950s, 237; ports visited by the USS Intrepid (CVA-11) during Sixth Fleet deployment in 1959, 242; the newly commissioned carrier Enterprise (CVAN-65) made a Mediterranean cruise in 1962 to show off the ship, 279-282

Miami, Florida
　　Hospitable city for naval personnel during World War II, 27; see also Naval Air Station, Miami

Miami (Florida) Naval Air Station
　　Lee assigned to maintenance division here in 1941, 20-23; officers and petty officers in 1941, 20-21

Michaelis, Captain Frederick H., USN (USNA, 1940)
　　As skipper of the Enterprise (CVAN-65) in 1963, qualities for the nuclear power program, 309

Middendorf, J. William, II
　　Lee's assessment of Middendorf as as dud when serving as Secretary of the Navy in the mid-1970s, 348

Midway, USS (CVE-63)
　　Lee rode this jeep carrier from San Diego to Pearl Harbor in March 1944, 62-63

Miller, Captain Gerald E., USN (USNA, 1942)
　　Lee's assessment of Miller, 123-124, 174, 279, 346; sent to Omaha on short notice in the late 1950s to help the Navy's effort for strong involvement in strategic target planning, 248, 269; efforts to prove submarine survivability, 254-255, 266, 274; involved in little league in Omaha, 255-256; helped Lee get air group command after serving together in Omaha, 275

Mills, Commander Richard H., USN
　　Trained new pilots to VB-15 in 1944, 73-74; as detailer in 1956, assigned former squadron mate Lee to undesirable duty, 215

Mini, Lieutenant Commander James H., USN (USNA, 1935)
　　Initial difficulty with carrier landings in the SB2C during World War II, 67-68; Lee's assessment of Mini, 73-74, 226; instituted training program for new pilots to VB-15, 73-74, 97; his plane was crippled during action at San Bernardino Strait in October 1944, 99

Missiles
　　Sidewinder air-to-air missile was favorably evaluated by VX-3 in the mid-1930s, 199; role of the Polaris ballistic missile in strategic target planning in the early 1960s,

247-249, 251, 254, 260, 266, 270, 273-274; Carrier Air Group Six squadrons planned to attack Cuban missile sites during the October 1962 incident, 289-291

Morris, Lieutenant Bert DeWayne, Jr., USNR
Anecdote about Morris, an actor and Lee's fellow VF-15 pilot on board the Essex (CV-9) in 1944, 104

Morse, Dr. Robert W.
As Assistant Secretary of the Navy for Research and Development in the mid-1960s, interviewed Lee to be his executive assistant, 339, 345-346; academic background, 345; assessed by Lee, 347-348; Lee's duties as aide, 349

Muller, Lieutenant (junior grade), USN
Assessed favorably as Lee's dive-bombing instructor in 1943, 47

N2S Kaydet
Stearman trainer that was flown by aviation cadets during primary training in 1943, 35-37, 42

Nagasaki, Japan
In the early 1950s, Lee toured by air the site of the second atomic bomb hit, 161

Naval Academy, U.S.
Lee refreshed himself on ship handling by practicing with the Academy's YPs in 1964 before taking command of his first ship, 317-318

Naval Air Stations
Norfolk NAS provided mediocre training for aviation machinist's mates in 1940-41, 18-19; Miami NAS was well run by Captain Gerald Bogan in 1941, 20-23; Los Alamitos, California, NAS was the site of primary flight training in 1943, 35-51; Cabaniss Field at Corpus Christi NAS provided basic instrument training for Lee in 1943, 41-42; Lee received advanced flight training at Kingsville, Texas, NAS in 1943, 42-44; Lee received dive-bomber training at Jacksonville NAS in 1943, 46-52; Lee was an assistant flight instructor at Jacksonville in 1943-44, 60-62; Bombing Squadron 151 formed and retrained at Manteo, North Carolina, Naval Auxiliary Air Station in early 1945, 116-119; Argentia, Newfoundland, NAS was the site of cold-weather testing of Navy planes in December 1946, 125-128; naval aviators studying in New York in the late 1940s flew periodically from Floyd Bennett Field in Brooklyn, 131, 139, 141; the staff of Carrier Division 15 surveyed a former Japanese airbase at Atsugi, Japan, in the summer of 1950 to determine its potential value as a U.S. naval air station during the Korean War, 152, 154; Jacksonville NAS was the home base for Attack Squadron 46 in the late 1950s, 223-225

Naval Aviation
   Lee worked on a variety of prewar aircraft as an aviation machinist's mate at Miami Naval Air Station in 1941-42, 20-29; preflight training at St. Mary's College, Moraga, California, in 1942-43, 28-33, 40-41; primary flight training at Los Alamitos Naval Air Station in 1943, 35-41; advanced training in Texas in 1943, 41-44; advanced training split between carrier and transport/patrol pilots, 44-45; operational training in dive-bombers in 1943, 46-52, 60-62; carrier landing practice, 47, 49-52; techniques for dive-bombing land and ship targets, 54-59; fighter sweeps during World War II, 88-90; pairing of fighters and scout bombers, 85-87, 98; aerial combat routine during World War II, 105-108; training of Bombing Squadron 151 in 1945, 115-119; training of Bombing Squadron 17, 1945-46, 120-129; difficulty in keeping naval aviation squadrons going because of the demobilization of trained personnel right after World War II, 120-121; Navy planes were cold-weather tested in Newfoundland in December 1946, 125-128; naval aviators studying in New York in the late 1940s flew periodically from Floyd Bennett Field in Brooklyn, 131, 139, 141; the escort carriers of Carrier Division 15 provided early support for the Korean War in 1950, 148-177; Attack Squadron 115 trained from May to December 1951, then operated in support of the Korean War in 1952, 178-186; night flying during the Korean War, 183; tacan, mirror landing system, and angled decks tested in the mid-1950s, 199, 204, 208; low-altitude flying tactics tested in the mid-1950s, 199, 204-205; the Bureau of Personnel established in 1957 a formal selection system for choosing aviation squadron commanders, 222; operations of Attack Squadron 46 in 1958-59, 222-243, 334; night flying in the late 1950s, 233-235; good support for dependents, 241; Air Group Six went aboard the new carrier _Enterprise_ (CVAN-65), made a Mediterranean deployment, and was on station for the Cuban Missile Crisis, 276-308; black shoe versus brown shoe rivalry, 342-344

Naval Forces Far East, U.S.
   This staff had to be temporarily augmented during the early days of the Korean War until permanent help could be arranged, 153-154

Naval Postgraduate School, Monterey, California
   Lee found his graduate work in nuclear engineering effects from 1952 to 1954 much more demanding than expected, 186, 188-195

Naval Research, Office of
   See Office of Naval Research

Naval Reserve Officer Training Corps (NROTC)
   Lee attended Columbia University from 1947 to 1949 under the auspices of this program, 130, 140-142

Naval Training Station, Norfolk, Virginia
See Norfolk (Virginia) Naval Training Station

Navigation
Discussion of the use of plotting boards and dead reckoning to help planes make it back an aircraft carrier, 90-92; scout bombers were often paired on missions with fighters to help with navigation, 98; ships of Amphibious Squadron Three on its way home from Yokosuka in 1964 tested themselves by navigating with sextants and then comparing results, 328-329

Navy Department
Discussion of the quality of Secretaries and other key position-holders in the mid-1960s, 346-348

Navy Special Weapons School, Norfolk, Virginia
Lee taught a series of introductory courses in atomic weapons here in the mid-1950s, 215-222

Neeb, Commander Lewis H., USN
Asked to review article on submarine survivability while on the Joint Strategic Target Planning Staff in the early 1960s, 254

Neefus, Colonel James, USMC
Officer on Carrier Division 15 staff in the early 1950s, served as liaison with Marine squadrons, 150, 159

Nelson, Lieutenant (junior grade) Loren, USNR
Kept on as a flight instructor in 1943 at Jacksonville Naval Air Station after graduating from flight training, 47, 62; sent as replacement pilot to VP-15 in 1944, 70, 72; wingman Nelson led his squadron skipper's crippled plane back to the Essex (CV-9) after San Bernardino Strait action, 99

Newfoundland
Argentia Naval Air Station was the site of cold-weather testing of Navy planes in December 1946, 125-128

Newport, Rhode Island
Site of General Line School for naval officers in the late 1940s, 144-148

New York City
Lee experienced culture of, and enjoyed living in New York and studying at Columbia University in 1947-49, 130-134, 137-138, 140-141, 143

New York Naval Air Station, Floyd Bennett Field,
Naval aviators studying in the New York area in the late 1940s flew periodically from this field, 131, 139, 141

Night Flying Operations
    Lee made his first night carrier landing on the Essex (CV-9) in October 1944 during the aftermath of Leyte action, 93-95; F4U-5Ns used for night operations during the Korean War, 183; the A4D was difficult to handle in night carrier operations in the late 1950s, 233-235

Nitze, Paul H.
    Secretary of the Navy who placed great faith in his aide in the mid-1960s, Captain Elmo Zumwalt, 346-347

Norfolk (Virginia) Naval Air Station
    Lee underwent unsatisfactory aviation machinist's mate training here in 1940-41, 18-19

Norfolk (Virginia) Naval Training Station
    Lee underwent boot training at Norfolk in the latter part of 1940, 15-17

North Korea
    See Korea, North

NROTC
    See Naval Reserve Officer Training Corps

Nuclear Power
    Vice Admiral Hyman Rickover's interviewing methods for prospective trainees in 1963, 297-307; training program in the mid-1960s, 311-316; instructors, 312-313

Nuclear Weapons
    Lee toured by air in the early 1950s the site of the second atomic bomb hit at Nagasaki, Japan, 161; in order to get a bigger budget, the Navy increased its atomic weapons capability in the mid-1950s, 216; Lee taught an introductory course on atomic weapons at Fleet Training Center, Norfolk, Virginia, in the mid-1950s, 215-222; in the early 1960s, the Joint Strategic Target Planning Staff devised the Single Integrated Operational Plan for the targeting of nuclear weapons, 247-274

Office of Naval Research, Washington, D.C.
    Lee was in charge of research on converting heat directly to electricity in 1959-60, 243-244, 246; Lee got bogged down by bureaucracy of civil service during duty here, 244-245

Ofstie, Captain Ralph A., USN (USNA, 1919)
    Popular as commanding officer of the Essex (CV-9) in 1944, 103

Omaha, Nebraska
    Description of environment and extracurricular activities at Offutt Air Force Base, 255-256

O'Rourke, Commander Gerald G., USN (USNA, 1945)
Suggested by the executive officer of the Enterprise (CVAN-65) in 1963 to be his replacement, but rejected by Vice Admiral Hyman Rickover, 297-298, 300-301, 303

Panoff, Robert
As a member of Vice Admiral Hyman Rickover's staff in 1963, conducted part of Lee's interview to enter the nuclear program, 299, 304

Parker, Vice Admiral Edward N., USN (USNA, 1925)
As head of the Navy contingent on the Joint Strategic Target Planning Staff in the early 1960s, 250, 257, 260, 269, 272; helped Lee get an air group command after serving on the JSTPS, 275

Pay and Allowances
Rates of pay for junior Navy enlisted personnel in the early 1940s, 25-26

Peleliu
New VF-15 pilot killed at Peleliu in September 1944 on first mission in an F6F, 84

Personnel
Difficulty in keeping naval aviation squadrons going because of the demobilization of trained personnel right after World War II, 120-121; the Bureau of Personnel established in 1957 a formal system for selection of aviation squadron commanders, 222; Lee was asked by Vice Admiral Hyman Rickover in 1963 to write a paper outlining how the officer complement of the carrier Enterprise (CVAN-65) could be reduced, 301-302

Petersen, Commander Forrest S., USN (USNA, 1945)
Assessed as typical of the type of officer Vice Admiral Hyman Rickover wanted for the nuclear power program, 309-310; in contention with Lee to become executive officer of the Enterprise (CVAN-65), 316-317

Philippines
VF-15 provided air support for the invasion of the Philippines in the fall of 1944, 84-85, 95; planes from VF-15 attacked a Japanese destroyer at Manila, 92-93; several Alamo (LSD-33) crew members contracted venereal disease during port visits in 1964, 325

Philippine Sea, USS (CV-47)
Used for attacks on North Korea during the Korean War, 165-166; operations off Korea in 1952, 180; night air qualifications held on board in December 1951, 183

Pirie, Vice Admiral Robert B., USN (USNA, 1926)
Interested in keeping aviation cadets and planes in good operating condition immediately prior to World War II, 21; responsible for prolonging the A-5/RA-5C in the 1960s, even though it was a lousy aircraft, 289

Planning
Headquarters of Commander U.S. Naval Forces Far East was used for planning and directing early Korean War operations in 1950, 151-153; tight security surrounded planning sessions in September 1950 in Tokyo for Inchon landings, 156-157; work of the Joint Strategic Target Planning Staff in establishing overall U.S. nuclear weapons planning in the early 1960s, 247-274; preparation for possible strikes against Cuba in October 1962, 290-291

Polaris Ballistic Missile System
Role in strategic target planning in the early 1960s, 247-249, 251, 254, 260, 266, 270, 273-274

Power, General Thomas S., USAF
As commander of the Strategic Air Command in the early 1960s, felt the Air Force should be given charge of the centralized war planning operation, including such Navy assets as Polaris, 249-251, 260-261; angered when aircraft carriers came out looking good in a survivability study, 253; directed submarine survivability study, 254, 273-274; assessed by Lee, 257-260

Preflight Training
At St. Mary's College, Moraga, California, in late 1942-early 1943, 28-33, 40-41

Promotions
See Advancement of Enlisted Personnel

Public Relations
The newly commissioned carrier _Enterprise_ (CVAN-65) made a Mediterranean cruise in 1962 to show off the ship, 277, 279, 281-282

RA-5C Vigilante
Lee thought this conversion from the A-5 Vigilante was a dog, 288-289

Racial Segregation
Poor or no educational opportunities for blacks in rural South Carolina in the 1920s and 1930s, 5-6; blacks in South Carolina largely relegated to farmhand role, 6-7

Reconnaissance
Aerial photos were used to help Air Group Six plan for possible bombing strikes against Cuba in October 1962, 290-291

Recruit Training
    Lee underwent boot training at the Norfolk Naval Training Station in the latter part of 1940, 15-17

Reid, Aviation Structural Mechanic Third Class H. M., USN
    Selected as an aviation cadet with Lee in 1942, but did not make it through the program, 28-29, 38

Religion
    Role in family and community life in rural South Carolina in the 1920s and 1930s, 8

Research and Development
    See Office of Naval Research

Rickover, Vice Admiral Hyman G., USN (USNA, 1922)
    Lee feels it was his academic credentials that first attracted Rickover's attention, 194-195; interview techniques, 297-307; admiration for Vice Admiral James Holloway, Jr., may have influenced Rickover's selection of the admiral's son for the nuclear power program in 1963, 310-311

Rigg, Lieutenant Commander James F., USN
    As commanding officer of VF-15 in 1944, criticized for having no initiation or training period for new pilots, 83, 97

Roach, Lieutenant Walter, USNR
    As executive officer of VB-151 in 1946, 117, 123

Rockwell, Theodore
    As a member of Vice Admiral Hyman Rickover's staff in 1963, conducted part of Lee's interview to enter the nuclear program, 299, 304

Ruble, Rear Admiral Richard W., USN (USNA, 1923)
    Assessed as Commander Carrier Division 15 in 1950-51, 151-153, 169; as operational commander, 160, 169-170; poor relationship with his chief of staff, Captain Henry Dietrich, 166-168, 170

SBC Helldiver
    Maintenance of this Curtiss dive-bomber at the Miami Naval Air Station in the early 1940s, 20, 22

SB2C Helldiver
    Replaced SBD Dauntless as standard U.S. Navy dive-bomber in mid-1943, 46, 52, 63; assessment of this plane, 64-66, 77-79, 188; SB2C's potential difficulties in carrier landings, 67-68, 70; didn't have enough power to keep up with F6Fs, 85-86; tendency to float when landing, 114-115

SBD Dauntless
   Lee's assessment of this plane that was used for dive-bomber training in mid-1943, 46-54, 64-66; Lee had a small accident while taxiing in an SBD during training, 47; Lee survived a midair collision between two SBDs at Jacksonville in 1944, 61-62

SNJ Texan
   Lee flew this North American trainer during advanced flight training at Kingsville Naval Air Station in 1943, 42

SNV Valiant
   Lee flew this Vultee trainer during advanced flight training at Corpus Christi, Texas, in 1943, 41

Safety
   Not a specific priority in naval aviation until well into World War II, 40-41; VB-15 skipper stressed safety during initial training for new pilots in 1944, 73-74; after a high number of casualties in VA-46 in the late 1950s, Lee instituted a stringent safety program that paid off, 226-227, 237-238, 242-243

Sable, USS (IX-81)
   Advanced flight students were required to make eight carrier landings on the Sable in the course of training during World War II, 47, 49-52

St. Mary's College, Moraga, California
   Lee attended preflight aviation cadet training here in late 1942-early 1943, 28-33, 40-41

Sasebo, Japan
   Provided liberty opportunities for U.S. Navy men during the Korean War, 160-161, 167, 176-177

Schwartz, Captain Walter W., USN (USNA, 1945)
   Lee's fellow student in nuclear power training in the mid-1960s was killed in a 1966 auto accident, 310-311

Shuff, Commander John W., USN
   Squadron commander killed during a night flying operation in the 1950s, 233, 235

Ship Handling
   Taught at the Navy's General Line School in the late 1940s, 144-146; Lee brushed up on ship handling with the Naval Academy's YPs in 1964, 317-318; Lee used a creative maneuver to enable a motor torpedo boat to be loaded in the Alamo (LSD-33) in 1964, 324-325; Lee built a device in the Alamo to make coming alongside another ship more easy, 332-333

Sicily, USS (CVE-118)
   Ordered to take on board Marine squadrons for deployment to Korean waters in July 1950, 150-151; operated as unit of Task Group 96.8 during Korean War, 155-156, 162-165, 173-177; Captain John S. Thach was a flamboyant, very capable commanding officer in 1950-51, 172-175

Sidewinder
   This air-to-air missile was favorably evaluated by VX-3 in the mid-1930s, 199

Silver Lance, Exercise
   The Alamo (LSD-33) won the Lancer Award for top performance during this amphibious exercise in early 1965, 336-337, 339-340

Single Integrated Operational Plan (SIOP)
   Air Force tried to control this joint service project in the early 1960s, 251, 257, 268; Lee faults the plan for not planning reserve assets, 253-254, 268; mechanics of putting together the plan, 261-263; target selection, 263-266

Sixth Fleet, U.S.
   The USS Intrepid (CVA-11) made a successful Mediterranean cruise in 1959 with VA-46 as one of the squadrons in the air group, 229-242; the newly commissioned carrier Enterprise (CVAN-65) made a Mediterranean cruise in 1962 to show off the ship, 277, 279, 281-282

Snakes
   Swim call in the Alamo (LSD-33) in the South China Sea in 1964 had to be curtailed because of poisonous sea snakes, 322-323

Snyder, Captain J. Edward, Jr., USN (USNA, 1945)
   Lee's recollections of Snyder as a technical assistant to Assistant Secretary of the Navy Robert Morse in the mid-1960s, 349-351

South Carolina
   Lee family farm near Florence in the 1920s and 1930s, 3-4, 9-11; rural public schools in the 1920s and 1930s, 5-8, 12; residual resentment about the Civil War in the 1920s and 1930s, 7-8; role of religion in rural life, 8

South Korea
   See Korea, South

Soviet Union
   Target sites set by the Joint Strategic Target Planning Staff in the early 1960s, 265

Stewart, Lieutenant Commander Marlar E., USN
   Characterized as a brilliant natural aviator, 201

Strategic Air Command (SAC)
SAC's influence pervaded the Single Integrated Operational Plan developed in the early 1960s, 251, 261, 269-270; didn't see the need to plan for reserve assets in strategic planning, 253-254, 268; dominated areas of the Joint Strategic Target Planning Staff in the early 1960s, 257; discussion of typical SAC officer, 257-258; strategic squadron provided intelligence for target selection, 263; fail-safe ability to recall planes in the event of an emergency, 267

Strategic Target Planning
See Joint Strategic Target Planning Staff

Submarines
Survivability studied by the Joint Strategic Target Planning Staff in the early 1960s, 254-255, 272-274

Tactics
Doctrine for carrier fighter combat in the Pacific in 1944, 107-108; methods of attacking ground targets in North Korea in 1952, 184-186; development of techniques for low-level atomic weapons delivery by A4Ds in the mid-1950s, 204-205; preparation for possible strikes against Cuba in October 1962, 290-291

Target Planning
In the early 1960s, the Joint Strategic Target Planning staff devised the Single Integrated Operational Plan for the targeting of nuclear weapons, 247-274; preparation for possible strikes against Cuba in October 1962, 290-291

Thach, Captain John S., USN (USNA, 1927)
Lee's recollections of Thach as commanding officer of the Sicily (CVE-118) in the early 1950s, 172-175

Tinian
VB-15 provided close air support during the invasion of Tinian during the summer of 1944, 75-76

Tokyo, Japan
Headquarters of Commander U.S. Naval Forces Far East used for planning and directing early Korean War operations in 1950, 151-153; tight security surrounded planning sessions in September 1950 in Tokyo for Inchon landings, 156-157

Training
Lee's boot training at Norfolk in 1940, 15-17; aviation machinist's mate school in 1940-41, 18-19; preflight aviation cadet training in 1942-43, 30-33, 40-41; primary flight training at Los Alamitos Naval Air Station in 1943, 35-41; advanced training in Texas in 1943, 41-44; advanced training split between carrier and transport/patrol pilots, 44-45; operational training in

dive-bombers in 1943, 46-52, 60-62; carrier landing practice, 47, 49-52; new arrivals to VB-15 in 1944 were given more than a week of training, 73-75; new pilots were forced to do their own training in VF-15 in 1944, 83; VB-151 pilots trained in North Carolina in early 1945, 116-119; Lee attended General Line School, a training program for non-Naval Academy officers, at Newport, Rhode Island, in 1949-50, 144-148; Fleet Training Center, Norfolk, Virginia, provided training on nuclear weapons effects in the mid-1950s, 215-222; nuclear power training program in 1963-64, 311-316; Lee brushed up on ship handling with the Naval Academy's YPs in 1964 before taking command of his own ship, 317-318

Typhoons
Lee's recollections of weathering a 1944 typhoon in the Essex (CV-9), 100-101

Ulithi Atoll
Liberty in this mid-Pacific atoll included a lot of drinking in 1944, 111-112

V-5 Program
Lee reenlisted as an aviation cadet in 1942, and attended preflight school at St. Mary's College in Moraga, California, 28-33, 40-41

Valley Forge, USS (CV-45)
Shakedown cruise to Guantánamo Bay, Cuba, in early 1947, 128-129; the only aircraft carrier in position to be of immediate assistance when the Korean War broke out, 129, 154-155, 165, 177

Venereal Disease
American naval officer caught gonorrhea from an American woman while on liberty in Japan during the Korean War, 182; as commanding officer of Attack Squadron 46 during a Mediterranean deployment in 1959, Lee gave young squadron members a talk on VD that paid off with lower instances of disease, 230-232; a few Alamo (LSD-33) crew members contracted VD on liberty in the Philippines in the mid-1960s, 325

Vietnam War
The Alamo (LSD-33) transported Marine landing groups up and down the coast of Vietnam in 1964, 321-324, 341; the Central Intelligence Agency provided motor torpedo boats to the Vietnamese for raids against North Vietnam in the mid-1960s, 323

VX-3
See Air Development Squadron Three

Watanabe, Dr. Michael
    Lee found Dr. Watanabe's quantum mechanics course at the Naval Postgraduate School in the early 1950s extremely difficult, 189-190

Weather
    The USS *Essex* (CV-9) went through a typhoon in the Central Pacific in late 1944, 100-101; Navy planes were cold-weather tested in Newfoundland in December 1946, 125-128; the USS *Alamo* enjoyed much more pleasant weather in 1965 when crossing the Pacific on a rhumb line than the great circle route, 337-338

Weinel, Rear Admiral John P., USN (USNA, 1939)
    Aviation flag officer assessed by Lee as being a top-notch operational commander, 279

Wellings, Captain Timothy F., USN (USNA, 1921A)
    As naval science professor at Columbia University in the late 1940s, gave his charges a great deal of personal freedom, 140

Yates, Captain Earl P., USN (USNA, 1944)
    Lee replaced Yates as executive assistant to Assistant Secretary of the Navy Robert Morse in 1965, 345

Yokosuka, Japan
    Site of U.S. naval facility that provided logistic support and liberty opportunities during the Korean War, 181-182; the *Alamo* (LSD-33) carried the ground equipment and personnel of a Marine air squadron to Yokosuka via the great circle route in 1965, 337-338

Zero
    U.S. Navy fighters generally compared unfavorably with this Japanese plane, 87, 126

Zumwalt, Captain Elmo R., Jr., USN (USNA, 1943)
    Lee's assessment of Zumwalt as aide to Navy Secretary Paul Nitze, 346-347

www.ingramcontent.com/pod-product-compliance
Lightning Source LLC
Chambersburg PA
CBHW082149070526

44585CB00020B/2145